All About Acol

The Allen & Unwin Books on Contract Bridge

By Ben Cohen & Rhoda Lederer
BASIC ACOL
ALL ABOUT ACOL
YOUR LEAD, PARTNER
THE A.B.C. OF CONTRACT BRIDGE
CURRENT CONVENTIONS MADE CLEAR

By Rhoda Lederer
ACOL-ITE'S QUIZ

By Robert Darvas & Norman de V. Hart
RIGHT THROUGH THE PACK

By Eric Jannersten
(English version by Rhoda Lederer)
CARDS ON THE TABLE
PRECISION BRIDGE

By Alan Truscott
(Conversion to British bidding by Rhoda and Tony Lederer)
MASTER BRIDGE BY QUESTION AND ANSWER

ALL ABOUT ACOL

BEING ALL YOU NEED TO KNOW ABOUT

THE ACOL SYSTEM

OF

CONTRACT BRIDGE

BY

BEN COHEN AND RHODA LEDERER

Second Edition

London

GEORGE ALLEN & UNWIN LTD

RUSKIN HOUSE   MUSEUM STREET

FIRST PUBLISHED IN 1969
SECOND IMPRESSION 1969
THIRD IMPRESSION 1971
FOURTH IMPRESSION 1972
SECOND EDITION 1974

This book is copyright under the Berne Convention. All rights are reserved. Apart from any fair dealing for the purpose of private study, research, criticism or review, as permitted under the Copyright Act, 1956, no part of this publication may be reproduced, stored in a retrieval system, or transmitted, in any form or by any means, electronic, electrical, chemical, mechanical, optical, photocopying recording or otherwise, without the prior permission of the copyright owner. Inquiries should be addressed to the publishers.

© *George Allen and Unwin Ltd, 1969*
ISBN 0 04 793022 5

PRINTED IN GREAT BRITAIN
in 10 on 11 pt Times type
BY HOLLEN STREET PRESS LTD
AT SLOUGH

DEDICATION

To all aspiring Acol players: also to all those who, being blissfully ignorant of the basic principles of the system which they profess to play, and thus continually frustrate their partners with their knavish tricks, we respectfully dedicate this book.

(With deep apologies also to the Prince of Denmark—R.L.)

To bid, or not to bid: that is the question:
Whether 'tis nobler in the mind to suffer
The calls and passes of outrageous partner,
Or to make bids against a sea of doubles
And, by revoking, lose them? To bid, to play:
No more; and by our calls to know we show
Our best suits from the thousand natural shapes
That hands are heir to—many's the combination
Devoutly to be wish'd. To bid, to play:
To play: perchance to win a good fat Rub.
For from that lead of King, what tricks may come,
When we have shuffled up this brand new pack,
Must give us pause: there's the finesse
That makes calamity of our long suit.
And who would bear the Yarboroughs and misfits
Opponent's wrong and partner's contumely,
The pangs of trumpéd Ace, declarer's scorn,
Kibitzer's nasty sneers, and all the tricks
Palooka partner to the unworthy gives,
When he himself might the whole contract break
With his bare ten-spot? Who would part-scores call
To grunt and sweat over the dreary cards,
But that the fear of cutting afterwards
The Acol-spoiling learner from whose mouth
No right bid ever comes, puzzles the will,
And makes us rather bear the one we have
Than risk the others that we know not of.
Thus Contract doth make cowards of us all,
And thus the simplest points of Acol bidding
Are sicklied o'er with the pale cast of thought,
And slam hands of great strength and moment
With this regard declarer plays awry,
To chuck both game and auction.

Contents

♠♡♣♢♠♡♣♢♠♡♣♢♠♡♣♢♠♡♣♢♠♡♣♢♠♡♣

Foreword

The increase in popularity of the game of Contract Bridge in recent years has been little short of phenomenal. Small home groups have found their numbers growing until they were literally forced to turn themselves into Clubs. Existing Clubs have expanded to the extent of frequently being hard put to it to accommodate the players turning up for regular rubber or duplicate sessions. Contract Bridge is no longer a relaxing recreation for the upper classes for, with the breaking down of the old class barriers and the introduction of sound education and equal opportunities for all, the game has become one of the major recreations in every walk of life. It is played in the homes, in the clubs, in the schools and in the universities. It is taught in many schools and evening institutes as well as in the clubs and schools of bridge, and is rapidly becoming a social 'must' for everyone.

Along with the growth in popularity of the game, the Acol System has also grown and spread. It is now by far the most widely used bidding system, not only throughout the British Isles, but in far more distant corners of the world. South Africa—New Zealand —even the U.S.A.—are coming increasingly under its spell. If you ask why this should be so, the answer is that Acol is so common sense, so reasonable, so effective, and yet so comparatively easy to learn, that more and more players are turning to it, whilst more and more learners and would-be players adopt it from the start.

Modern Contract Bridge literally bristles with new devices, gimmicks, and conventions. Many of these are diametrically opposed to each other, and a novice left to himself to decide which to use, or which is compatible with which, would become hopelessly confused at the outset of his career, and even experts have come sadly to grief over this same hurdle. For those who elect to play the Acol System, perhaps this most formidable of all obstacles is overcome. No longer is there any need to worry about what Uncle Fred or Aunt Daisy may decree—or even what a particular group of experts may propound—for they can rely on the fact that the sponsors of modern Acol have considered every new gimmick and convention in existence, and if a particular one has not been adopted as a part of the Acol System there is a good reason for its exclusion. Like the manufacturer of a first-class car, Acol has always been, and always will be, aware of anything new, and will have considered it, and either adopted or rejected it, according to whether it enhances or detracts from the efficiency of the system as a whole.

You see, there never was any 'Mr Acol', in which the system differs from the great majority of others. There are many illustrious names in the world of Contract Bridge, and a large proportion of the accepted systems bear the names of one or more of them— Baron—Barton—Culbertson—Goren—to mention only the first few that come to mind. The Acol System, on the other hand, is not the brain-child of any one man. Acol is the name of a road in Hampstead and, in a house there in the early 1930s, a group of enthusiastic experts met and played, and tried out various forms of bidding. From this emerged the Acol System, the kind of bidding these experts elected to use because it seemed to them to produce the best results in the long run. A very long run it has been too—the best part of forty years—and it is a run which is likely to last as long as the game of Contract Bridge itself.

Since those days the Acol school of thought, for that is really what it is, has increased in popularity even more rapidly than Contract Bridge. One might almost say that it is not so much a system as a collection of sifted, approved, and workable mechanisms fitted together into one complete smooth-running machine. It has too many authors to name a quarter of them, owing much to various earlier systems such as Baron and Culbertson, and having adopted the best ideas of many well-known players like Blackwood, Flint, Gerber, and a host of others. As with our first-class car again, many of the components for which are made by different manufacturers, the Acol System is the final assembly of various parts. All these components have passed the chief designer's eagle eye, have been tested and proved to work well together and to complement each other, whilst other parts, however inherently brilliant, have been excluded as not being the most effective for the whole.

There are, of course, occasional instances where alternatives may be used, for who would quibble as to whether our car's body-work were grey, blue, or green? The basic principles of the Acol System have been tried and tested in the crucible of both rubber and tournament bridge at the highest levels in the world. Though now beyond the age of discretion, and even reaching early middle-age, the Acol System is still sufficiently young to have had the advantage of starting its life with a good and well-tried armoury. This has been added to over the years, and will doubtless be added to again if new ideas which are both compatible as well as effective come its way.

Change to Acol, which many early Acolites will remember, was really the grandfather of this new book. In due time *Acol Without Tears*, the child of *Change to Acol*, took over, and now *All About Acol* is the third generation and direct descendant of its two fore-runners. *All About Acol* is the implementation of the policy of improvement, as well as the bringing up-to-date of the older product. Like father like son, and existing Acolites will undoubtedly recog-nise in *All About Acol* many of the features of the previous two books for, it goes without saying, the fundamental principles of the Acol System remain unchanged. But they will also recognise various new features which have proved effective, which fit into the basic framework of the system without disturbing it and which, in fact, add to its efficiency. To borrow from our car manufacturer again, 'When better ideas are available ACOL will use them. In the meantime you have the very latest model in *All About Acol*'.

Let others spend endless precious minutes before each session explaining all their bids—what they do about this—what they do about that—what is meant by such-and-such, or how to construe a particular bid or bidding sequence. You may have to listen to what they say and try to understand it so that your own bidding or defence is not hampered, and you may have to face reading long and closely-written sheets before embarking on a tournament for the same reason. But at least be in the envious position yourself of being able to say quite simply 'I play Acol'—which implies the most up-to-date form of Acol, and know that everyone will under-stand what you are doing. The most you should have to do is name your chosen slam convention, the strength of your opening No Trump, or your method of combating pre-emptive opening bids!

There is an old adage that assures us that two heads are better than one, and doubtless it would be equally true to say that three heads are better than two. The third head concerned with *All About Acol* has been that of Mervyn Morgan, to whom the authors wish to express their deep and lasting gratitude for the hours of unstinted labour he has done on their behalf. First he sifted through *Acol Without Tears*, making copious notes of spots where clarification, revision, or regrouping seemed to him to be needed. Subsequently he went right through the revised draft for *All About Acol* making still further constructive suggestions, many of which have been adopted. All this, mark you, not from next door, the next town, the next county, or by way of a simple telephone call, but by air mail and cable from twelve thousand miles away in New Zealand, the extreme opposite end of the English-speaking world. Without his help this volume would have been considerably the poorer.

B.C. and R.L.

1968

Chapter 1

Hand Valuation and Definitions

FIRSTLY, how certain are you on the important question of hand valuation? Let us go over the various guides you can use until your experience grows.

There are four yardsticks by which the strength of a hand may be measured, high card point count, distributional count, quick tricks and playing tricks. The point count referred to throughout this book is the Milton Work high card, or honour, point count, i.e.,

Ace .... 4 points
King .... 3 points
Queen .... 2 points
Knave .... 1 point

In assessing a hand with a view to bidding in No Trumps, 10s should be counted as $\frac{1}{2}$ point, and additional values may be allowed for good 'fillers'.

When a suit contract is contemplated a distributional count is added to the high card count. As opener, or prospective declarer, one point for each card over four in the prospective trump suit may be added, and one point for each card over four in a second, or side suit. Thus, applying the Milton Work and distributional counts to this example hand, you would count nine high card points for the ♠A-K-Q, four for the ♡K-J, two for the ◇Q, and one each for the fifth and sixth spades, a total of 17 points.

♠ A K Q 7 4 3
♡ K J 3
◇ Q 7 4
♣ 2

A different distributional count is applied when assessing a hand as responder to partner's opening bid, as in this case the fit with opener's suggested trump suit assumes great importance. Provided you hold four-card trump support (known as primary trump support) for your partner's bid suit, you add points for *shortages in side suits*. For a void add three points, for a singleton add 2 points, and for a doubleton add 1 point. For example, as responder to a 1♡ opening bid you count four points for the ♡K-J, three for the ◇K, and 2 for the spade singleton, a total of 9 points. It is easy to see that, played in hearts the spade singleton is likely to be an asset whereas, if partner opens 1♠ it is worse than worthless,

♠ 9
♡ K J 9 7
◇ K 7 6 5
♣ 8 5 4 3

and the hand then counts 7 high-card points only.

You will have noticed, of course, that opener, on the first example, did not count additional points for his club singleton. You can't have all this and heaven too, and if you add points for long cards you cannot also add them for short suits as well!

The quick trick count is used only on the very big hands, so is seldom necessary. It must, however, be learned for use with those rare and wonderful rock-crushers which seem to come our way on all too infrequent occasions. When counting quick tricks only honour cards in combination are reckoned, and no suit can contain more than two quick tricks. No one hand, therefore, can contain more than eight. The scale is as follows:

A-K	$= 2$ Q.T.	K-x	$= \frac{1}{2}$ Q.T.
A-Q		K-J-x	$= \frac{1}{2}$ Q.T. and
A-J-10	$= 1\frac{1}{2}$ Q.T.	Q-J-10	a + value
K-Q-J		2 + values	$= \frac{1}{2}$ Q.T.
A	$= 1$ Q.T.		
K-Q			

Note that an ace and king in the same suit count as two quick tricks, whereas if these two cards are in different suits the ace counts one, and the king on its own counts $\frac{1}{2}$, or $1\frac{1}{2}$ Q.T. only, though the king, if supported by its queen, counts 1 Q.T. So in the following hand, the ♠A-K counts 2 Q.T., the ♡K-Q counts 1 Q.T., the ♢A-Q counts $1\frac{1}{2}$ Q.T., and the ♣K counts $\frac{1}{2}$ Q.T., a total of 5 Q.T.

♠ A K 7 6 5
♡ K Q 8
♢ A Q 9
♣ K 10

Finally, there is the playing trick count, about which you will need to know when you are thinking, for instance, of opening with an Acol Strong Two, which requires eight playing tricks.

A playing trick may be defined as a card with which you expect to win a trick if you or your partner become declarer, as distinguished from a defensive trick, and in estimating these one is permitted to assume, unless something in the auction has suggested the contrary, that the suit will break reasonably. Thus a hand with a seven-card suit headed by the four top honours can reasonably be expected to win seven tricks with that suit as trumps, and an outside ace would make up the eighth. A seven-card suit headed by A-Q-J can reasonably be counted as six playing tricks as, with any luck, you will lose only one trick in it.

Though these methods of valuation give an extremely good working guide, they can never be more than arbitrary. Obviously a hand which was dealt a given number of honour points will continue to contain that number until they have been played, but before that, their value can constantly vary in the light of the bidding as it develops. For instance, a king held in a suit subsequently bid by your left-hand opponent can no longer be considered worth its face-value of 3 points, whilst a king held in a suit bid on your right is worth more, being more likely to win a trick. A singleton king is often worthless if held in your opponents' suit, though it can be counted as a valuable 3 points if it is in a suit bid by your partner.

So much, then, for the methods of valuation themselves. The reason for them, of course, is to enable a partnership to judge their combined trick-taking capacity, as an approximate guide to which you may find the following table helpful:

Combined values

								Combined values
To make the 10 tricks required for a major suit game								26 points
„	„	„	11	„	„	„ „ minor „	„	28/9 „
„	„	„	9	„	„	„ „ No Trump game		25/6 „
„	„	„	12	„	„	„ Little Slam in a suit		31/3 „
„	„	„	12	„	„	„ „ in No Trumps		33/4 „
„	„	„	13	„	„	„ Grand Slam in a suit or No Trumps		37 „

Now let us go on to examine some of the features which go to make up the Acol System.

Acol is an approach-forcing system, which means that many bids call for a reply and some insist on one.

In the realm of opening bids, the Acol Light Opener, supported and protected by the system of limit bids and non-forcing rebids, is added at the lower end of the scale of normal openers, and is one of its most potent weapons. The No Trump openings are made on very precisely limited point counts, and for this reason are limit bids. Indeed all No Trump bids (except the few conventional ones dealt with separately) whether original, responding, or when used as rebids by either opener or responder, are limit bids. All direct raises of suit bids are also limit bids, being rigidly limited in terms of playing strength. All original bids at the one-level are, within the confines of a fairly wide field (a possible range of approximately 9-20 points) limit bids because the hand has not been opened with a stronger bid. In the same way, simple responses are limited by the fact that responder has not made a forcing bid.

Except for strategical reasons, particularly in tournament play, the generally accepted range for an opening 1 N.T. is 12-14 points not vulnerable and 15-17 points vulnerable. Opening bids of two in any other suit than clubs—the Acol Strong Twos—proclaim hands of strength and quality, too strong for a one-bid and not strong enough for Two Clubs. They are forcing for one round.

The Acol System's big forcing bid is the cypher-bid of Two Clubs, though this bears no relation to the Club-holding. It promises a minimum of five quick tricks in a game-going hand and is unconditionally forcing to game unless the Two Club bidder rebids 2 N.T.

It would be as well, perhaps, at this stage, to define some of the above, as well as other terms which will be used throughout this book, rather more clearly, as they constitute the framework on which the Acol System is based. This framework is standardised, certainly in Great Britain and largely in other countries, and the introduction of sequences which violate it is more likely to produce disaster than benefit! The correct application of these bids is fundamental to the whole system—many unfortunate contracts would be avoided and many more good ones reached if all the players who claim to play Acol understood completely what they were doing.

You will find most of these terms covered even more fully in the chapters devoted to each of them. In the meantime, however, the following brief descriptions will give you an overall picture of the basic principles of the Acol System.

1) THE LIGHT OPENING BID is, as already pointed out, one of Acol's most potent weapons. It is a means of getting into the attack early as well as directing partner's lead if you become the defenders, and may be made on as little as 9 or 10 honour points *as long as the hand contains a safe rebid.* This rebid will be either in the suit opened (in which case it will probably be a six-card suit), or in a second five-card suit. When you come to examine these hands in Chapter 2 you will see that they seldom, if ever, count less than a total of 12 points once the long card, or distributional points, have been added to the high card points.

It is, perhaps, worth stressing once again that the Acol Light Opener is used *in addition to,* and not instead of, a normal opening bid such as will be familiar to any player accustomed to an approach-forcing system.

2) THE SIGN-OFF, when used by opener as his rebid, is the protection offered to the light opening bid. If the opening has been made on a hand of good 'shape', that is, a six-card suit, opener can sign off by returning to this suit at the lowest available level, so telling his partner that he has nothing to add to what he has already shown. Responder should respect this message, though this does not mean that he should allow the auction to die if his own hand is worth another try. If he does bid again, however, he will be doing so in

the knowledge that his partner has announced a minimum hand and will probably pass at the earliest opportunity, or continue signing off in his long suit until responder gives up!

3) THE LIMIT BIDS, a corner-stone of the Acol System, are bids which announce immediately the full values held. They are once-and-for-all bids—'this much I've got and no more'. They may be made as direct suit raises or No Trump responses (Chapter 3), as opener's or responder's rebids (Chapters 8 and 9), or as opening No Trump bids (Chapter 4). In whatever situation they are used they carry the same clear message which is that this is the only bid the hand is worth, and a player who has once made a limit bid should *never* bid again except in response to a forcing bid from his partner, to 'correct' to what he considers the best final denomination or occasionally, on a maximum for his bid, to accept a strong invitation to go on to game.

The limit bids work equally well whether opener has bid on a light, normal, or strong hand. Far from being shut-out bids, they can encourage him to go on, as the limit bid will have given him an accurate assessment of the combined values of the two hands, as well as an immediate pointer towards the best final denomination. A limit bid is *never* forcing and, just as the limit-bidder will not bid again unless his partner in turn forces, or to 'correct' if necessary, so the responder to a limit bid is under no obligation to rebid if he thinks that the best final contract has been reached. He is, however, expected, if he does not think it best to pass, to make one final bid naming what he considers the best contract. For example, opener's rebid of 1 N.T. is a limit bid. Responder may pass this, make a forcing bid or, failing either of the alternatives, himself decide the final contract. It is no use his bidding 2♢ and hoping his partner will go on to 3 N.T. or 5♢— he won't. If responder thinks either should be bid, he must bid it himself.

$$1♢ \quad —1♡$$
$$1\,NT—?$$

4) A FORCING BID is one which unconditionally demands a response from partner, whatever his holding, and however much he may dislike the idea of having to bid on his hand. Strong Two opening bids (Chapter 11) and Two Club openings (Chapter 12) both demand that responder should keep the auction open. Either member of a partnership may force in various ways, to ensure another turn to bid, or to make certain that at least a game contract, if not a slam, is reached. Whatever the situation, a player whose partner makes a forcing bid must never take it upon himself to pass—one of the surest ways of creating lack of partnership confidence! It goes without saying, however, that an opponent's intervening bid over the hand which has forced lets responder off what may be a painful

hook, since the auction will be open back to his partner anyway. In these circumstances responder may take the opportunity to pass unless he has something constructive to say.

5)   A SACRIFICE BID is one made quite deliberately with the knowledge that the contract cannot, or is highly unlikely, to be made. It arises when a partnership is prepared to incur a penalty rather than permit the opposition to score a game or slam. It is, for instance, cheaper in terms of points at Duplicate to go down seven tricks doubled and not vulnerable (1,300 points) than it is to allow the opponents to score a vulnerable Little Slam in one of the major suits (1,430 points). The pre-emptive bids come into this category, being weak opening bids or overcalls made at a high level with the deliberate object of obstructing the opponents, and possibly shutting them out of the auction altogether.

6)   A PREFERENCE BID is one given by a player when he returns at the lowest available level to the first of two suits bid by his partner.

1♠—2◇
2♡—2♠
or
1♠—1NT
2♡—2♠

This does *not* rank as a raise of partner's suit, and is merely a 'correction' to the lesser of two evils. Had the original response been 1 N.T. instead of 2◇, responder's 2♠ rebid would still be a weak preference. It might show no more than two or three small spades as compared with a doubleton or singleton heart.

It follows that there must be a means of showing active preference, amounting to real support, for one of partner's suits, and for this

1♠—2◇
2♡—3♠

a *jump preference* bid is used. The values and fit for a raise of partner's second suit, hearts, could be shown quite simply by a responder's rebid of 3♡, from which you will see that the jump preference bid of 3♠ shows not just a weak preference, but a very decided choice, as well as being an actual raise in the suit. The jump bid is *not* forcing, though obviously it is highly encouraging, so should never be made on a minimum hand—minimum, that is, for the situation existing at the time.

7)   A DELAYED GAME RAISE is a waiting bid. It is one which may be used when, facing partner's opening bid, responder needs to hear opener's rebid before taking a decision as to the best final contract. The most usual spot for it is when responder is too strong for a three-level limit bid which opener might pass, but not quite strong

1♡—2◇
2♡—4♡

enough for an immediate forcing bid. Alternatively responder's values, though worth a final game contract, do not contain primary trump support for opener's suit. In such circumstances responder delays his raise to game level until he has heard opener's rebid. Should this be strong instead of in the sign-off category, responder may well be in a position to explore for a slam. If it is a sign-off the chances of a slam become remote and opener is simply put to game in his suit.

8) A QUANTITATIVE BID is best defined as one which is natural, limited, and non-forcing. In practice, however, the term is used for an invitational bid made by a member of a partnership who is hoping to reach a slam contract but is in difficulty for an expressive bid on his hand. The classic situation is a quantitative raise of an opening No Trump bid direct to the four-level, which indicates that if the opening 1 N.T. were based on a maximum, not a minimum, there should be a good play for a slam. Opener is invited to bid 6 N.T. if he fancies his chances in the light of his knowledge that responder is not quite strong enough to be sure that a slam should be bid.

1NT—4NT

There are, however, many other situations where such a bid may be used. In this sequence, for example, it is safe to assume that responder's 2♢ was a waiting bid, and the prelude to a delayed game raise. When opener makes the strong rebid of 3♡, responder, himself unable to bid a conventional 4 N.T. (too short of first-round controls) bids a quantitative and highly invitational 5♡, asking opener to bid the Little Slam if he has anything in reserve for his bidding thus far.

1♡—2♢
3♡—5♡

Acol Light Opening Bids and the Sign-off

ACOL players believe firmly in the principle that the safest form of defence is attack, which is the reason for the development of the *Acol Light Opening Bids*. Used in conjunction with the *Sign-Off Rebids* and *Limit Bids*, these light openings frequently impede the opposition to such an extent that they miss their own best contract. These bids can, too, often pave the way to most profitable 'sacrifice' contracts.

It cannot be stressed too strongly that these light opening bids do not replace normal one-level suit bids. They merely increase the range of these at the lower end of the scale whilst the upper limit remains, as before, more or less indeterminate, and limited only by the fact that the hand could not be opened with an Acol Strong Two or Two Club bid, both of which require far stronger hands.

In this chapter we shall be dealing only with hands suitable for opening suit bids at the one-level, and particularly with the Acol Light Openers and the subsequent rebid. We shall not be discussing normal full-strength, or even strong, opening one-bids and it should be sufficient to remind you that a normal one-level opening can be made on a count of 12 or more honour points with a four or five-card trump suit. The only criterion is that the hand should contain an honest rebid, either to develop the attack or to provide a safe line of retreat.

Hard and fast rules about opening bids are impossible to formulate except with particular types of hands. You must accept that the point count is not the be-all and end-all as a guide to your bid. You can hold 20 points so distributed that the hand qualifies for a Two Club bid, for a Two No Trump bid, or only for a one-bid. The important point here is that opening one-bids *are* limited, even if no rigid limits can be set. They are limited by the shape or distribution, or the honour content that makes them unsuitable for a stronger bid. They can come near to these stronger bids, in which case their strength will be shown later by the appropriate rebid. At the other end of the scale, they can come near to being too weak to open at all, which will be shown by a sign-off rebid. When you find yourself responding to a one-level suit bid, therefore, remember that at least some negative inference can be drawn from the fact that only a one-bid was made.

ACOL LIGHT OPENING BIDS

Let us now get down to the business of examining the Acol Light Openings in detail. As we have already said, this is an attacking weapon, and increases the lower range of normal opening one-bids. It can be made on a count of as little as 9 honour points as long as the hand contains the vital requirement of a safe line of retreat. This can be in the form of a six-card suit or two reasonably good five-card suits, either of which holding will provide a safe rebid, and on which it is often a good strategical move to open the attack. Remember at this point that a player who opens the bidding first or second in hand with a one-level suit bid promises that his hand contains a sensible rebid.

A rebid in the suit opened at the lowest available level should be understood by responder as a sign-off, that is, a warning that you have nothing further to add to your original bid. Responder should now be in a good position to judge whether his own hand warrants any further action, or whether to pass the two-level rebid. Similarly, when the rebid is made in a second five-card suit at the two-level, this must not be taken as showing anything other than another possible spot to play the hand. More of this in a moment but, in the meantime, remember that if you open the auction with, for instance, a bid of 1♣, your opponents cannot tell whether this is showing a light, normal, or strong hand. Good opponents will not intervene lightly at the two-level, especially if vulnerable, so that by the time the bidding has gone, perhaps like this, fourth hand may

E.	S.	W.	N.
1♣	—	3♣	?

find it difficult, if not quite impossible to come into the auction. Here is a hand from a duplicate pairs event which illustrates this point:

Dealer: East
North-South Game.

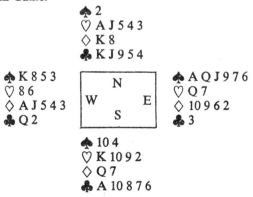

At tables where East opened a typical Acol Light 1♠, the vulnerable South was unable to make an intervening bid. When his pass was followed by a 3♠ limit bid from West, North in his turn was snookered, as he could not come in at this level without incurring serious danger—remember that East might have held *all* South's honour points without stepping beyond the limits of an opening 1♠. But East was minimum, and so exercised his right to pass his partner's limit bid, so there the contract rested, exactly nine tricks being made for a score of +140. At other tables, where East did not open, or West responded to 1♠ with 2◇ instead of 3♠, North-South found their heart fit, and East-West either had to bid to 4♠ (doubled and one down, −100) or allow the even more costly vulnerable game score of 620 points to be chalked up against them.

This hand alone proves our point that it pays to open the attack early. So on 9 or 10 honour points, if your hand contains a six-card suit (for which you may add 2 distributional points) attack immediately, as the suit provides its own safe rebid.

♠ K 7 5
♡ Q 10 7
◇ A J 9 7 5 3
♣ 5

Here is another example. If you open 1◇ on this hand you have a safe rebid of 2◇, in addition to which you have suggested a good lead to your partner in the event of your becoming the defenders. Even more than that, you may well have ruined any chance of your opponents bidding and making 3 N.T. on a 'blind' lead from your partner.

The next important point we come to is that, in the Acol System, a simple change-of-suit rebid at the two level is *not* forcing. It is, therefore, just as safe to open the bidding on many equally light hands, containing two five-card suits, as the rebid in the second suit can be passed by responder. He has a choice between rebidding his own suit, passing the second suit bid if he has a weak hand and prefers this second suit, or merely giving preference to the first bid suit. Thus as in the case of opening on a six-card suit, once again the partnership is very unlikely to get into trouble whilst they may reap great rewards.

♠ A J 9 5 2
♡ K Q 10 8 6
◇ 9 3
♣ 7

Only 10 honour points (increased to 12 by two distributional points for the fifth spade and heart), but it contains two excellent five-card majors, a bid in either of which might easily lead to a successful game contract. On the other hand, an opening bid of 1♠ may well obstruct the opposition whilst causing no trouble to responder. If he bids 2♣ or 2◇ you can safely rebid 2♡, confident that he will not become excited by the change of suit, which merely suggests an alternative possible trump suit, and that he can, in fact, pass 2♡ or return you to 2♠ if he himself is minimum.

This does not mean that you should open the bidding on any 9 or 10 point hand containing two five-card suits. Switch the suits in the previous example and now, if you open 1♠ and responder bids 2♡, your only possible rebid would be 2♠ which, on this straggly five-card suit, would be most misleading. It would be equally unthinkable to rebid in diamonds, which you must do at the three-level over 2♡, as this is a forcing bid

♠ A J 9 5 2
♡ 7
◇ K Q 10 8 6
♣ 9 3

reserved for much stronger hands. If, to avoid this pitfall, you open 1◇, then again you are in trouble if the response is 2♣. A rebid of 2♠ might well be disastrous as responder, to give you preference to diamonds, would have to raise to the three-level, and a rebid of 2◇ over 2♣ would be as misleading as 2♠. Nor are any of the following examples suitable for opening bids as, in spite of their count, they contain no sensible rebid :

1) ♠ A Q 8 6 2   2) ♠ A K 6 2
    ♡ 9 5 4   ♡ Q 5
    ◇ K 7   ◇ Q 6 5 4 2
    ♣ 9 6 2   ♣ 7 6

3) ♠ 9 2   4) ♠ K 9 7 5 2
    ♡ Q 7 6 4 2   ♡ A 7 2
    ◇ 3   ◇ K 5 3
    ♣ A K 6 5 2   ♣ 9 6

Note that, in the case of No. 3, if the two five-card suits were adjacent—say hearts and diamonds or diamonds and clubs—a one-level opening in the higher-ranking would be in order, as the second suit could be rebid at the two-level. Similarly if they were clubs and spades, you could open 1♣ and rebid 1♠ over a red-suit response. This, then, is the clue—on these very weak hands, if one of the two suits is not rebiddable, you should not open unless the two suits are adjacent or both black, as you will have no safe rebid.

There is an exception to the rule that you must be prepared to make a rebid when you open the bidding, and that is if you are third or fourth in hand after your partner has passed. When we come to responding to opening bids you will see that a change-of-suit response is a one round force *unless* responder has previously passed. This is why, before your partner has had a chance to bid—or pass—you must be prepared to rebid. *After* he has made an original pass you guarantee nothing, and it is often a good move to open on hands such as the above at favourable vulnerability. But these are more advanced situations so, in the meantime remember that if, as first or second in hand, you feel the urge to make an opening bid, let the deciding factor be whether or not the hand contains a safe rebid.

OPENER'S SIGN-OFF REBIDS

The sign-off rebid, which we've mentioned several times already, is the safeguard which enables Acol players to make use of the attacking weapon of the light opening bid without undue risk to the partnership. Either a simple rebid at the lowest available level in the suit opened, or a two-level rebid in a new suit promises no added values, and either may be passed by responder if he thinks that the best final contract has been reached. Here are some examples which are the easiest way of making the situation clear.

♠ A J 9 7 6 4
♡ K 8 6
◇ Q 6 2
♣ 7

Open 1♠ and sign off in 2♠ whatever your partner responds. But if, for instance, the bidding went 1♠ —2♡—2♠—3◇ you should not repeat your spades again, but give partner preference to his hearts, as fairly obviously he dislikes your suit whilst you do not really dislike either of his!

1♠—2♡
2♠—3♣
?

On this sequence, return responder to his hearts— you have already signed off by rebidding 2♠ so now are merely giving preference, not a raise, in hearts. 3♡ is a return to responder's suit at the lowest available level, and is not an encouragement to him to go on to game unless he has a good deal of extra strength.

1♠—2♡
2♠—3♡

Here your most forceful second sign-off is to pass. Responder knows that you made a weak rebid in the first place, so you must just take it that he prefers to play in hearts.

1♠—2◇
2♠—2NT
?

Responder's second try is a limit bid showing 11-12 honour points (see Chapter 3). It is non-forcing so you have a choice of passing or 'correcting' to what you think will be the best final contract. This, in your opinion, will be 3♠ which you bid in the knowledge that your partner will pass. As a corollary to this, if you thought that, in view of partner's second bid, you had a play for game, you would have to bid it yourself—responder will not bid it for you.

♣ 7
♡ A J 9 8 6
◇ K Q 7 5 3
♠ 9 8

Here's a two-suited example—with the suits adjacent you have an opening of 1♡ on which, if responder bids 1♠ or 2♣, you can rebid 2◇ without misleading him. If the same holdings were in clubs and spades instead of the red suits, you would open 1♣ and rebid 1♠ over a response of 1◇ or 1♡.

From the above it should be clear to you that a sign-off rebid may well be the end of the auction. Here, if the opposition does

1♣—2♡
2♣—?

not come to life, and we have already seen how difficult this may be, responder, if not himself fairly strong, is likely to see the red light and pass. From this it follows that if you have a good or strong opening bid rather than a light opener you must at all costs try to avoid an

♠ A Q J 7 4

♢ A K 5
♣ K Q 4

apparent sign-off rebid. You will learn how to deal with a hand such as this in Chapter 8 (Opener's Rebids) but meanwhile note that, although you have only one suit you must on no account rebid 2♣, which might well be passed when there is a virtually certain game on between the two hands.

It follows also that you must become Acol-minded about the revaluation of your hand in the light of your partner's responses.

♠ A Q J 8 6 2
♡ K 10 4 2
♢ 7 5
♣ 8

Here, for example, we have very much the same hand as in earlier examples, and rightly open 1♠. If responder bids either 2♢ or 2♣ it contains nothing but a sign-off rebid of 2♠. If he should respond 2♢ and, over your 2♠, rebid 3♣, then it is rapidly becoming one of those rare hands on which you begin to wish you hadn't opened! If this should happen, remember that there is an element of risk in practically every bid, but that for the one occasion on which you may come to grief there will be fifty on which you gain. Instead of a minor suit response, however, your partner might bid 2♡, and though nothing can improve your honour point count, the value of the hand rises immediately. You would not dream of signing off with 2♠, for with short clubs and diamonds and a first-class heart fit you no longer *wish* to sign off, so you raise your partner's bid to 3♡.

A word about intervening bids before we leave this section. If the opponent on your left intervenes over your opening bid, this may affect your partner's response. In this first sequence, South's bid

N.	E.	S.
1♣	2♢	2♡

at the two-level will be substantially the same as it would have been without the intervention, and you can make your appropriate rebid undisturbed. If, however, the intervention forces South to bid at the three-

N.	E.	S.
1♣	2♡	3♢

level, he can be relied on to hold *either* support for the opening bid *or* compensating values. You can, therefore, safely afford to make your own rebid, whether a sign-off or not, at the three-level. A further

N.	E.	S.	W.
1♠	2♢	2♡	3♢

intervening bid from West means that the auction will remain open round to South again, which releases opener from the obligation to rebid. As North you can, therefore, sign off by *passing*, and any 'free' rebid over West's intervention should confirm values above those required for a light opening bid.

CHOICE OF BID

Opener's choice of bid, when he has more than one suit he may want to show as in the example hands earlier in this chapter, really comes in 'Opener's Rebids', but you will not want to wait until Chapter 8, where these are fully discussed, to get an idea of why you choose a particular suit in preference to another for your opening bid. Here, then, is some guidance on the subject. The following can hardly be called rules, because they cannot avoid being conflicting and overlapping at times, and the over-riding point is always to make the most natural bid open to you on the hand in question. Within these terms of reference, therefore:

1) Bid the longer suit before the shorter, i.e., a six-card suit before a five-card suit.

2) With suits of equal length bid the higher-ranking before the lower-ranking, i.e., spades before hearts, *except* if the two suits are spades and clubs, in which case bid clubs first.

3) Bid the stronger suit before the weaker, i.e., A-K-Q-x-x before Q-J-x-x-x. This, however, is of very secondary import- ance to No. 2 above, which takes precedence in almost every instance, particularly where five-card adjacent suits are concerned.

Set out in terms of suit-length, we get the following as at least a rough guide:

Suit length

1) 6—6 or 5—5	If adjacent, bid the higher-ranking first unless spades and clubs, when bid clubs first. If not adjacent, strength of hand and sensible rebid will have to be taken into consideration.
5—4	With adjacent suits in a strong hand worth an 'opener's reverse' (see Chapter 8) bid five-card suit first. In a weak hand it is sometimes necessary to bid the four-card suit first, particularly if the five-card suit is not worth rebidding as a sign-off. If the four-card suit is weak ignore it, as it is of value only in support if bid by partner. With non-adjacent suits bid 5-card suit first.

2) 6—5   Bid the longer suit first unless the hand is weak
    7—6   and the suits are adjacent. Rebid in the shorter
    7—5   suit, indicating that both suits are rebiddable
            because your opening was made in the longer
            (See examples on p. 120).

3) 6—4   Bid and *repeat* any six-card suit before showing
            a four-card suit *unless* the four-card suit is a major
            which can be shown at the one-level (1◇—2♣—
            2◇ BUT 1◇—1♡—1♠ on a hand 6—4 in
            diamonds and spades).

4) 4—4—4—1   Bid the suit below the singleton unless the single-
              ton is in clubs, when bid 1♡ (Chapter 8).

5) 4—4   With adjacent suits bid the higher-ranking first
            except with spades and clubs, when bid clubs
            first. (Counting the suits as forming a circle, clubs
            rank as adjacent to spades.) With spades and
            diamonds, and holding *three* hearts (i.e. heart
            support), bid spades first. With three *clubs* (i.e.
            club support), bid diamonds first. These last two
            choices are based on the hope that this will best
            facilitate the rest of the auction.

The above, of course, all pre-suppose biddable suits, that is, suits
which opener is prepared to suggest as the possible trump suit, and
not those so weak that they are of value only in support of partner.

1) What opening bid would you make on the following hands?

    a) ♠ K J 9 6 4 2: ♡ A 6 5: ◇ 7: ♣ K 9 4:
    b) ♠ K 5 3: ♡ Q 10 9 8 7 2: ◇ A 4: ♣ 8 3:
    c) ♠ Q 4: ♡ K 10 9 6 3: ◇ A 5 4 3: ♣ J 3:
    d) ♠ 5: ♡ 6 4: ◇ A Q J 10 6 3 2: ♣ K 4 3:
    e) ♠ K 5: ♡ K J 9 6 3: ◇ K Q 8 4 2: ♣ 3:

2) You open 1♠ and partner responds 2♡. What is your rebid on these hands?

    a) ♠ K J 10 8 4 3: ♡ A 4: ◇ K 9 3: ♣ 6 3:
    b) ♠ A K Q 10 7 6 5: ♡ Q 9 7 5: ◇ K: ♣ 9:
    c) ♠ K Q 10 9 6: ♡ Q 4: ◇ K Q 10 8 3: ♣ A:
    d) ♠ A Q 9 6 4: ♡ J 4: ◇ K 4: ♣ A Q 9 6:
    e) ♠ A K J 9 4 2: ♡ —: ◇ Q J 9 3: ♣ A 4 3:

3) What opening bid would you make on the following hands, and what would you rebid if partner responds 2♣?

    a) ♠ K 10 8 4 2: ♡ A Q 9 6 5: ◇ Q 5: ♣ 4:
    b) ♠ 8 6: ♡ 5: ◇ A K 10 9 7 3: ♣ Q J 9 8:
    c) ♠ 5 3: ♡ A K Q 5 4: ◇ 8 4 3: ♣ 10 6 2:
    d) ♠ A K Q 6 3 2: ♡ 8 6: ◇ 7 4: ♣ Q 3 2:
    e) ♠ K 4: ♡ 9 6: ◇ A Q J 8 5 3 2: ♣ 8 3:

4) What opening bid would you make on the following hands?

    a) ♠ A 7: ♡ A K Q 8 2: ◇ Q J 10 6 4: ♣ 7:
    b) ♠ A 7: ♡ Q J 10 6 4: ◇ A K Q 8 2: ♣ 7:
    c) ♠ A K J 6: ♡ A K Q 8 2: ◇ Q 5: ♣ 6 3:
    d) ♠ 9 7 5 4: ♡ A K Q 8 2: ◇ A K: ♣ Q 3:
    e) ♠ A J 5 4: ♡ K 9 7 6 4: ◇ A J: ♣ 6 3:
    f) ♠ A J 5 4: ♡ K Q 10 6 5 4: ◇ J 10: ♣ 6:

ANSWERS TO REVISION QUIZ ON CHAPTER 2

1) a) 1♠   Your six-card suit provides a safe sign-off rebid.

   b) 1♡   Here again, you can safely rebid your six-card heart suit.

   c) Pass You have nothing you can honestly rebid on this hand, so you must not open the bidding.

   d) 1◇   You can bid, rebid, and continue to rebid, in diamonds.

   e) 1♡   Here both your five-card suits are reasonably good so you open with one of the higher-ranking of two adjacent suits, that is, hearts, and later bid your diamonds.

2) a) 2♠   You made an Acol Light Opener, and can only rebid in your six-card suit.

   b) 4♡   You had nearly a 2♠ opening bid here. Partner will not take your jump to game in his suit as a shut-out if his hand is strong for his bid.

   c) 3◇   This was a full-strength, not a light, opener, and your diamonds are good enough to show at the three-level, especially as ♡ Q 4 is by no means a misfit with partner's hearts.

   d) 3♣   Partner will know your spades are longer than your clubs or, with two equally long black suits, you would have opened 1♣.

   e) 2♠   Although you have 15 points, you are not strong enough to bid anything else, especially with a complete misfit in partner's hearts.

3) a)   You would open 1♠ and, over 2♣, rebid 2♡. As the change of suit is not forcing, partner may pass or just return you to spades.

   b)   You would open 1◇ and raise 2♣ to 3♣. You really do not want to sign off here and anyway, clubs are a wonderful fit.

   c)   Perhaps not quite a fair one—as you would not open in the first place you will not have to rebid!

   d)   You would open 1♠ and rebid 2♠. You have nothing else to say.

   e)   Here again, you would open 1◇ and rebid 2◇, and continue repeating diamonds till partner gets the message.

4) a) 1♡   The higher-ranking of two equal and adjacent suits which presents no problems as to a sensible rebid.

   b) 1♡   Again this order of bidding ensures a sensible rebid. Many learners find it hard to give up opening 1♢ (with all the pretty honours!) in favour of the higher-ranking suit.

   c) 1♡   This is an exceedingly good hand, for which reason it is safe to open in its longest suit and 'reverse' (see Chapter 8) into the four-card spade suit on the next round.

   d) 1♡   Conceal the spades, even though the hand is as strong as (c) in terms of honour points. The spades are of interest only if partner bids them.

   e) 1♠   One of the hands on which you have to break *some* rule! The heart suit is not rebiddable, though you must open on this hand. If you bid 1♠ you can rebid 2♡ over 2♣ or 2♢, and the only risk you run is that you will be given weak preference to spades—which you do not actually prefer!

   f) 1♡   The six-card suit is rebiddable, so there is no need at all to risk misleading partner by starting with 1♠.

Chapter 3

The Limit Bids

HAVING got clear in our minds the important basic principle of the Acol light openers guarded by the non-forcing rebids, let us now turn to the LIMIT BIDS, a cornerstone, and one of the main features, of the Acol System. Limit bids can be made in suits or in No Trumps, by opener or responder, or as second-round bids by either. In whatever situation they are used their essential purpose remains unchanged, to bid the hand to the full extent of its values telling partner 'This far I can go and no farther. I shall not bid again unless forced'. Within these terms of reference both members of the partnership lose no time in assessing their combined strength or weakness, as the case may be.

RESPONDER'S SUIT LIMIT BIDS

The first law relating to a suit limit bid by responder, that is, a direct raise in the suit bid by his partner, is that four-card trump support is held. The reason for this is that the Acol System permits the free use of opening bids based on four-card suits (always provided, of course, that sufficient honour strength is held to compensate for the shortage in trumps). Four trumps in either hand, a total of eight, gives the balance of power in the suit, and is the lowest number likely to make a comfortable 'fit' and to give declarer control of the hand. This is the simple basis of the responding suit limit bids and, in particular, in the majors. Note also that once responder makes a direct suit limit raise, to whatever level, he is announcing his full values within very precise limits as well as denying the values to make a stronger bid (see Chapter 7).

When responder answers his partner's one-level opening suit bid he does not know whether opener has bid on a minimum hand, that is, an Acol light opener, something just short of an Acol Strong Two bid or Two Club hand, or something in between such, for example, as a four-card suit and 16 or 17 honour points. But opener knows, and when his partner makes a limit bid response he will be in an excellent position to judge what action, if any, to take next, since he will know within narrow limits the combined strength of the two hands, in addition to the fact that there is at least a four-card trump fit facing him. Let us take the same opening

♠ A Q J 8 6 2
♡ K 10 4 2
◇ 7 5
♣ 8

hand that we used in Chapter 2 and consider it in the light of responder's possible limit bid in reply. Look at the situation from opener's point of view and remember that, once responder has answered with a limit bid, opener is not so much concerned with signing off, *but with deciding the best final contract which his partner has said he leaves to opener's own judgement.*

The basic requirement for a suit limit bid being primary, or four-card trump support, the following is responder's guide :|

      5— 9 points .... raise a one-bid to the two-level
      10—12   „   ....   „ „   „   „ „ three-level
      13 points or more ... bid in a new suit (see Chapter 7).

Remember that these counts include both honour and distributional points and that, precise though they are, other factors must be taken into consideration. An ace-queen, for instance, held over an intervening bid of that suit must be worth more than its face-value of 6 honour points.

♠ 9 5 4 3
♡ A 7 3
◇ K 6 2
♣ 9 7 5

Here's a typical hand for the weakest responding limit bid, a raise to the two-level. If partner opens 1♠ you have a count of 7 honour points, as well as the necessary four-card trump fit. Look at this and the opening hand together. Played in spades declarer can very easily lose one heart, two diamonds, and a club, and will need to catch the ♠K and find the ◇A 'right' even to make his contract. But your opponents will be hard put to it to double a 2♠ contract, and may well be equally hard put to it to discover that they have a game on for themselves in another suit.

♠ K 7 5 3
♡ 7 6 3
◇ 8
♣ K J 7 6 4

Here's another typical example—combined honour and distributional count of 9 points. Raise to 2♠ and declarer, holding the original hand, will be extremely unlucky to lose more than one club, one diamond, and three hearts, for 2♠ made.

Looking at it from opener's side of the table, when he hears the humble response of 2♠ it should not take him long to add this message to his own hand, itself of minimum strength, and to pass.

♠ K 9 4 3
♡ 8 6
◇ A Q 8 6 4
♣ 9 2

Now let's top it up a bit. Facing a 1♠ opening this hand is worth 11 points in all, a raise to 3♠. Again opener, being minimum, would refuse the chance to bid again and would pass. To make 3♠ he needs *either* to find the ♡A 'right' *or* to lose not more than one trick in diamonds, a very fair chance. If both are right then, of course, it must be your lucky day and you will make ten tricks because the hands fitted so perfectly; but on balance one of two chances is likely to be wrong and 3♠ is what you will make.

Opener, obviously, would only pass on a minimum hand, and if you work out a few normal hands with 13-14 honour points instead of only 10 you will find that far more often than not he'll be able to make ten tricks which means that, on such a hand, he would accept the invitation of the 3♠ raise and bid the game. Similarly with a strong opening hand facing even only a raise to the two-level, he would go on, or at least make another try (see Chapter 10).

In the original version of Acol the raise from one of a major to the four-level (1♠—4♠) was a strong limit bid, not to be taken as a shut-out if opener were strong for his bid. In practice, however, it was found that many slams were missed in this way as opener, possibly short of first-round controls, feared to investigate further. Modern technique has, therefore, developed various new ways of dealing with these responding hands such as the 'Swiss' 4♣—4◇ convention, details of which you will find in Chapter 7. So in the meantime let us consider the direct raise to game level as it is used to-day.

Nowadays such a bid is used purely pre-emptively, and is only a limit bid in the sense that distributionally there may be a play for game, though the thing of main importance is to block the opposition bidding. The indications are exceptionally good trump support, a poor high-card count, but 'shape' by way of voids or singletons.

♠ 7
♡ J 8 6 4 3 2
◇ 5
♣ K Q 10 7 6

This hand, containing a total of 10 honour and distributional points, is a typical example of a hand suitable for raising opener's 1♡ direct to 4♡. This will exert the utmost possible pressure on fourth-in-hand who, if he wants to show spades, will have to do so for the first time at the four-level. Even if there has been an immediate overcall of the 1♡ opening (1♡—1♠—4♡) fourth-in-hand may be unable to judge correctly whether or not his side can play in game.

If your hand qualifies for a responder's limit bid in either major it is better to make this response straight away rather than to make a change-of-suit response. Note the word 'qualifies', because there are many occasions when a responding hand with four-card trump

♠ Q 9 8 7
♡ 8 4
◇ A Q 9 6 5
♣ J 10

support will be *too strong* for a limit bid, and these you will be meeting later. In the meantime note that, with a hand like this, when partner opens 1♠ you should raise to 3♠, not bid 2◇. Or with this next example, raise your partner's opening 1♡ to 2♡

♠ K Q 8
♡ Q 9 5 3
◇ J 9 8 5 2
♣ 5

rather than show the diamond suit. The direct raise has the great merit of informing opener immediately of your combined strength—or weakness—as well as being as pre-emptive as it is possible to be on the hand.

We have spoken of these limit bids so far as though they applied only to the major suits. This is not true, although with the minor suits the situation is somewhat different. The limit bids to either the two or three-level can be used in exactly the same way when the opening has been a club or a diamond, but a minor suit game requires eleven tricks, and opener may well pass even a raise to the three-level when he would not pass a raise to three in hearts or spades. So unless you have previously passed (see Chapter 7), it is generally tactically sounder to respond by showing a four-card major if one is held, as this may pave the way for a final contract of 3 N.T. But if your best and only sensible response is a direct raise of opener's minor suit, make this raise, and opener himself may be able to convert to No Trumps or at least make some other effort. As you will see in Chapter 6, it is possible that opener has been forced to make a 'prepared' minor suit opening, in which case he will rebid in the appropriate number of No Trumps. On a strong opening based on a natural good minor suit, a limit raise may be all he wants to hear to bid to game in it.

A jump to the four-level in response to a minor suit opening bid is, of course, a purely pre-emptive measure based on weakness, particularly in the majors, as it cuts out any chance

♠ 8
♡ 7 4
♢ Q J 10 7 5
♣ K Q J 8 6

of the partnership playing in 3 N.T. In the same way a direct jump to the five-level may cause havoc in the opposition ranks. It would be well worth raising either 1♣ or 1♢ to four of that suit on this hand, and if you top it up by the addition of another three honour points it would probably pay high dividends to jump direct to the five-level.

It is very important to get this distinction between the limit bids in the majors and the minors quite clear, and also to understand how the *latter* may be affected by your position at the table. Bear in mind three important rules of the Acol System:

1) Any direct raise of opener's one-level suit bid is a limit bid showing four-card trump support.

2) A change-of-suit response made by a player who has not yet had a chance to call, at which he might also have passed, is a one-round force, which is why an opening bidder must be prepared to rebid as first or second in hand.

3) A simple change-of-suit response by a player who has already passed is no longer forcing and may be passed by opener.

Now compare the following examples, which should make the

♠ 9 7 5
♡ K J 8 4
◇ K 9 8 3
♣ 5 3

position clear:— If partner opens 1♡ in any position, raise to 2♡. If he opens 1◇ as first or second in hand, make the possibly constructive response of 1♡. Having previously passed, however, raise 1◇ to 2◇ in preference to bidding 1♡ which might well be passed out when there is this excellent diamond fit available.

♠ Q 9 5 3
♡ K Q 8
◇ 10 9 8 2
♣ 5 3

If partner opens either 1◇ or 1♡ as dealer or second in hand, bid 1♠. Once having passed, raise 1◇ to 2◇ in preference to bidding 1♠ which opener might pass. It is even better to raise an opening 1♡ to 2♡ in this position, even though the hand is not strictly qualified for a limit bid in hearts, because you do not want to risk a pass from opener on a hand which clearly belongs in hearts. *Not* previously having passed there is no reason to promise four-card heart support when you can bid an honest 1♠.

♠ 9 5
♡ J 9 8 6
◇ K Q 9 6 2
♣ K 3

Whether you've previously passed or not, raise an opening 1♡ to 3♡. This is a perfect opportunity to tell your partner that you hold four-card trump support and a count of 10-12 points. If, having passed, your partner opens 1◇, it is only common sense to raise him to 3◇.

Before we go on to the limit bid responses in No Trumps let's just summarise what we have learned so far about the limit bids.

Firstly, immediately responder makes a limit bid, several things happen. The 'captaincy' of the bidding has been firmly planted on the opening bidder. Responder has got his whole hand off his chest in one bid and has announced that he will not bid again except in reply to a forcing rebid from his partner, or to 'correct', if given a choice, to the best final denomination. This last alternative includes his right to accept or refuse a strong *invitation* made by his partner on the next round to bid on to game. (See ps. 47-8).

Secondly, opener knows within close limits the combined strength of the two hands and must accept the responsibility of deciding the best final contract. There are and always will be difficult decisions to be made. A very lucky 'fit' plus fortunate distribution may result in making a game which has not been bid or, alternatively, a game which has been bid may come to grief on the rocks of adverse distribution. Far more often, however, when the limit bids are accurately and intelligently used, the right contracts will be reached, the right games bid, and the right hands left in part-scores.

Last and by no means least, the limit bid will have cast the highest possible pre-emptive barrier across the auction which, whilst not taking opener and his partner beyond their depth, will obstruct the opponents' bidding to the fullest possible extent.

When in doubt it is better to over-value your hand than to under-value it. That is to say, when you are not quite sure whether a responding hand is worth a raise to the two or to the three-level, it is better to err on the high side. In cases where you wish you might raise 1♠ to 2½♠, raise to 3♠, not merely to 2♠. This will not happen very often because generally some feature of the hand will tip the scales in favour of one bid or the other, but when in real doubt, make the higher bid. The reason for this is that the higher bid has a higher pre-emptive value. The weaker your partner's opening the less your combined hands contain, leaving all the more for your opponents. Make life as hard for them as possible! Particularly when contemplating a limit bid over an intervening bid from your right-hand opponent—which in itself warns opener of a concentration of strength on his left—call up to the highest possible limit with obstruction in view. Remember that it will pay you to go down one, even doubled and vulnerable, to prevent an unvulnerable game being bid and made against you, and that you can afford two down doubled and vulnerable in exchange for their vulnerable game.

One final word before we go on to the next item on our programme. One of the many reasons why Acol's system of limit bids is so highly successful is that these responses give little or no information to the opponents.

1♠—2♠	1♠—3♠	1♠—2NT	1♠—2NT
4♠	4♠	3NT	4♠

These brief sequences and many others like them, in preference to a complicated and revealing sequence going all around the mulberry bush before arriving at the same contract, tell the opposition virtually nothing except in a general way that some particular suit and a variety of other cards are held. No weakness or spot where attack is least likely to be appreciated has been shown up, which may well make the difference between making the contract or going down, or may assist towards reaping those vital overtricks that every duplicate player prizes so highly.

RESPONDER'S NO TRUMP LIMIT BIDS

Within the terms of reference set out below, that is, when a responding hand does not qualify for a suit limit bid or for a possibly more constructive change-of-suit bid, the values for No Trump limit bids in response are as follows:

1 N.T.   5—9 honour points in a hand which cannot bid a suit at the one-level and is not strong enough to bid at the two-level. The 1 N.T. response *denies* primary trump support, and is little more than a keep-open bid in case partner is

very strong or has a second possible trump suit to show which might fit the combined hands better.

2 N.T.   11—12 honour points in a more or less evenly-balanced hand with no more constructive bid available. Used as a response to a major suit opening, 2 N.T. will *always* deny four-card trump support.

3 N.T.   13-15 points, again on a hand unable to produce a more constructive bid. It is most likely to be one with four-card support for a minor suit opening and good stops in the other suits. It is a strong limit bid but *not* a shut-out, and opener is free to judge his further action, if any, in the light of the information received.

Note the differing responses on the following hands, none of which is strong enough for a change-of-suit bid at the two-level—which would promise 8 or more points:

♠ Q 10 6	1♣—1♡	1◇—1♡	1♡—2♡	1♠—1NT
♡ Q 9 8 5				
◇ 7 6				
♣ K 9 3 2				
♠ Q 10 6	1♣—2♣	1◇—1NT	1♡—INT	1♠—1NT
♡ Q 9 8				
◇ 7 6				
♣ K 9 8 3 2				
♠ 9	1♣—1♡	1◇—1♡	1♡—2♡	1♠—1NT
♡ Q J 8 7 5				
◇ 7 6 2				
♣ K 9 8 3				
♠ 9 3	1♣—1◇	1◇—2◇	1♡—1NT	1♠—1NT
♡ Q 7 2			(not 2◇)	(not 2◇)
◇ Q J 9 6 4				
♣ J 7 2				

The examples above have all referred to hands qualified for no better than a one-level response, either in a suit or 1 N.T. Before going further we should like to stress once again that a response of 1 N.T., in addition to being a 'keep open' bid, is an immediate denial of primary trump support for the suit bid by partner. A one-level suit response promises no more honour strength (5—9 points) than 1 N.T. would do, though it may at this stage conceal a great deal more. A two-level suit response (1♡—2◇) promises a minimum of 8 honour points with a biddable suit, or possibly 7 honour points with a six-card suit (see Chapter 7).

In the table of values for these No Trump limit bids you will see that 10 points is missing, being too good for a 1 N.T. response and not good enough for 2 N.T. With 10 honour points, therefore, responder must judge whether to produce a change-of-suit response (which may not be possible), under-bid his hand by saying 1 N.T. or overbid it by saying 2 N.T. Note that this will not apply if the opening bid is 1♣, and may not apply if it is 1◇ (see Chapter 6 on the prepared minor suit openings and the responses concerned), as the values required for a 1 N.T. response facing either of these opening bids are different, 8—10 points opposite a 1♣ opening and 7—9 points opposite 1◇.

Opening   Response

♠ Q 9 8 7	1) 1♣—1♠
♡ K J 7	2) 1◇—1♠
◇ K J 5	3) 1♡—1♠
♣ 7 6 3	4) 1♠—3♠

There is never any problem when a responding hand contains primary trump support for opener's major suit, or when a one-level response in another suit is available. In this next example, however, in spite of its 10 honour points, the quality of the whole is poor. It is wiser to take a pessimistic view at this early stage to the extent of responding only 1 N.T. (except in the case of the 1♣ opening, when it is the truth). If opener follows 1 N.T. with another forward try you can then come to life.

♠ Q 3 2	1) 1♣—1NT
♡ K J 4	2) 1◇—1NT
◇ K J 5	(See Ch. 6)
♣ 7 4 3 2	3) 1♡—1NT
	4) 1♠—1NT

♠ Q 9 8	Respond 2 N.T.
♡ K J 9	to any one-
◇ K J 9	level opening
♣ 10 9 8 6	bid.

This is the same hand as the one above as far as honour points are concerned, but its whole quality has changed. It is no longer threadbare as the intermediates are all good, for which reason it is better to err on the high side and bid 2 N.T., for which it is, in any case, only ½ point under strength.

♠ Q 5 3	1) 1♣—1◇
♡ Q 10 8	2) 1◇—3◇
◇ A Q 9 7	3) 1♡—2◇
♣ Q 10 8	4) 1♠—2◇

The two examples above were of hands on which it was impossible to compromise by bidding a suit at the two-level. Here is a hand on which it is possible to get out of all trouble by bidding your suit at either level, as necessary, with no fear of misleading opener.

Now we come on to the hands containing a genuine 2 N.T. limit bid response. This is a useful bid because, as well as being highly pre-emptive, it shows the honour count held, 11—12 points, indicates that responder has no sensible change-of-suit response to make, has not got primary trump support, at any rate for a major suit opening, though he has a bit of 'something in everything'. The 11—12 points required are the same whether opener has bid a major or minor suit though, as you will learn in Chapter 7, it is possible for your response to vary according to your position at the table, that is, whether or not you have previously passed—you would not open the bidding on an evenly-balanced 11 points, though you would probably open 1 N.T. on 12 points, and certainly would do so if not vulnerable.

	Opening	*Response*
♠	K 7 6	1♣—1♡
♡	Q 9 8 4	1♢—1♡
♢	A 7 4	1♡—3♡
♣	Q 10 8	1♠—2NT

Over a minor suit opening you have a choice between responding 1♡ or 2 N.T. The former is the better and more constructive choice *unless* you have previously passed (see Chapter 7). Facing an opening 1♡, as before, there is no problem, a 3♡ raise being in order. Over 1♠ use the 2 N.T. limit bid in preference to 2♡.

♠	K J 7 6	1♣—1♠
♡	J 6 5	1♢—1♠
♢	A 7 4	1♡—1♠
♣	Q J 10	1♠—3♠

These are the possibly more helpful responses *unless* you have previously passed, in which case, though the raise of 1♠ to 3♠ would, of course, remain unchanged, it would be better to show the full values held by the 2 N.T. limit bid in response to a *red* suit opening. However, if opener, third or fourth-in-hand, opens 1♣, the 1♠ response is still the wiser choice. Remember that it is correct to open 1♣ holding the two *black* suits, so a response of 2 N.T. might prejudice a spade contract. Another factor which has important bearing is that a player will seldom if ever open up the auction as third or fourth-in-hand with a sketchy bid of 1♣, and will either hold spades as well or a hand strong enough to rebid on his own in comfort. The 1♣ opening lets the opposition in to compete for a part-score too easily for this opening to be a wise move on a weak hand.

♠ K 7 6   Respond 2 N.T.   Whatever partner's opening bid,
♡ Q J 8   to any one-   even 1♣, 2 N.T. is the best response
♢ A 7 4   level opening   on a hand of this sort. 3♣, the only
♣ Q 9 8 4   bid.   possible alternative, might well be
                                       passed out when there is a good
play for 3 N.T. Responder has 'something in everything', and his
club holding must 'boost' opener's, whether his bid is natural or
'prepared'.

Lastly in this section we come to the 3 N.T. limit bid, showing
13—15 honour points. This is a bid to be avoided if it is at all
possible to find another expressive of the hand in question, as its
high level is apt to inconvenience subsequent slam exploration by
opener. It goes without saying that, since with 13 points, there will
have been no previous pass, the only occasion for the use of this
bid will be in response to a dealer's or second-in-hand opening. Just
occasionally, however, hands will crop up on which there is no
sensible alternative, for which reason it is included in the system.
The 3 N.T. response is *not* a shut-out bid, even if it may be
difficult to bid on over it, and opener can go on for a slam if he
thinks that the combined values warrant it.

♠ J 10 9   Whatever suit partner opens, including 1♣, there is
♡ A Q 8   no satisfactory response here except 3 N.T. One could,
♢ Q J 8   of course, respond 2♣ to 1♢, 1♡, or 1♠, intending
♣ Q J 8 4   to convert the opener's rebid to 3 N.T., but this leaves
                 the way far more widely open for the opposition to
find a cheap 'save'. In any case it is a hand which lends itself well to
a No Trump contract, and responder might as well say so straight
away. In the case of responding to a 1♣ opening, with no alternative
suit to show, it would be folly to make the non-forcing limit bid
of 3♣ which stands a great risk of being passed out when 3 N.T.
is 'cold'.

♠ Q 7 5   If partner opens 1♣ or 1♢, respond 1♡, not 3 N.T.
♡ A J 10 5   Similarly if he opens 1♠, respond 2♣ and in either
♢ K 8   case make sure game is reached by rebidding 3 N.T.
♣ A 10 6 4   unless opener's own rebid is a strong one suggesting
                 a slam try on responder's part.

So try to avoid using this 3 N.T. response except on hands of
4-3-3-3 pattern whose strength cannot be shown in any other way.
When a responding hand shows promise of a slam, a forcing-to-game
switch should be preferred. This may safely be made in a short
suit provided adequate support for opener's suit is held, and also
provided the short suit is lower-ranking than opener's, so that the
final contract can always be returned cheaply to opener's suit. This
is more fully covered in Chapter 9 on responder's rebids. In the

meantime remember that all limit bids, whether in No Trumps as above, or in the suit opened, as earlier in this chapter, are once-and-for-all bids. They deny the ability to bid more strongly as well as announcing a specific minimum.

Let us now, however, return to the original light opening hand

♠ A Q J 8 6 2
♡ K 10 4 2
♢ 7 5
♣ 8

from Chapter 2, quoting it again for easy reference. You open 1♠ to which partner responds either 1 N.T. or 2♠, both weak limit bids. There is no sensible course for opener to take except to convert 1 N.T. smartly to 2♠ or pass the 2♠ response. This hand facing 5—9 points will not yield a game. But the return to 2♠ is no longer a sign-off bid, as it was in Chapter 2 when responder made a change-of-suit response—it is opener's decision as to the best final contract in the light of the values shown by responder.

OPENER'S INVITATIONAL REBID AFTER LIMIT BID IN RESPONSE

The important point to remember here is that no limit bid is forcing. In other words opener, following a limit bid from his partner, is under no obligation to bid again. But this does not mean that the auction will necessarily be dropped at this point, because opener himself may decide to issue a strong invitation to his partner or to make a forcing bid which responder must again answer. It is, unfortunately, taking matters somewhat out of order to deal with opener's rebids here when Chapter 8 is devoted entirely to this aspect of bidding, but to avoid unnecessary confusion note the following.

Facing responder's suit limit bid, opener may make either a Trial or a Cue bid (Chapter 10) both of which are one-round forces to which responder must, of course, reply. Facing responder's No Trump limit bid somewhat different positions can arise. For

1♡—1NT
3♡

example in this first sequence responder has shown lack of primary support for hearts in a hand which may contain from 5—9 points and in this particular case, because responder did not choose to respond with the equally cheap bid of 1♠, no biddable spade suit. Opener in his turn shows a good strong hand with at least a six-card heart suit and *invites* his partner to raise to game in spite of his limit bid if there is any justification for doing so. This, of course, will be if responder holds a near maximum for his 1 N.T. response instead of 5 or 6 points, and some sort of heart fit.

1♡—1NT
2NT

In much the same way here, opener is showing a good hand on which he is just short of the values to bid game direct—probably 17 or 18 points—and asks responder to bid 3 N.T. with 8 or 9 points, though permitting him to pass if he doesn't fancy the chances.

In such situations the implications of opener's rebid are clear. After responder's limit bid it is opener's responsibility to judge whether or not to let the bidding rest or go further. If he can bid game direct he should do so without putting the onus of choice on responder. Alternatively on a weak opening hand and weak response he may either pass the limit bid or convert to what he thinks will be a better part-score contract at the lowest available level. If he does neither of these things he is either too strong or not strong enough to be sure of the best final contract, in which case he passes the decision back to responder.

♠ A K J 8 5   You open 1♠ in response to which your partner
♡ J 10 4   bids 2♠. Pass—you will be very lucky if your
◇ K 7   combined hands fit so well that you make ten
♣ J 10 8   tricks. If instead of 2♠ responder bids 3♠, accept
               his invitation and bid 4♠. If the original response
is 1 N.T., pass. There will be a *maximum* combined count of 22 points and, with quite a suitable hand for this denomination, 1 N.T. may well be easier to make than 2♠. If the response is 2 N.T. raise to 3 N.T., assured of a combined count of 25 points.

♠ A Q J 9   You open 1♠. If responder bids *either* 1 N.T. *or*
♡ K 8 7   2♠, issue an invitation by rebidding 2 N.T. This
◇ J 10 9   will show a 17-18 point hand with almost certainly
♣ A Q 8   only a four-card trump suit, and also just in-
               sufficient strength to plump for 3 N.T. or 4♠
without being sure of maximum support from responder. In other words it is too good to pass without a further try and responder can pass 2 N.T., raise to 3 N.T., or convert to either 3♠ or 4♠ once he has revalued his hand in the light of the information received. If the original response is 3♠ instead of a weaker bid, rebid 3 N.T., leaving responder to judge whether to pass or convert to 4♠.

♠ A K J 8 6 2 You open 1♠ which responder raises to 2♠. No
♡ K 10 4   messing about this time—bid 4♠ direct. If instead
◇ A Q 5   the original response is 1 N.T. bid 3♠ invitationally,
♣ 6   showing approximately seven playing tricks with
               spades as trumps and asking responder if he can
see his way to bidding 4♠. If the original response is 2 N.T., rebid 4♠, for which the hand is far better suited than for a No Trump contract.

1♡—2NT   Before we go on please note that, if you are using
3♡—3NT   the system accurately, a bidding sequence such as
or 4♡   this simply cannot happen. Opener's 3♡ rebid is
          neither invitational nor forcing, but his considered
opinion as to the best final contract in the light of his partner's
response. The only possible excuse for responder's second bid would
be if he had accidentally miscounted his hand in the first place!

OPENER'S FORCING REBID AFTER 2 N.T. RESPONSE

You will doubtless have noticed that whenever the responder's limit
bid of 2 N.T. has been mentioned it has been qualified by the words
'when no more constructive change-of-suit bid is available'. This is
because, though the 2 N.T. response is extremely useful on many
occasions, it is one which can cause difficulties to opener. In other
words, though to a lesser extent than the immediate response of
3 N.T., 2 N.T. is to be avoided if a more constructive change-of-suit
bid can be made.

It is also important to remember than any new suit bid at the
three-level is a one-round force. Compare this sequence with the
          one in the previous section where the three-level
1♡—2NT   rebid in opener's original suit was neither invita-
3◇   tional nor forcing. Here 3◇ is forcing, the reason
for which is not far to seek—opener may find himself in an extremely
embarrassing position if he fears that his new suit rebid may be
passed. There will, of course, be hands from time to time on which
the opening bid is based on 'shape' rather that a good honour count,
and on such occasions opener may well wish that his rebid were not
forcing! But these will be greatly outweighed by the times on which
the best result will be obtained by treating the three-level bid as a
one-round force.

♠ A K J 6 5   You open 1♠ and if responder raises to 2♠ you
♡ K 8   bid 4♠ direct. If his response were 2♡ instead
◇ A Q 10 6 3   you have every intention of rebidding 3◇, a new
♣ 9   suit at the three-level and a one-round force (see
               Chapter 8). So now when the response is an
immediate 2 N.T. you still bid 3◇, a bid which *demands* an answer,
even if this is only 3 N.T. Obviously if responder has 11-12 points
you want to play in at least a game though at this point are not
sure what the best denomination is going to be.

♠ 8
♡ A Q 10 7 6
◇ A Q 9 6
♣ A J 7

Consider also the plight of opener who, having bid 1♡, hears the response of 2 N.T. There may well be a slam available if responder has a diamond fit but, unless the 3◇ rebid is forcing, opener is faced with an impossible situation. Does he jump to 4◇, rebid 4♡, or 'shoot' 3 N.T. with no idea of what the best denomination really is, or at what level the hand should be played?

♠ A J 10 6 3
♡ Q 7 4
◇ 6
♣ K J 9 6

At the lower end of the scale you open 1♠ third-in-hand and get the one response you want least to hear—2 N.T. Since 3♣ would be forcing and a rebid of 3♠ as likely to be disastrous as safer, let partner struggle in his 2 N.T. Do not try to rescue him as any effort along these lines is fraught with danger!

Being a one-round force only, the three-level rebid does not commit the partnership to an astronomical minor suit contract. In

1♡—2NT
3◇—?

the sequence already quoted, for example, responder can rebid 3 N.T., and if opener decides to take this out into 4◇ asking for preference, responder can pass. Alternatively he could give an immediate raise of the 3◇ bid to 4◇ or make a simple preference bid of 3♡, either of which opener could pass if this seemed to him the wisest course.

There are many situations in which responder, having made a change-of-suit response in the first place, can use the point-showing limit bid on the next round. These are covered in Chapter 9.

REVISION QUIZ ON CHAPTER 3

1) What response would you make to your partner's opening 1♠ on the following hands?

    a) ♠ Q 7 6 3 : ♡ J 3 : ◇ 1 0 9 7 4 2 : ♣ K 3 :
    b) ♠ K J 9 3 : ♡ K 4 3 : ◇ 6 5 : ♣ K 9 4 2 :
    c) ♠ 1 0 9 8 5 4 : ♡ 3 2 : ◇ K Q 1 0 7 6 : ♣ 4 :
    d) ♠ K J 9 4 : ♡ 5 : ◇ Q J 9 6 5 4 3 : ♣ 4 :
    e) ♠ K Q 1 0 : ♡ K Q J 9 6 4 : ◇ 6 3 : ♣ 5 4 :

2) What response would you make to your partner's opening 1♡ on the following hands?

    a) ♠ Q J 9 : ♡ Q 4 : ◇ J 9 7 3 : ♣ 1 0 9 8 6 :
    b) ♠ K 9 8 : ♡ K 4 : ◇ Q J 5 4 : ♣ Q J 3 2 :
    c) ♠ Q J 7 : ♡ J : ◇ Q 1 0 6 3 2 : ♣ 7 4 3 2 :
    d) ♠ Q 5 4 2 : ♡ J 1 0 : ◇ Q 5 4 3 : ♣ Q 7 5 :
    e) ♠ A Q 9 : ♡ J 1 0 3 : ◇ Q J 6 3 : ♣ Q J 9 :

3) Having opened the bidding with 1♡, what would you rebid if partner's response is 1 N.T.?

    a) ♠ K 7 5 : ♡ Q 1 0 9 7 4 2 : ◇ K 3 : ♣ A 4 :
    b) ♠ K 4 : ♡ A K Q 9 6 5 : ◇ A 4 2 : ♣ 7 4 :

What is your rebid if partner's response to 1♡ is 2 N.T.?

    c) ♠ J 4 : ♡ A K J 9 6 3 2 : ◇ A 4 : ♣ 1 0 9 :
    d) ♠ Q J 4 : ♡ A K Q 6 2 : ◇ Q J 4 : ♣ J 1 0 :
    e) ♠ J 6 : ♡ A K Q 9 7 : ◇ J 9 7 : ♣ J 6 4 :

What is your rebid if partner's response to 1♡ is 3 N.T.?

    f) ♠ Q 4 : ♡ K J 1 0 9 7 5 3 : ◇ A 4 : ♣ Q 5 :
    g) ♠ Q 9 3 : ♡ A K Q 5 4 : ◇ 9 6 2 : ♣ K 4 :
    h) ♠ 9 : ♡ A K J 9 6 : ◇ A J 9 4 2 : ♣ K Q :

4) You open 1♡ to which your partner responds 2◇. What is your rebid?

    a) ♠ K 7 : ♡ A K J 9 7 6 : ◇ 8 : ♣ K 9 8 7 :
    b) ♠ J 7 : ♡ A Q 1 0 9 7 6 : ◇ 8 2 : ♣ K 1 0 8 :
    c) ♠ J 7 : ♡ A K J 9 7 6 : ◇ A 8 : ♣ K Q 9 :

ANSWERS TO REVISION QUIZ ON CHAPTER 3

1) a) 2♠   A simple Limit Bid in spades, by far the best and most expressive bid on this hand.

   b) 3♠   This is the stronger Limit Bid, of course, and tells your partner you are too strong to bid 2♠ and not strong enough to bid more.

   c) 4♠   A purely pre-emptive bid based on trump support and 'shape'.

   d) 3♠   If opener has a fit with you in diamonds, this will merely be an asset towards a spade contract.

   e) 2♡   There is nothing odd about this one—a perfectly straightforward take-out into your own good suit.

2) a) 1 NT On 6 points you must keep the bidding open, so use this weak limit bid.

   b) 2 NT A Limit Bid showing just what you have—a balanced hand with 11-12 points.

   c) 1 NT Your hand is unsuitable for No Trumps but you are not strong enough to show a suit at the two-level. All you can hope for is that partner can show a second suit.

   d) 1♠   Some players would bid 1 N.T., but 1♠ is better style and more constructive *unless* you've previously passed, when the 1 N.T. response is wiser.

   e) 3 NT You have 13 balanced points and no other constructive bid, so bid your limit at once.

3) a) 2♡   Rebid your six-card suit as, facing responder's limit bid, you are now responsible for selecting the final contract.

   b) 3♡   You are too strong for a mere 2♡ bid. Tell your partner that your hearts are long and strong and that you had better than a light opener. He will pass if he is minimum, but will raise to 4♡ if he possibly can.

   c) 4♡   Facing a known minimum of 11 points you want to be in game. You prefer hearts to No Trumps and the final contract is up to you.

   d) 3 NT You have something in every suit and your hearts should be most helpful.

e) Pass Pass in sleep, as they say. Partner's balanced 11 points plus your 12 are unlikely to produce game and you have no reason to think 3♡ would be a better contract than 2 N.T.

f) 4♡ Obviously a better bet from your point of view. Responder, having bid No Trumps, certainly will not have worse than a doubleton in your suit.

g) Pass 3 N.T. should be as good a contract as any other.

h) 4◇ Apart from being allergic to No Trumps, you have two good suits, either of which could produce slam, let alone game, if you find the right fit. Partner must bid again, even if only to return you to 4♡. The 4◇ bid is forcing and responder must either raise to 5◇ or give preference to 4♡.

4) a) 3♡ This strongly invites partner to bid 4♡ though he is permitted to pass if absolutely minimum for his bid and with no heart fit.

b) 2♡ The simple signing-off rebid, as you have no ambitions towards a game contract.

c) 3♣ The new suit at the three-level is a one-round force which may be made on a short suit to facilitate finding the best final contract.

Chapter 4

One No Trump Opening Bids and Responses

THE No Trump opening bids and responses are as vital a part of the Acol System as are the light opening bids and limit bids. We are discussing them next, not as a matter of priority, but because it is not possible to cover everything simultaneously!

Unlike opening suit bids, openings of either 1 N.T. or 2 N.T. can both be regarded as limit bids as, like the No Trump responses covered in the previous chapter, they are made on clearly limited and defined counts. The 2 N.T. opening is fully dealt with in Chapter 13 so, in the meantime, we confine ourselves to the 1 N.T. bid and the responses to it.

Standard Acol advocates an opening bid of 1 N.T. on a balanced hand of 12-14 points not vulnerable and 15-17 points vulnerable, which is known as 'variable'. In practice, however, you will find that there are many different schools of thought as to the values required and that there are, in fact, many more variations than the one above. Many rubber bridge players, even in this day and age, favour a 16-18 point No Trump whatever the score, but there is much to be said in favour of either 'variable' or 'weak throughout', which means 12-14 points at all times. Perhaps the ultimate choice should be left to individual temperament, though at Match Pointed Pairs particularly the advantages of using 'weak throughout' can be tremendous. For one thing, the frequency with which suitable hands for it occur gives its adherents wide scope for the use of this most pre-emptive of all opening one-bids. It is often difficult for the opposition to intervene against it, and it can be extremely awkward to deal with in the 'protective' position.

A word of explanation here—when you come to the raises of opening No Trump bids you will see that, facing a 12-14 point opener, it is correct for responder to pass on anything up to 10 points in a balanced hand. This in turn means that, when fourth-in-hand after two passes, a player will not know whether he is competing against a combined 22 or even 24, points or whether his partner, who has passed the 1 N.T. opening, has a share of the goodies, and this can make life very difficult. Furthermore, left undisturbed, the 1 N.T. contract can be most difficult to defend, and many a declarer has sneaked away with his 90 points for 1 N.T. bid and made when the opponents have two, or even three of a suit 'on'. Even the loss of 100 points for one down vulnerable scores well at M.P.Pairs against the opponents' 110 for 2♡ or 2♠. On the other hand, it is no use denying that a vulnerable 1 N.T. bid on 12 points, doubled and left in, can result in the most almighty 'bottom', being a tempting target for opponents with the balance of the strength. This is a risk which many experts are fully prepared to take, being of the opinion that, for the once you will get into trouble, you will gain a dozen times, and surely this is a very fair exchange! If you don't like the nervous strain of what *may* happen, then stick to 'variable', but remember that then you will very likely be opening one of a minor suit which can easily be over-called by your opponents. True you will not risk your 'bottom', but you will miss many a more than compensating 'top'.

From now on we shall not speak of vulnerable or unvulnerable opening No Trump bids, but of weak or strong. Weak is 12-14 points, and strong is 15-17. If you learn the mechanics of both you will be equipped to deal with any variation you may meet, or may be required to play when with a strange partner. It is not very difficult to adjust the values required for the various raises or responses to a slightly different opening strength.

Whatever the agreed strength of the opening No Trump, it should be used for hands within its qualifying range which are 4—3—3—3 in pattern, or perhaps 4—4—3—2. There are also strategic positions where the bid can be made with a five-card suit, of which you will find one example below.

♠ A 7
♡ K 10 6
♢ K J 8 5 4
♣ Q 7 3

You will remember that, as opener or second-in-hand, if you open one of a suit, you promise a sensible rebid which, on this hand, you have not got. In Chapter 8, when we come to opener's rebids you will find that a *rebid* of 1 N.T. (1♢—1♠—1 N.T.) requires 14-15 points, and a rebid at the forced level of two (1♢—2♣—2 N.T.) requires 15-17 points. You can get out of an awkward situation such as this by opening 1 N.T. which requires no rebid except to answer any forcing response from your partner. The following hands are, however, far more typical for the bid :

♠ K J 7 6	♠ J 8 6	♠ K 6
♡ Q 9 8	♡ A Q 3	♡ A 7 6 2
♢ A 9 3	♢ K 10 8 7	♢ K Q 5
♣ K 8 4	♣ Q 9 6	♣ 10 9 7 4

In each case, if you add another honour card to bring them into the

15-17 point range, they would make excellent strong No Trump opening hands.

It follows, of course, that once you and your partner have agreed your opening No Trump range, you step outside it at your peril. A responder expecting his partner to hold a maximum of 14 points will not raise on 10 points and, if opener has, in fact, 16 points, a perfectly sound game contract will be missed. Conversely, if your agreed range is 15-17 points, you can expect responder to gauge his responses accordingly. He will raise you direct to 3 N.T. on 9+ points, and you may come sadly to grief if you have opened in the 12-14 point range.

Before we go on to the responses to 1 N.T. opening bids, refresh your memory as to the basis for them, which was set out briefly in Chapter 1. Given a fair share of the good breaks, 25 points between two more or less evenly balanced hands stand an excellent chance of producing the nine tricks required for a No Trump game, and the counts are calculated on this basis. Good 'intermediates' such as 9's and 10's (the latter being counted as $\frac{1}{2}$ point in No Trump bidding) and useful suit length must be given full weight.

DIRECT RAISES IN NO TRUMPS

Accuracy is the key-note of these opening No Trump bids and direct No Trump raises. You will see that it is occasionally possible to get into 3 N.T. on a combined 24 points—a figure which most expert card-players would agree is reasonable—and a lucky distribution or finesse has often brought home the bacon on fewer points than this. You're unlikely to stay out of 3 N.T. on 25 points, though conversely, bad breaks and losing finesses can well upset the apple-cart on even a good many more points.

The values required for direct raises in No Trumps are a matter of simple arithmetic. On an evenly balanced hand in itself suitable for No Trump play, and bearing in mind the target-figure of 25 points for a game, responder should add his point count to opener's known *minimum*. If the total comes to within 2 points of 25 (remember that the opening bid has a permissible 'spread' of 3 points), then raise to 2 N.T., an invitation to opener to bid the game, which you are just not strong enough to do yourself, if he has the maximum, or near maximum, for his bid. If the total comes to 25 or more, you bid 3 N.T. direct unless, of course, it is so very much more that you suspect a possible slam (33-34 points between two evenly balanced hands) when you can take much stronger action. We shall be dealing with these situations later. In the meantime, if opener bids:

1 N.T. weak	Responder:	
(12-14 points)	Raises to	2 N.T. on 11-12 points
	„ „	3 N.T. on 12+ points
and if opener bids 1 N.T. strong	„ „	2 N.T. on 8-9 points
(15-17 points)	„ „	3 N.T. on 9+ points

Opener bids 1 N.T. weak (12-14 points)

Responder holds:

♠ Q 6 3	♠ Q 6 3	♠ A 6 3
♡ Q 2	♡ Q 2	♡ Q 2
◇ K J 8 6	◇ A Q 8 6	◇ A Q 8 6
♣ Q 9 6 2	♣ J 9 6 2	♣ J 9 6 2
12 (opener's minimum) +10=22 which opener cannot make up to game values. Pass.	12+11=23 so raise to 2 N.T. invitationally.	12+13=25 so raise to 3 N.T. direct.

Opener bids 1 N.T. strong (15-17 points)

Responder holds:

♠ Q 6 2	♠ Q 6 2	♠ A 6 2
♡ Q 2	♡ Q 2	♡ Q 2
◇ K 9 8 6	◇ K 9 8 6	◇ K 9 8 6
♣ 9 8 6 2	♣ J 10 9 6	♣ J 9 8 6
15 (opener's minimum) +7=22 which opener cannot make up to game values. Pass.	$15+8\frac{1}{2}=23\frac{1}{2}$ so raise to 2 N.T. invitationally.	15+10=25 so raise to 3 N.T. direct.

WEAK TAKE-OUT RESPONSES

A take-out in a suit at the two-level (except conventionally in clubs which we shall deal with in the next chapter) is a *weak* bid. It doesn't matter whether the opening No Trump itself is weak or strong, except that this will influence responder's view of whether or not he should make a weak take-out. But whatever the strength of the opening bid, a response of 2♠, 2♡, or 2◇ is in the nature of a rescue operation, being made on an unbalanced hand containing a long suit—at least five and more probably six—more likely to be of value if used as trumps than in a No trump contract. If responder sees the likelihood of a game in a suit contract he will take stronger action (see p. 59), so the weak take-out is reserved strictly for hands with which responder, knowing his partner's limits, sees no chance for game, but prefers the suit contract to No Trumps.

♠ 10 8 7 5 4 3
♡ 7 2
◇ 7 5
♣ Q 7 5

Whatever the strength of the opening 1 N.T., take out into 2♠ which, if used as trumps, are bound to be valuable whereas opener, left to play in 1 N.T., can never hope to get anywhere. The story would be the same if the suit were either hearts or diamonds—take out at the two level.

♠ 8
♡ Q 8 7
◇ K J 9 7 5 3
♣ 8 7 6

Again here, whatever the strength of the opening 1 N.T., take out into 2◇ which should be safe whereas in No Trumps it must be highly doubtful. You will see that in both these examples there is no question of the combined hands reaching game values, either in points or with distributional points coming into the picture.

In both the above examples the suit used for the 'rescue' was of six cards. In cases where responder has only a five-card suit correct judgement is, perhaps, a little more difficult. Compare the following on which admittedly you cannot be certain that your chosen action will be for the best, but on which the probability is that it is wisest:

♠ J 8 6
♡ 9
◇ A K 8 5 3
♣ J 7 6 4

Facing a weak No Trump game is extremely unlikely and 2◇ will almost certainly be a safer contract, so take out. Facing a strong No Trump, however, raise to 2 N.T. invitationally, in spite of the heart weakness.

♠ Q 6
♡ J 7 5 4 2
◇ Q 10 7 3
♣ 8 7

Facing either a weak or strong No Trump it is probably wiser to pass. You have no reason to suppose that the hand will play more safely in hearts than in 1 N.T.

♠ 7
♡ J 10 8 4
◇ A 9 5 3 2
♣ 6 4 2

Again, whatever the opening 1 N.T., pass. If you turn back to p. 54 of this chapter you will remind yourself of the difficulty the fourth player may have in deciding whether or not to compete. If you bid 2◇ you only tip him off as to your weakness. In any case, opener has not yet been doubled, and though he may not make seven tricks, he has just about as good a chance as you have of making 2◇.

A response of 2♣ to an opening 1 N.T. is conventional (see Chapter 5) so this means, of course, that you cannot bid 2♣ intending it purely as a weak take-out. If, therefore, your hand is such that you would prefer to play in a low club contract, the correct procedure is to bid 2♣ as your first response and then go on to repeat 3♣ over your partner's rebid. This will tell him that your

2♣ bid was a weak take-out and nothing more. For this reason a weak responding hand with no better than a five-card club suit should never disturb 1 N.T., so that the 2♣ bid and 3♣ repeat should only be used on a six, or even seven-card club suit and 'tram tickets'.

There is never any onus on responder to dredge up a reply to a No Trump opening bid if he can see that a game contract is impracticable or that a safer suit contract is not being missed. On evenly balanced hands he should pass or raise, according to his strength, or take out into a suit either weakly or strongly, again according to his strength. This, of course, is because opener's strength is strictly and precisely limited, not unknown as it is in the case of a suit opening, so that there is no urgency to keep the auction open in the hope that a better fit or a higher contract may be reached.

From opener's side of the table, if responder raises 1 N.T. to 2 N.T., opener should pass if holding the minimum for his bid, or accept the invitation to go on to 3 N.T. if better than minimum. In some cases this may depend on the quality of the hand apart from actual honour points, for example:

♠ Q 5 2
♡ K 4 3 2
♢ A 7 5
♣ A 4 3

You open 1 N.T. weak on this 13-point hand and responder bids 2 N.T. You have absolutely no 'stuffing' so, unless responder has his maximum of 12 points, you are hardly likely to be able to make nine tricks. Pass—but add a knave somewhere and you must bid 3 N.T. regardless.

♠ Q 9 8
♡ K 9 7 6
♢ A 7 5
♣ A 9 6

Here the intermediates are excellent, and it would be dangerous to pass a 2 N.T. raise. 9's and even 8's can develop a trick-taking capacity far more quickly than 4's and 3's!

Finally, if responder makes a weak take-out into two of a suit, opener should always respect the warning that his partner has a weak hand unsuitable for play in No Trumps. For this reason he should *never* rebid 2 N.T., though just occasionally, if maximum and his partner's suit bid hits the jackpot of a good four-card fit, he can raise to three of the suit.

STRONG (JUMP) TAKE-OUT RESPONSES

Obviously when partner opens 1 N.T., many responding hands will be too good for a weak take-out into a suit at the two-level, though clearly better fitted for a suit game contract than for play in No

Trumps. These will be 'shape' hands with a good suit to suggest as trumps as well as a point count high enough for a game contract, and these are shown by a jump bid in the suit. It includes clubs this time, and is game-forcing, either in the suit or to 3 N.T.

There is a distinction between the jump take-out in the majors and in the minors. In the case of the majors, responder would prefer a game contract in four of his suit, but in the minors five is a lot to make. As responder you should, therefore, either be prepared to stand opener's conversion to 3 N.T. or to go on to game in your minor suit if you make a jump bid in clubs or diamonds. In principle, therefore, it is better to reserve the jump bid in a minor as a warning to opener of some weakness elsewhere which may prove dangerous in No Trumps, or as a possible prelude to a slam contract. Otherwise bid 3 N.T. direct without putting the onus of decision on opener.

From the other side of the table, opener should raise a jump to either 3♡ or 3♠ to four with as good as a three-card fit, but with only a doubleton he may rebid 3 N.T. Thus if the bidding goes 1 NT—3♠—4♠, responder will be sure of at least three-card support and can investigate further for a slam if he feels this may be a likely resting-place. In the minors opener's decision may be a little more difficult, but most particularly if he himself has a marked weakness in one of the other three suits, should prefer a raise of responder's suit to a rebid of 3 N.T. This may cause the occasional poor result at M.P. Pairs (where 3 N.T. + 1 gives a much better score than even five of a minor bid and made plus one) but is likely to produce many safer contracts.

♠ K J 9 7 6 3
♡ A 4
♢ J 9 4
♣ 7 2

Even with distributional points added, this hand only comes up to 10 points. Opposite a weak No Trump take out into 2♠, which is likely to be an easier contract than 1 N.T. Opposite a strong No Trump bid 3♠.

♠ 7 6
♡ 4
♢ K J 10 6 4 2
♣ A 9 8 6

Opposite a weak No Trump bid 2♢. Opposite a strong No Trump bid 3♢ and pass if opener rebids 3 N.T. This should stand an excellent chance of making as, apart from the likelihood that opener has at least one honour in diamonds, the hand contains a certain outside entry.

♠ 10 6
♡ 7 4
♢ A K J 9 7 4
♣ 9 8 7

Opposite a weak No Trump take out into 2♢. Opposite a strong No Trump raise to 3 N.T., the deciding factor here being that you have no possible wish to play in 5♢.

♠ K Q 10
♡ A Q 6
♦ K J 10 8 7 3
♣ 5

Whatever the strength of the opening No Trump, bid 3◇. If it is a weak 1 N.T. and opener rebids 3 N.T., pass. If he raises instead to 4◇ try a cue-bid of 4♡ to test the possibilities of a diamond slam. If the opening No Trump is strong a slam is an interesting idea from the word go.

♠ J 9
♡ A 9 7 3
♦ K J 6
♣ K 8 6 3

From opener's side of the table, having bid 1 N.T. on this hand, raise a jump response of 3♡ to 4♡. If, however, the response were 3♠, rebid 3 N.T., leaving it to responder to judge whether to remove to 4♠ or pass 3 N.T.

♠ A Q
♡ K J 8
♦ K 8 6 5
♣ 7 6 4 2

It goes without saying that there will be times when judgement rather than strict adherence to rules must take over. Having opened 1 N.T. you are in no trouble if partner responds 3♡, as you merely raise to 4♡. If, however, he responds 3♠ you must judge whether to raise to 4♠ on the doubleton or rebid 3 N.T. with one suit (clubs) 'wide open'. If responder prefers the idea of a spade contract when he is missing his own ♣ A-Q, then surely it is better to let him play in spades, of which he is hardly likely to hold less than six to the ♠ K-J, than to insist that you want to play in No Trumps. Raise to 4♠.

ADVANCE CUE BIDS

There is one other opener's rebid which falls into place here, and that is an advance cue bid. If you play your Acol with a partner who is prepared to learn as much as you will know when you have absorbed this book, then read on. But otherwise you might as well skip this section, as nothing but disaster is likely to result from making an advance cue bid if you are playing with someone who will not know what you are talking about! In any case it is not an essential part of the Acol System, but merely an adjunct to it.

You will find more about these bids in Chapter 10 but, in the meantime, an advance cue bid is one which shows a first-round control when the trump suit has not been agreed by a direct raise.

1 NT—3♡
4♡

In this sequence, opener raises to 4♡, confirming the trump fit, and now if responder wants to go on to investigate a slam he is welcome to do so—but must start at rather a high level, especially as he does not yet know anything about opener's hand except that it contains 12-14 points and heart support. Such a situation can often be eased by the use of an advance cue bid, an opener's rebid in another suit, the meaning of which is that opener's hand is maximum, contains an excellent trump fit, and also first-round control of the suit in which the advance cue bid is made. It costs the partnership nothing in bidding-space as responder's original jump bid was forcing to game anyway, and may facilitate the rest of the auction considerably if responder is slam-minded.

♠ K 9 4
♡ Q 10 8 7
♢ K J 6
♣ A J 8

You open 1 N.T. to which your partner responds 3♡. It costs nothing at all to rebid 4♣ on this hand instead of a mere 4♡. 4♣ shows a maximum (14 point) opening, excellent heart support, and the ♣A. (You would not open 1 N.T. with a club void, so it must be the ace.)

One word of warning here, concerning the negative inference to be drawn from the fact that opener rebids 3 N.T. or raises responder's suit instead of making an advance cue bid. A 3 N.T. rebid will, of course, have shown that responder's suit is not opener's favourite. A raise of responder's suit instead of an advance cue bid should be understood as a warning that opener's hand is not maximum and responder, if he decides to make further slam investigations, must do so with this knowledge.

JUMP TAKE-OUT RESPONSE TO GAME LEVEL

An immediate take-out of the 1 N.T. opening bid into four of a major denotes a very unbalanced hand containing a long major suit and very little else. The bid announces that the hand is worthless except when played in the suit named by responder.

♠ 7
♡ A J 10 9 8 7 3
♢ 7
♣ J 9 7 5

There is no point in forcing with 3♡ here, and then taking out opener's possible 3 N.T. rebid into 4♡, when you know that the hand must be played in hearts and that, distributionally, there is a good chance of making game on it. Bid the game direct, which also has the highest possible pre-emptive value against your fourth-in-hand opponent who might well have his eye on a spade contract.

An immediate jump to 4♢ is purely pre-emptive, and made on a hand which is virtually a 'blizzard' except for something like seven or eight to the ♢K-Q. A jump to 4♣ cannot be made, as this bid is the 'Gerber' convention explained in Chapter 5.

A somewhat stronger hand in either clubs or diamonds should be bid direct to game in the suit, both as a pre-emptive measure against an opposition get-together in one of the majors, and because it seems the most possible game contract.

♠ 9
♡ 8 6
◇ A 4
♣ K Q 9 8 7 5 4 2

It is unlikely that a jump to 5♣ will mean a missed slam on this hand, as partner's No Trump opener will have to take care of a minimum of five losers. It is also a contract with excellent chances of success, especially against a blind opposition lead.

REVISION QUIZ ON CHAPTER 4

1) Playing weak No Trump throughout, what do you open on the following hands?

    a) ♠ K 9 4: ♡ Q 10 2: ◇ A J 9 4: ♣ Q J 6:
    b) ♠ K J 10: ♡ Q 10 9 8: ◇ K J: ♣ A J 4 3.
    c) ♠ Q 4 3: ♡ Q J 4: ◇ Q 7 4: ♣ A K 6 3:
    d) ♠ A Q 4: ♡ 8 7 4 2: ◇ K Q 10: ♣ A Q 10:
    e) ♠ Q 10 4: ♡ Q 9 3: ◇ A K 9 5 2: ♣ Q 4:
    f) ♠ A Q: ♡ A Q: ◇ 10 9 8 7 4: ♣ J 10 9 8:
    g) ♠ A K 7: ♡ 9 5 4 3: ◇ A K 6: ♣ J 4 2:
    h) ♠ A Q 6 2: ♡ K 9 3: ◇ 7 4 3: ♣ K 10 6:
    i) ♠ A K 5: ♡ 10 7 3 2: ◇ A 6 2: ♣ A Q 5:
    j) ♠ 7 6 3 2: ♡ A Q 6: ◇ K 6 5: ♣ A Q 5:

Now what do you open on them if you are vulnerable and playing 'variable'?

2) Partner has opened 1 N.T. (12—14 points). What do you respond on the following hands?

    a) ♠ Q 7 6 5 3 2: ♡ 7: ◇ 8 4 2: ♣ K 7 3:
    b) ♠ Q 7 6: ♡ K J 9: ◇ A 3: ♣ Q J 9 8 5:
    c) ♠ Q 9 2: ♡ K 7 3: ◇ K 5 4: ♣ A 6 3 2:
    d) ♠ Q 10 9: ♡ K 10 9: ◇ K 9 4: ♣ A 10 3 2:
    e) ♠ A Q 6: ♡ K Q 10: ◇ 7 4: ♣ K J 10 8 7:
    f) ♠ 7: ♡ A Q 10 9 6 4 3: ◇ Q 7 5 3: ♣ 4:
    g) ♠ 7: ♡ 6 2: ◇ K Q 9 6 5 4 3 2: ♣ 8 4:
    h) ♠ 7: ♡ A 7: ◇ K Q 9 6 5 4 3 2: ♣ 9 4:
    i) ♠ Q 9: ♡ J 3: ◇ K J 8 4 2: ♣ 7 6 4 3:
    j) ♠ K Q 10 9 8 3: ♡ 7: ◇ A Q 4: ♣ K J 9:

3) You open 1 N.T. (12—14 points) on the following hands, to which your partner responds 3♡. What would you rebid?

    a) ♠ A 10 7: ♡ Q 9: ◇ K J 10 6: ♣ Q 6 4 3:
    b) ♠ A 10 7: ♡ Q 9 6: ◇ K J 10: ♣ Q 6 4 3:
    c) ♠ A 10 7: ♡ K J 6 3: ◇ K J 9: ♣ Q 6 4:
    d) ♠ A 10 7: ♡ A J: ◇ J 10 9 8: ♣ Q 9 8 6:
    e) ♠ A 10 7: ♡ A J: ◇ 8 6 5 3: ♣ K 7 6 2:

ANSWERS TO REVISION QUIZ ON CHAPTER 4

1) a) 1 NT A balanced 13-point hand is ideal for the bid.

   b) 1♣ It is better to open 1♣ than 1♡, as 1♣ gives the better chance of finding a fit with your partner.

   c) 1 NT Bid the whole hand at once—1 N.T. is far more pre-emptive than your alternative of 1♣.

   d) 1♡ With 17 good points you cannot bid 1 N.T. and you can afford to show the heart suit.

   e) 1 NT 13 points and a good 5-card minor. This is a good strategic bid on such a hand.

   f) 1 NT If you fall into the trap of opening 1◇, what can you possibly rebid?

   g) 1◇ This is a moment for a 'prepared' 1◇, hoping that your partner will bid hearts. If he bids 2♣ you will have to rebid 2 N.T.

   h) 1 NT If you feel tempted to open 1♠, ask yourself how you propose to rebid this hand.

   i) 1♡ Almost the same hand as in (d) above, and just to see if you remembered.

   j) 1♣ Too strong for 1 N.T., not strong enough for 1♠—(see Chapter 6).

Now bidding these hands again using the 15—17 point No Trump when you are vulnerable:

   a) 1◇ Open your 4-card suit in preference to 1♣.

   b) 1 NT A perfect strong 1 N.T. opener.

   c) 1♣ Not strong enough for 1 N.T. so bid 1♣.

   d) 1 NT Still within the limits for a strong No Trump which you bid in preference to the weak heart suit.

   e) 1◇ A bit difficult, because your only rebid is going to be 2◇ but you must open something.

   f) 1◇ Other than passing on this 13-point hand, you must break some rule to find a bid, and this seems the least of a number of evils.

   g) 1 NT No trouble this time.

   h) 1♣ You dare not open 1♠ as this leaves you no sensible rebid, so you open 1♣ *and rebid in No Trumps.*

   i) 1 NT Automatic—17 points, well balanced.

   j) 1 NT Again automatic—a well balanced 15 points.

2) a) 2♠   A simple weak take-out into your long suit.

   b) 3 NT You have the full necessary count plus a most valuable five-card suit.

   c) 2 NT Opener's minimum of 12+your 12=24. Leave the decision to him.

   d) 3 NT The same arithmetic, but your 'intermediates' are strong enough for 3 N.T.

   e) 3♣   You are far too strong to make a weak take-out and partner must now bid 3 N.T. or raise your clubs.

   f) 4♡   A direct bid to game in the majors means a long suit and practically nothing else.

   g) 4◇   This is highly pre-emptive on a hand with no defence in the major suits.

   h) 5◇   Stronger by just that ace, but still worth a game bid in diamonds rather than a try at No Trumps.

   i) Pass You have no reason to suppose that eight tricks with diamonds as trumps will be easier to make than seven tricks in No Trumps.

   j) 3♠   A straight-forward jump take-out into a good suit in which you would prefer to play. Partner will keep open by raising or bidding 3 N.T.

3) a) 3 NT The response is, of course, forcing to game, but your shortest suit is hearts. Tell your partner that you have a stop in the other suits without very much heart support for him.

   b) 4♡   You still have a hold on the other three suits, but if your partner feels a heart contract might be safer than one in No Trumps you have nothing against this.

   c) 3♠   An advance cue bid showing the ♠A (first round control), complete agreement of hearts as trumps and a maximum (14 points) for the opening bid.

   d) 3 NT You have no reason to suppose the hand will play better in hearts than in No Trumps.

   e) 4♡   You have only a doubleton heart it is true, but what you have are good ones. You also have virtually no stop in diamonds which might prove disastrous, so on balance it is likely to be safer to let partner play in hearts than to insist on No Trumps.

Chapter 5

One No Trump and The Club Suit

We have now covered the various responses, both weak and strong, to an opening bid of 1 N.T., except those in the club suit, the reason for the previous omission being that both 2♣ and 4♣ responses to partner's 1 N.T., whatever the agreed strength of the opening bid, are conventional. The correct handling of the responses in clubs, particularly in the case of 2♣, which crops up so frequently, is so important that we are devoting a whole chapter to these bids and the subsequent sequences.

A response of 2♣ to an opening bid of 1 N.T. requests opener to show a four-card major suit if he has one. The object of this is to find a trump suit 'fit' in which the hands can be played more safely than in No Trumps. This may well prevent the hands being torn to pieces—a most humiliating situation which can easily occur when responder happens to have no stop in opener's own weakest suit.

This bid was first invented by the late Ewart Kempson and then further developed by J. C. H. Marx. From there it crossed the Atlantic and was further elaborated and publicised by Samuel M. Stayman as a part of his system, and it is a tribute to the American genius for advertising that the 2♣ response to 1 N.T. has become almost universally known as 'Stayman'. A name, however, is really not necessary, and once a player has announced that he plays Acol it should be implicit that he uses a 2♣ bid in response to his partner's opening 1 N.T. as a means of fit-finding, which is a part of the Acol System.

2♣ RESPONSE TO 1 N.T.

The 2♣ response to an opening bid of 1 N.T. is quite distinct from the weak take-out 'rescue' bids into two of any other suit examined in the previous chapter. The difference is that the 2♣ bid is used when responder would like to *discuss* the best final denomination with his partner whereas, with a suit take-out, either weak or strong, he is telling, not discussing.

There is no limiting qualification imposed on a responder who wants to use this fit-finding bid and it may, in fact, be used on anything from a Yarborough to a rock-crusher provided responder can himself see a sensible course of action in the face of any opener's rebid.

We shall be going into these situations in the following pages but, in the meantime, it must be stressed that a player who has bid 2♣ in response to his partner's opening 1 N.T. has taken charge of the bidding, which must be dropped or allowed to develop along the lines he subsequently indicates.

OPENER'S REBID AFTER 2♣ RESPONSE TO 1 N.T.

Opener's choice of rebid when his partner responds 2♣ to his opening 1 N.T. is simple:

a) Holding *one* four-card major suit he bids it at the two-level (1 NT—2♣—2♡).

b) Holding *two* four-card major suits he bids the spades first (1 NT—2♣—2♠) and can later, if expedient, show the hearts. This is merely a matter of following the Acol principle of bidding the higher ranking of two equal and adjacent suits first.*

c) Holding no four-card major, he rebids 2♢ *irrespective of either his diamond holding or his precise point count* (1 NT—2♣—2♢). This is of paramount importance, as it leaves responder free to make what will now be a weak take-out bid at the two-level on a weak hand, whilst not preventing him from rebidding more strongly if his hand is worth it.

RESPONDER'S SECOND ROUND BIDS

Responder's next bid is equally simple. The initiative belongs to him and:

a) If opener's rebid suits his hand he can pass or raise, according to his strength (which includes possibly passing opener's rebid of 2♢).

b) If opener's rebid is not what responder had hoped to hear he can convert to 2 or 3 N.T. according to his strength, make a weak take-out if he is able to do so at the two level (1 NT—2♣—2♢—2♠) or jump-bid his own best suit if strong.

c) On somewhat rare occasions he can make use of a conventional forcing rebid of 3♢ over opener's 2♢ (1 NT—2♢—3♢) which asks opener to describe his hand further (see p. 73).

*Nowadays many players, by partnership agreement, show hearts before spades when holding two majors, which may change the subsequent auctions as described on p.69. This method is used mainly by expert tournament players as the preliminary to an escape route if responder is very weak or the 1 N.T. is doubled.

    d) If responder's only asset is a long weak club suit he can
       rebid this at the three-level (1 NT—2♣—2♠—3♣) show-
       ing that his 2♣ was, in fact, the preliminary to a weak
       take-out in that suit and not a fit-finding bid.

These rules are not nearly as complicated as they sound, and will
become quite clear if you go through the following examples. They
are based on common sense allied to a quite simple convention
which will get you out of many a sticky No Trump contract into a
far safer trump suit. The opening No Trump examples are based on
a 12-14 point hand, and responder's bids are geared to this. If a
strong No Trump is being used the responding values might justify
a different bid.

♠ K 9 7
♡ K 8 6 5
◇ A 9 7
♣ K 8 6

You open 1 N.T. to which your partner responds
2♣. Holding a four-card heart suit you rebid 2♡.
Exchange the hearts and spades, and you would
respond 2♠. You will realise if you think about it
that a response of 2♡ *denies* holding four spades,
though a response of 2♠ does not necessarily deny four hearts
as well.

♠ K 9 7
♡ A 9 7
◇ K 8 6
♣ K 8 6 5

This is the same hand again with the suits changed
round. When partner responds 2♣ to your 1 N.T.
you rebid 2◇, to deny holding either four hearts
or four spades.

♠ K 9 7 6
♡ K 10 6 5
◇ A 9 8
♣ K 7

It would be somewhat misleading to open 1♠ on
this hand, intending to rebid 2♡ so, if you are
using a 12-14 point No Trump, you can open
1 N.T. Partner responds 2♣ and you rebid 2♠,
the higher-ranking of your two equal and adjacent
majors. Your partner rebids 2 N.T. Now you know a number of
things. Responder was interested in your major suit holdings, and
his interest faded when you showed spades—in fact he must have
been hoping you would show hearts. His hand must be stronger
than he would need for a weak take-out into 2♡ or he would have
passed 1 N.T. or bid 2♡ straight away. You can, therefore, read
him for something like 11 points, spade weakness, and a four-card
heart suit, so now it becomes expedient to show your hearts,
particularly as you are not too happy about your club stop. Bid
3♡ over the 2 N.T. Responder, knowing that you have at least eight
cards between the majors, can take his choice between passing 3♡,
converting to 3 N.T., or raising to 4♡.

Now let us turn to responder's side of the table and look at a variety of hands on which the use of the 2♣ response may prove invaluable. As with all conventions, however, it is important to know when *not* to use it. Used injudiciously it can give much gratuitous information to the opposition, who will be quick to take advantage of the fact, for example, that declarer has less than four cards in any particular suit. 1 NT—2♣—2♢ tells the opposition as well as responder that opener has not more than three cards in either major, and 1 NT—2♣—2♡ that he has less than four spades. This is, of course, negative information, but it may be the one thing necessary to suggest the best line of defence. So unless responder feels sure that the discovery of a suit fit is likely to be a great benefit he should pass or give a direct raise in No Trumps according to his strength. The occasions on which not to use the convention are:]

a) On balanced responding hands suitable to play in No Trumps. This covers all responding hands, weak or strong, when there is no reason to suppose that a suit contract will be an improvement on No Trumps.

b) On hands containing a clear-cut take-out into a suit, either weak or strong.

c) On hands where responder may find himself in an embarrassing position on the second round because of opener's possible reply to the 2♣ bid.

♠ A 7 6 5 4
♡ J 9 6 3
♢ J 10 7
♣ 4

This hand is obviously better equipped for a low-level suit contract than for No Trumps. Opposite 1 N.T., therefore, bid 2♣ and *pass* if opener rebids either 2♡ or 2♠. If, however, he rebids 2♢, take out into 2♠, which now becomes the weak take-out you could have made in the first place if it had not been wiser to investigate for a possible spade *or* heart fit.

♠ J 9 6 3
♡ A 7 6 5 4
♢ J 10 7
♣ 4

This is the same hand with the major suits exchanged, and is also the same story. Bid 2♣ and pass opener's rebid of either 2♡ or 2♠. If he rebids 2♢, convert to 2♡, in the knowledge that a spade fit has not been missed.

♠ J 10 7
♡ J 9 6 3
♢ A 7 6 5 4
♣ 4

The same again except that now the five-card suit is diamonds. It is not possible for responder to use the 2♣ bid because there is nothing sensible he can say if opener rebids 2♠. His choice, therefore, lies between passing 1 N.T. and taking out into 2♢.

the former probably being the better course, as no one likes playing in two of a minor, particularly at M.P.Pairs!

♠ J 9 8 6 5 4   Bid 2♣ opposite 1 N.T. and pass opener's rebid
♡ J 10 6 4   of either 2♡ or 2♠. Over 2◇ take out into 2♠.
◇ 6 3   Do not make the mistake of bidding 2♠ on the
♣ 4   first round, without giving yourself the chance of
                 discovering a 4-4 heart fit.

♠ 9 8 6 5   This horrible hand will be even more horrible as
♡ 8 6 5 3   dummy for a declarer trying to play in 1 N.T.! Bid
◇ 8 7 5 4 2   2♣ and pass *any* opener's rebid, including 2◇. A
♣ —   four-card fit in either major would be a blessing,
but if opener has no more than six cards between the majors he is morally bound to hold at least three if not four diamonds, so the pass of his 2◇ rebid merely becomes the weak take-out you could have made in the first place if you had not given yourself the chance to discover a possible 4-4 fit in either hearts or spades.

♠ 9 8 7 5   The same hand except that now the void is in
♡ 8 7 6 4   diamonds which makes all the difference. This time
◇ —   you must not bid 2♣ in an effort to save partner
♣ 8 7 5 4 2   from playing in No Trumps because there is
                 nothing at all you can do if his response is 2◇.

♠ Q 9 8 6   Here again, if you bid 2♣ you *may* discover a
♡ Q 8 6 4   comfortable 4-4 spade or heart fit, but if opener
◇ J 2   rebids 2◇ there will be nothing you can do but
♣ K 8 6   shoot yourself—or wait for him to do so when he
                 has struggled with the final contract. Presumably you would convert 2◇ to 2 N.T. and if opener raises to 3 N.T. he will be playing at game level on a maximum of 22 points.

♠ Q 10 7   *If* opener responds 2♡ to 2♣ everything in the
♡ Q 9 5 4 3   garden will be lovely, but you are in a hopelessly
◇ K 9 5   embarrassing position if he responds 2♠. So your
♣ 8 4   choice is between passing 1 N.T. and taking out
                 into 2♡. You have no particular reason to think the latter would be a happier contract at this stage, so your best choice is to pass—you will never know until you see the two hands together anyway.

In other words you must not use the 2♣ fit-finding bid on a responding hand unless you are sure you will be able to pass opener's 2◇ rebid without regret or find another sensible rebid of your own.

♠ K 9 8 6
♡ Q 10 7
◇ Q J 6
♣ Q 10 9

In contrast to the above, this is an evenly balanced hand with something in everything and, therefore, perfectly suitable for a No Trump contract. Counting, you will remember from Chapter 1, 10's as $\frac{1}{2}$ point for No Trump bidding, it contains 11 points, and 1 N.T. should be raised invitationally to 2 N.T. Add as little as another knave and 10 and you should raise direct to 3 N.T.

Finally we come to the last of our weak responding situations, that is, when responder's only asset is a long weak club suit:

♠ J
♡ 9 7 4
◇ 10 8 4
♣ Q 9 7 5 4 2

Bid 2♣ in response to opener's 1 N.T. and repeat 3♣ over whatever rebid he makes. The hand is useless except played with clubs as trumps, and the 3♣ rebid is your method of showing that, had this been possible, you would have made a weak take-out into 2♣ in the first place.

Now let us go on to some stronger examples, which should make it clear that this versatile convention does not limit you to stopping in little part-score contracts. Indeed you will find that it is often the only way in which you can discover the right or safest game either in a suit or in No Trumps.

♠ K Q 5 4
♡ 6
◇ K 7 5 3
♣ Q J 10 4

Strong enough to raise 1 N.T. to 2 N.T., but clearly that heart singleton is a worry. Bid 2♣ and, if opener rebids 2♠ raise him to 3♠, inviting him to go to game in spades if he fancies his chances. If he bids 2♡ convert to 2 N.T., in the knowledge that he has at least a four-card heart stop. If he bids 2◇ you will have to chance it and bid 2 N.T. anyway, but with your own heart shortage it is more than probable that he has a good stop in the suit. If the opening No Trump were of the strong variety, by the way, you would not be content with a possible part-score contract. Opener's rebid of 2♠ should be raised to 4♠ or his 2♡ converted to 3 N.T. Add even another knave, and you would raise 2♠ to 4♠ opposite to a weak No Trump, or rebid 3 N.T. if opener's rebid is in diamonds or hearts.

♠ Q J 9 7 5 4
♡ Q J 10 3
◇ 8
♣ A 3

Here is a slightly different situation. Facing even a weak No Trump you want to be in game if partner has a fit for either of your majors, so bid 2♣ and if he rebids 2♡ or 2♠ raise direct to four of that suit. If, however, he bids 2◇ you would still *like* to be in game, but are not quite so confident. Rebid 3♠ which is very highly invitational but not forcing. Opener will raise to 4♠ if he can find any excuse for doing so, or perhaps convert to

3 N.T., though he is at liberty to pass 3♣ if he feels he must.

♠ 9 7
♡ A 10 9 7 6
♢ A J 8 6
♣ J 10

This hand is too strong for a weak take-out into 2♡ though not strong enough for a jump to 3♡. It contains the values for a raise to 2 N.T., though the two doubletons make this a somewhat unattractive idea. Bid 2♣ and if opener rebids 2♢ or 2♠ convert, even though you do not much like it, to 2 N.T. If he bids 2♡, however, raise invitationally to 3♡. Exchange the ♠9 for the ♠K, and a 2♢ or 2♠ rebid should be converted to 3 N.T. whilst a 2♡ rebid should be raised direct to 4♡.

♠ Q J 8 6 4
♡ 7 3
♢ 6
♣ A K 8 5 4

This responding hand is of excellent 'shape' but needs a spade fit to make it worth a game contract, so bid 2♣. If opener rebids 2♠ raise to 4♠. If he rebids 2♢ or 2♡, then the chances do not look quite so rosy. Again rebid 3♠, from which opener will know that without the fit you are doubtful of just where to go.

Before passing on let us make it quite clear that many bidding situations are, and will remain, controversial. Different authorities take different 'views' and as an instance one compares the following two sequences:

	a)			b)	
	1 NT—2♣			1 NT—2♣	
	2♢ —2♠			2♡ —2♠	

The argument is that in (a) the 2♠ bid is a weak sign-off on a hand which probably contains five spades and four hearts whereas in (b) responder cannot hold four hearts so can have no reason to bid 2♣ in the first place, so that his 2♠ should be treated as constructive. This is a specious view until you remember that responder may have a variety of reasons for his 2♣ bid. Paramount will be his hope of finding a trump fit and, if this is lacking then, in his opinion, the combined hands will not be worth a game contract, in which case he signs off in 2♠. If doubtful, he can bid 3♠ invitationally, as we suggested on the last example above. So the best one can honestly say for sequence (b) is that the 2♠ rebid will show at least a five-card suit in a hand which is slightly better than it need be for an immediate weak take-out into 2♠—a hand on which he would have liked to have bid 2½♠ if he were allowed to do so.

RESPONDER'S FORCING 3♢ REBID

Another invaluable bid, even if the need for it crops up but rarely, is an extension to the 2♣ fit-finding response, a responder's forcing rebid of 3♢ when opener has denied the holding of a four-card major, mentioned on p. 68. The need for this arises when responder is two-suited in the majors, is determined to play at game level in one or the other, but has received a 2◇ response to his exploratory 2♣.

Once opener has rebid 2◇, responder knows that the 1 N.T. hand does not contain a four-card major, but it must contain at least one *three*-card major. Wanting to play in whichever fits his partner's hand best, responder can use a forcing rebid of 3◇, asking opener to clarify his hand still further.

In reply to the 3◇ force, opener should show the better of his two major suits, preferring length to honour strength. That is to say, with three hearts and two spades he must bid 3♡, or with three spades and two hearts he must bid 3♠. Holding equal length in both, he should bid the one containing the greater strength.

♠ A Q J 8 7
♡ K Q 10 9 8
◇ 6
♣ 3 2

1 NT—2♣
2◇ —3◇
?

Here responder's count and 'shape' justify a game contract facing a 1 N.T. opening bid, but clearly 4♡ or 4♠ would be more attractive than 3 N.T. The obvious starting-point for investigation is a response of 2♣ and, if opener rebids either 2♡ or 2♠, responder would bid game in that suit. If opener bids 2◇, however, responder still wants to play in hearts or spades and uses a 3◇ rebid to find out which opener prefers. Note, by the way, that this 3◇ also works as a transfer bid, as the opening No Trump bidder will become declarer. His hand will remain concealed and the lead will come up to, and not through it.

Remember that the key-note of this 2♣ convention, of which the 3◇ bid above is a part, is its fit-finding efficiency. It can convert a dangerous No Trump contract into a comfortable part-score or game in a suit once the best denomination is discovered.

RESPONDER'S 2♣ WHEN 1 N.T. IS DOUBLED

It seems appropriate, before closing this chapter, to clarify one or two other points which often seem to cause confusion.

Firstly, if the opening 1 N.T. is doubled—a business double intended primarily for penalties and not for a take-out—a 2♣ bid by opener's partner is used as a natural weak take-out and not as a conventional fit-finding request. The reason for this is that if North holds the values for his opening bid and East the values for a double, then the most probable holding for South will be a weak hand, and his most usual need will be to suggest a suit in which his partner can play more safely than in 1 N.T. doubled.

N.	E.	S.	W.
1 NT	x	2♣	

N.	E.	S.	W.
1 NT	—	—	x
—	—	2♣	

Similarly if the double comes from West in the protective position, South's subsequent 2♣ is again a weak take-out. South doubtless refrained from bidding 2♣ on the first round as he did not want to have to rebid the suit at the three level later. Once the double has been passed round, however, he feels that the hand will play more safely in 2♣—which, of course, may also be doubled—than in 1 N.T.

Lastly, if the opening 1 N.T. is immediately overcalled by a *natural* 2♣ intervention, a double by South takes the place of the 2♣ fit-finding bid he cannot now bid himself.

N.	E.	S.	W.
1 NT	2♣	x	

Any other natural intervening bid can be doubled by South strictly for business. If the opening 1 N.T. is overcalled with a conventional 2♣ or 2◇, probably the best counter is also to double, this time to show partner a scattered 8 or 9 points if no more constructive bid is available. This is a matter of partnership agreement but many authorities, especially if the intervening bid is of the 'Astro' type, recommend passing to await developments. See *Current Conventions Made Clear*.

THE GERBER CONVENTION

An immediate response of 4♣ to partner's opening 1 N.T. has a special conventional meaning, and is one which fills a long-felt want. True to the Acol principle of incorporating bids or conventions which do not conflict with its basic framework, the Gerber Convention is now added to your weapons.

The 4♣ response is an immediate announcement of interest in a slam and, at the same time, a request to partner to show the number of aces held. Opener's responses to 4♣ are on the step principle:

4◇	....	no ace
4♡	....	one ace
4♣	....	two aces
4 N.T.	....	three aces
5♣	....	four aces

As it is almost inconceivable that the 4♣ bidder is going 'slamming' on an aceless hand, in practice the 5♣ response to show four aces leaves free a subsequent rebid of 5♣ by the original bidder to ask for kings on the same step principle. Any responder's rebid other than 5♣ to ask for kings is a sign-off and should be left undisturbed by the opening No Trump bidder.

1 NT—4♣
4♡ —4 NT

In this first sequence the 4♡ rebid shows one ace which is, presumably, insufficient for responder's needs, and he signs off in 4 N.T., which becomes the final contract. It is, of course, possible that responder had hoped

♠ K
♡ K Q J 10 8 7 5 2
♢ 9
♣ A 7 6

to play in 6♡ if, for instance, he held a hand like this. When he discovers that two aces are missing he can simply pass the 4♡ reply to his enquiry. Had his suit been spades instead of hearts he would have converted to 4♠.

You will note, by the way, that 'Gerber' can involve the same dangers as 'Blackwood' particularly when the long suit is clubs. On the hand above, for example, with the hearts and clubs exchanged, it would not be possible to take out opener's 4♡ rebid into 5♣, as this would be a request to show kings. As with any other convention, therefore, 'Gerber' must be used judiciously, with an eye to the subsequent bid in relation to the possible responses to the original 4♣ bid.

1 NT—4♣
4♡ —5♣
5♠ —?

In this sequence the 4♡ response has again shown one ace which must be good enough for at least a little slam, because responder now goes on to 5♣ asking about kings. 5♠ shows two, so opener's hand is now pinned down to one ace and two kings, a total of 10 out of his 12-14 points. Whatever else opener has, his extra points can only be in queens or knaves, and responder must judge the best final contract.

As with the case of a player who has responded 2♣ to his partner's opening 1 N.T., so when he responds 4♣, it must be remembered that he has taken charge of the bidding which must be allowed to develop along the lines he indicates. His discretion as to the best final contract must be accepted by opener.

Finally, let's apply another 'Gerber' sequence to the example hand above, though replacing the ♠ K with the ♠ A : —

1 NT—4♣
4♠ —5♣
5♠ —?

When opener replies to 4♣ with 4♠, responder knows that there are no aces missing. 5♣ then elicits the information that opener has two kings which, incidentally, accounts for 14 points, so he cannot have even another knave. But this does not matter, as there will be thirteen tricks 'on top'. Bid 7♡ at rubber bridge (for the honours) and 7 N.T. at duplicate.

Note how this convention facilitates the rest of the auction. Without it responder would have to start off with a 3♡ force to which opener's almost inevitable rebid would be 3 N.T., making subsequent investigations far more complicated. An immediate 4 N.T. response would, of course, be out of the question, as it would be a non-forcing quantitative bid, not a conventional one.

1)   What do you bid over partner's opening 1 N.T. (12-14 points)?

    a) ♠ A J 9 2: ♡ K 10 3 2: ◇ 10 9 8 6 3: ♣ —

    b) ♠ A J 9 6 2: ♡ 4 3: ◇ K 10 4 3: ♣ 6 2:

    c) ♠ 8: ♡ K 10 9 4: ◇ K Q 8 6 4 2: ♣ Q 4

    d) ♠ K 9 6 5 4: ♡ Q 9 6 2: ◇ 4: ♣ J 9 8:

    e) ♠ K Q 9 5: ♡ K Q 9 5: ◇ 7 4: ♣ A 10 3:

2)   Over partner's weak 1 N.T. opening bid you respond 2♣ and partner bids 2♡. What is your next bid?

    a) ♠ 7: ♡ Q 10 8 4: ◇ A K 6: ♣ K 10 7 3 2:

    b) ♠ K J 6 3 2: ♡ 6: ◇ Q 7 4: ♣ K 10 7 3:

    c) ♠ Q 10 9 4: ♡ A 4: ◇ K J 9: ♣ A 9 8 2:

    d) ♠ K 10 9 6: ♡ Q 10 9 6: ◇ A 8 6 4: ♣ 4:

    e) ♠ K Q J 9 5: ♡ K Q 7 4: ◇ Q 4: ♣ Q 4:

3)   What do you bid over partner's opening 1 N.T., weak, and how do you plan to continue the bidding?

    a) ♠ K Q 10 9 7 4: ♡ A Q 7 2: ◇ 6 3: ♣ 3:

    b) ♠ Q 7 5 4: ♡ K 6 3 2: ◇ A J 4 2: ♣ 2:

    c) ♠ Q 3 2: ♡ K 8 4 3: ◇ A 6 3: ♣ K J 6:

    d) ♠ Q 4 2: ♡ 7 6 3: ◇ 8 2: ♣ K J 7 6 2:

    e) ♠ A 7: ♡ K Q J 6: ◇ A K Q J 7 6: ♣   :

ANSWERS TO REVISION QUIZ ON CHAPTER 5

1) a) 2♣   Then pass anything partner says, including 2◇.
   b) 2♠   A simple weak take-out bid.
   c) 2♣   Pass 2♡ or 2◇ and bid (rather reluctantly) 2 N.T. over 2♠.
   d) 2♣   Pass 2♠ or 2♡; bid 2♠ over 2◇.
   e) 2♣   Over 2◇ raise to 3 N.T. Raise either major to four.

2) a) 4♡   A perfect fit and enough strength to raise to game.
   b) 2♠   This now becomes a weak take-out. If partner had bid 2♠ you would have passed.
   c) 3 NT   As you have not found the spade fit you hoped for, raise direct to game.
   d) 3♡   You have found the fit you hoped for, but are not quite strong enough to go direct to game yourself.
   e) 4♡   Do not make the mistake of showing your spades with the known 4-4 fit in hearts.

3) a) 2♣   first, and if partner shows either major, you plan to raise direct to game in it. If he bids 2◇ you will bid 3♠.
   b) 2♣   You plan to pass 2◇ and raise either major to three.
   c) 3 NT direct. Evenly balanced—enough points.
   d) No bid. You cannot make a weak take-out into 2♣ as you don't want to rebid 3♣.
   e) 4♣   The 'Gerber' request to partner to show aces. If he shows two your plan is to bid 7◇ direct at Rubber Bridge (for the honours) and 7 N.T. at duplicate. You could enquire about kings with a 5♣ bid on the way, just in case his N.T. were made up with queens and knaves, of course.

Chapter 6

'Prepared' Minor Suit Opening Bids

THE Acol attitude towards 'prepared' opening bids is important for, with the emphasis at all times on bidding as naturally as possible, prepared bids, that is, openings in a suit in which you do not really want to play, are only admitted to the system because occasions do arise when no other sensible bid is possible.

In the wider sense of the word all opening bids are prepared, in that they are made with the need for a descriptive rebid in mind. But the Acol System does not advocate the over-use of preparedness which can, when carried as it so often is to unnecessary lengths, result in bidding your partner's cards for him—the very antithesis of the principles of the system, where every bid is aimed at bidding your own cards simply and fully.

It is fair to say that 1♣ is the most abused opening bid of all. Far too many players have developed the habit of using it almost at random when they can think of nothing better to do, even on innumerable hands which contain a perfectly good opening bid which can be followed by a sensible rebid. Most such players seldom, if ever, use a 'prepared' 1♦ opening—1♣ will do whatever the cards, or lack of cards, held in the suit. There is, though, a difference between the two, not to mention the need for both, however seldom or however reluctantly you use either.

Correctly used, prepared minor suit opening bids of 1♣ or 1♦ occur in Acol in only two situations. The first is if you are using a strong (15-17 point) No Trump and pick up a balanced hand of 12-14 points which is too strong to pass and not strong enough to open 1 N.T. Nor is it strong enough to risk opening a four-card major as the hand would then contain no sound rebid at the two-level. In such circumstances you may resort to a 1♣ or 1♦ opening, whichever suit fills the bill, because you must *never* make a prepared minor suit opening bid with less than three cards in the suit, one of which must be a high honour. Using a 12-14 point No Trump, of course, you could open 1 N.T. on this sort of hand in the first place, and with 15 or more points you can usually open one of your four-card suit and rebid in No Trumps at the lowest available level.

The second situation in which a prepared minor suit opening may be necessary is when playing a 12-14 point No Trump and, as occasionally happens, you pick up a 15 point hand, or possibly even a 16 point one in which your four-card suit is really not biddable—when it is, in fact, only worth bidding as support for your partner's response. Then, once again, you may be forced into opening 1♣ or 1♢.

The reason why you should hold three to a high honour in the minor suit you select is to protect yourself from the danger of being given a two or even a three-level limit raise in the suit. If you have a minimum of a three-card holding, the worst that can happen to you is that you will play in the suit on a 3-4 fit, whereas if you allow yourself to make a 1♣ or 1♢ opening on a doubleton, you either face the possibility of playing in a 2-4 fit, or of rescuing yourself into a possibly disastrous No Trump contract, or making your partner feel that it is acutely dangerous for him to use a limit response in the minors—which may well be the only sensible thing he can do. This also is why the Acol System permits you the choice between opening in either of the minors, not only in clubs.

Allowing for the use of a prepared minor suit opening even in these circumstances is a violation of the natural quality of Acol bidding, as you are opening in a suit in which you do not want to be taken seriously. It is, however, an evil which must be endured in order, occasionally, to save yourself from an even more misleading opening bid, so it is important to let your partner know what you have done as quickly as possible. Remember this vital rule—having opened the auction with a prepared minor suit bid, your rebid *must be in No Trumps* unless responder elects to bid your four-card suit, in which case you may raise according to your strength. The latter will, of course, have been conditioned by the strength of the opening No Trump being used. The object of this is not only to try to avoid misleading your partner more than has already been necessary, but to protect you from subsequently being given preference to a suit which you do not, in fact, prefer, a most ignominious position in which to find yourself!

Finally, before we go on to some examples, if both minors qualify under the heading of 'three to a high honour', open 1♣ in preference to 1♢, as 1♣ allows responder the maximum possible freedom in his choice of bid.

♠ 10 8 6 4
♡ A Q 7
♢ K Q 3
♣ K J 5

This is a perfectly good strong No Trump opener but, if you are using 12-14 points, it is too strong. Nor is the spade suit really biddable in such a balanced hand. Open 1♣ and bid 1 N.T. if partner responds in a red suit, *not* 1♠, which would announce a club-spade two suiter. If partner responds 1♠, however, raise to 3♠.

♠ 8 6 4 2 A very similar hand, but strengthened to 17 points,
♡ A K 7 an excellent 1 N.T. (strong) opener. It is, of course,
◇ K Q 3 far too strong for a 12-14 point No Trump, but this
♣ K Q 5 time, because of the outside values, you can safely
open 1♠, as you will be in no trouble with finding an expressive rebid—2 N.T. over any change-of-suit response at the two-level. If responder insists on playing in spades he will have at least four-card support, and you will have an excellent chance of making your contract.

♠ A Q 7 3 Here again you open 1♣ if you are not playing a
♡ Q 8 3 12-14 point No Trump because you are not strong
◇ K 7 3 enough to open 1♠ and rebid 2 N.T. over a two-level
♣ Q 10 3 response. But rebid 1 N.T., not 1♠, if partner's
response is 1♡ or 1◇. Raise 1♠ to 2♠.

♠ 8 6 4 2 Hardly a hand for bidding as two-suited in the majors
♡ J 6 4 3 yet, with 15 points, it would be unthinkable not to
◇ A K 8 open. A prepared bid of 1♣ should not be considered,
♣ A K as there are only two cards in the suit. Open 1◇ over
which responder can show either hearts or spades at the one-level, so no major suit fit will be missed. If he bids 2♣ missing his own ♣ A-K, it is a safe bet that he will have points in hearts and spades and you can make an honest and safe rebid of 2 N.T.

♠ J 7 4 2 Here again open 1◇ in preference to 1♣. There is no
♡ A Q 6 honour, let alone a high one, in clubs, and it will
◇ A K J serve you right if you open 1♣ and responder raises
♣ 8 4 3 you to 2♣ on six or seven honour points and four
small clubs! If you open 1◇ you can rebid 1 N.T. if the response is 1♡, raise 1♠ to 3♠, or rebid 2 N.T. over 2♣.

As far as your partner is concerned, your opening bid of 1♣ or 1◇ may be either prepared or genuine—time will show which—but responder should treat it as genuine when framing his reply, and await further information. Compare the following, assuming that the prepared opening is needed because of the No Trump range in use.

♠ K J 7	♠ K 9 8 6	♠ K 8 7	But: ♠ A Q 9 8 6
♡ K 9 8 6	♡ K J 7	♡ Q 9 8 6	♡ K 6
◇ A 9 6	◇ A 9 6	◇ A 9 6	◇ 8
♣ A 8 4	♣ A 8 4	♣ A 8 4	♣ A J 10 7 4

1♣—1♠	1♣—1♠	1♣—1♡	1♣—1♡
1 NT	3♣	2♡	1♠
or	or	or	or
1♣—1♡	1♣—1♡	1♣—1♠	1♣—1♠
3♡	1 NT	1 NT	4♣

To summarise, therefore:

a) Never use a prepared minor suit opening bid if you have a more natural opening bid allowing for an honest rebid. This will be influenced by the strength of the opening No Trump being used.

b) Never use a prepared minor suit opening with less than three cards, one of them a high honour, in the suit.

c) Having made a prepared opening, rebid in No Trumps *unless* responder bids your four-card suit, in which case raise this according to your strength.

We have already pointed out that responder, lacking any definite information to the contrary, should treat a 1♣ or 1◇ opening as a natural bid to which he should respond naturally. He has, however, the choice of all three other suits for a one-level response to 1♣, and of both majors to 1◇. Because of this wider choice it follows that a response of 1 N.T. to either 1♣ or 1◇ can be used more positively than as a mere keep-open bid when the opening has been 1♡ or 1♠. The Acol System, therefore, uses a 1 N.T. response to 1♣ to show 8-10 honour points, not the 5-9 you would expect over a major suit. Over 1◇ it shows 7-9 points. So in both cases opener's rebids in No Trumps (see Chapter 8) can be devalued. After 1♣— 1 NT., for example, a 17-18 point opening hand becomes worth a direct raise to 3 N.T. as the combined minimum of the two hands will be 25 points.

REVISION QUIZ ON CHAPTER 6

1) If you are using the variable No Trump (12-14 points not vulnerable, and 15-17 points vulnerable), what do you open if not vulnerable on the following hands?

a) ♠ 9 8 5 3: ♡ A Q 4: ◇ K Q 5: ♣ K J 3:
b) ♠ 7 6 3 2: ♡ K Q 9: ◇ A Q 10: ♣ A Q J:
c) ♠ Q 10 8 6: ♡ J 10 6: ◇ A Q 3: ♣ A K 4:
d) ♠ K Q 6: ♡ 8 6 4 3: ◇ K J 10: ♣ A J 4:
e) ♠ J 9 6 3: ♡ J 10 6 4: ◇ A Q: ♣ A K 4:
f) ♠ K 8 6 3: ♡ K 9 8 4: ◇ A Q: ♣ 9 5 3:

And what if you are vulnerable on these?

g) ♠ 9 5 3 2: ♡ A Q 6: ◇ K Q 7: ♣ K 10 8:
h) ♠ K J 4: ♡ 8 6 4 3: ◇ A J 9: ♣ K Q 10:
i) ♠ A K Q: ♡ K 8 6: ◇ A 6 4 2: ♣ A 9 6:
j) ♠ K Q 6: ♡ J 9 8 7: ◇ A Q 4: ♣ A Q 5:
k) ♠ J 8 4 2: ♡ J 9 6 4: ◇ A Q: ♣ A Q 4:
l) ♠ J 8 4 2: ♡ J 9 6 4: ◇ A Q 4: ♣ A Q:

Now reverse the vulnerability. What do you bid, vulnerable, on hands (a) to (f) above?

What do you bid unvulnerable on hands (g) to (l) above?

ANSWERS TO REVISION QUIZ ON CHAPTER 6

1) a) 1♣   One point too strong for an unvulnerable No Trump and the spades really are not biddable.

b) 1♠   The spades may be equally unbiddable, but the rest of the hand is so strong that you can afford to make this opening.

c) 1♠   This is a biddable suit within the meaning of the Act.

d) 1 NT   No comment except that this is an automatic bid.

e) 1♣   Too strong for 1 N.T. and 1♣ is safer than one of either of the majors, which will be excellent in support of partner—or as an undisclosed menace to the opposition.

f) 1 NT   You really cannot give such a false picture of your hand as to bid one of your majors, especially as this would give you no sensible rebid.

g) 1♣   Not strong enough for a vulnerable No Trump and apart from the weakness of the spade suit, you would have no available rebid.

h) 1♣   Again, not strong enough for a No Trump but this time it is your heart suit that is too weak and which offers no rebid.

i) 1♢   In spite of its 20 points this is an unpleasant type of hand, the concentration of points in the spades making it top-heavy. You don't really want to be in game unless partner can make a 'free' response, and you're far too strong for 1 N.T. whatever the score.

j) 1♡   Too strong for a 15-17 point No Trump, and the hearts are perfectly biddable, especially when your honest rebid will be in No Trumps.

k) 1♣   You will be happy to support either major if bid by partner, and if he bids 1♢ you will bid 1 N.T.

l) 1♢   Only two clubs in the hand, so do not use a 'prepared' club, but a 'prepared' 1♢, and rebid in No Trumps or support either major.

Now reversing the vulnerability, let us see what difference this makes to the opening bids. On (a) to (f) vulnerable, and using the 15-17 point No Trump: —

a) 1 NT   15 points—just right.

b) 1♠   Too good for 1 N.T., so bid the spades and rebid in No Trumps.

c) 1 NT If partner bids 2♣ asking for a major suit take-out you
will bid 2♠.

d) 1♣   Not strong enough for 1 N.T., and the hearts are really
only interesting as support on a hand of this medium
strength.

e) 1 NT With 15 points you can get the whole hand off your
chest with one bid again, as well as having a good
response to partner's possible 2♣.

f) Pass You cannot honestly, allowing for a sensible rebid,
open one of anything!

On (g) to (l), unvulnerable, using 12-14 points for a No Trump:—

g) 1 NT 14 points—a maximum for the bid, but still the bid
best fitted for the hand.

h) 1 NT As above, with no further comment.

i) 1◇   The first hand that calls for the same bid, whether
vulnerable or not, and for the same reasons.

j) 1♡   Again, the same bid, and for the same reasons.

k) 1 NT A 4-4-3-2 distribution such as this comes within the
scope of a No Trump, and the point-count is right.

l) 1 NT No need on these hands to make a 'prepared' bid of any
sort. One of the virtues of using 'weak throughout' is the
frequency with which you can bid 1 N.T., dispensing
again and again with the unnatural bids.

Chapter 7

Change-of-Suit Responding Bids

WE now turn to the large group of responding hands on which the limit bids will be of no avail. Either there is insufficient trump support for a direct suit raise, the hand is not fitted for a No Trump response at any level, it is too strong for a limit bid which might be passed by opener, or circumstances demand pre-emptive action. These will be the hands on which a change-of-suit response is needed, and though some of them have already been mentioned in the previous pages, you will find them gathered together here under one chapter heading, for convenience of reference.

Responding hands which must be bid by way of a change-of-suit come into various categories, both weak and strong. Such changes of suit, except in pre-emptive cases, and unless the bidder has previously passed as mentioned in Chapter 3, are *forcing for one round*. The simple response and the response after a previous pass are, therefore, quite distinct and this distinction may well make a difference to the correct response on a particular hand. We will deal now, however, with the simple situations and come on to the variations later in the chapter.

SIMPLE CHANGE-OF-SUIT RESPONSES

A simple change-of-suit response can be made merely as a keep-open measure, provided it is at the one-level only. At this low end of the scale it does not promise any greater strength than a 1 N.T. response would do, that is, something between 5-9 honour points. On the other hand, it may conceal values only just below those required for an immediate force or, for example, a delayed game raise (see p. 87) when exploration is necessary. A change-of-suit bid at the two-level should be stronger, requiring a minimum of 8 honour points and a five-card suit, or possibly 7 points if the suit is of six-card length. There are occasions when responder must bid a four-card suit at the two-level, but in this case more honour strength is needed, to compensate for the shortage in the suggested new trump suit.

♠ 10 9 7
♡ K 10 7 6
◇ A 9 2
♣ 10 7 5

If partner opens the bidding with 1♡, raise to 2♡. If he opens 1♣ or 1◇, bid 1♡, which does not raise the level of the auction. If he opens 1♠ bid 1 N.T. as, though the hand is too good to pass, it does not qualify for a bid at the two-level.

♠ 10 9 7
♡ Q 4
◇ K 9 6 5 3
♣ Q 8 2

If partner opens 1◇ raise to 2◇. If he opens 1♡ or 1♠ bid 1 N.T., as the hand is not strong enough to show the diamonds at the two level. Over an opening 1♣, however, make a simple change-of-suit response of 1◇.

♠ 10 9 7
♡ K Q 9 6 5
◇ A 10 8
♣ 6 4

Over an opening 1♣ or 1◇ respond 1♡. Over an opening 1♠ respond 2♡. Similarly, if the red suits were exchanged, respond 1◇ to 1♣, or 2◇ to 1♡ or 1♠.

♠ 10 9 7
♡ Q 6
◇ A J 9 8 7 6
♣ 6 4

Over 1♣ respond 1◇. Over 1♡ or 1♠ respond 2◇ as, though the hand contains only 7 honour points, it has a good six-card suit which it would be folly to conceal in favour of the alternative bid of 1 N.T.

♠ K J 8
♡ A K 10 9
◇ 6 4 3
♣ Q 8 4

To 1♣ or 1◇ respond 1♡. To 1♠ respond 2♡, the only sensible bid as the hand does not contain primary spade support or the suitable cards for a No Trump limit bid. 2♡ is, in effect, a waiting bid, as clearly the hand is worth another bid facing partner's opening, and what this will be depends upon opener's rebid.

You will see that a response at the one-level may contain a very modest minimum or a good deal more. A response at the two-level contains a less modest minimum, and opener can rebid his own hand with this knowledge.

DELAYED GAME RAISE

As we've already pointed out, a simple change-of-suit response, in itself forcing for one round, may be the prelude to a stronger bid such, for instance, as a delayed game raise. This bid really comes under the heading of a responder's rebid (Chapter 9), but it must be taken here, as an understanding of it is the key to a number of first round responses.

The indications for a delayed game raise are good trump support, good honour strength and/or 'shape', and yet not sufficient strength for an immediate game-forcing response. It is a waiting bid because responder, although he intends the hand to be played in at least a game contract, is not yet sure just where he is going and needs to hear his partner's rebid before making up his mind. Thus the first response is exploratory and, unless opener's rebid makes a slam a reasonable proposition, responder's rebid will merely be a jump to game level in opener's suit.

N.   S.   *South:*   Here South is not strong enough for an
1♠—2♣   ♠ K 10 5 4   immediate force, though he is much too
2♠—4♠   ♡ 5 4   strong for any level of limit bid, which
        ♢ K J 10   might well cost a missed slam. A waiting
        ♣ A Q 8 7   bid of 2♣ is, therefore, the best response,
                    followed by a jump rebid to 4♠ if opener
rebids 2♠ or two of either red suit. When opener's rebid has been 2♢ or 2♡, this will clearly show South's strength *plus* the fact that his hand contains four-card spade support, because responder will be giving this strong support to a suit which has not been rebid.

N.   S.   *South:*   On this hand too, if North opens 1♠
1♠—2♢   ♠ K Q 9   South wants to play in game but is not yet
2♠—4♠   ♡ K J 7 2   sure *what* game. The spade support,
        ♢ A Q 9 8   though good, is only three-card, so does
        ♣ 9 6 5   not qualify for an immediate raise anyway.
                    Once again the best course of action will be
to make a waiting bid, this time of 2♢—*waiting* to see whether North will rebid his spades in which case South has very adequate support and can rebid 4♠. If, however, North makes a strong rebid, there is ample time to investigate a possible slam, let alone game. Note also that had North opened 1♡ instead of 1♠, South is far too strong for an immediate heart raise, so once again should bid 2♢ and await developments.

Thus a delayed game raise does away with the need to force lightly, and allows a slow approach with time for exploration where it will do most good. It may be used whenever the suit you bid is not very big and the support for opener's suit not necessarily of limit bid standard. The yardstick is in the region of 13-15 points in a hand not strong enough to force immediately whilst responder fears that, because of some other feature in the hand, the best contract may be missed if a direct raise to game in opener's suit is made.

It must also be emphasised that a delayed game raise is only used on a responding hand containing either a good or reasonable fit for opener's suit. In the former case the first-round change-of-suit response is used as a prelude to the strong raise to game level on the second round, and in the latter it is used because responder would like to hear opener's suit *rebid* before he can consider his holding in it good enough for a raise to game.

THE 4♣—4♢ 'SWISS' CONVENTION

The 'Swiss' convention, which is used in conjunction with opening one-bids in the *majors,* has one thing in common with the delayed game raise—it is not a substitute for an immediate force. At no time should either of these bids be used if a responding hand *does* qualify for a forcing bid, so in other words, the use of either denies a suitable hand on which to force.

There are various different forms of this convention in use, details of which can be found in *Current Conventions Made Clear* by the same authors. Meanwhile here is, if not the simplest form of all, the one most widely used nowadays, which works extremely well in conjunction with the Acol System.

Using 'Swiss', a direct raise of a 1♡ or 1♠ opening bid to the four-level, which used to be a very strong limit bid, is now used purely pre-emptively. In practice it was found that, when responder's hand contained two or three aces though insufficient strength to force, opener was likely to be short of first-round controls and, therefore, being ignorant of responder's assets in this respect, generally felt disinclined to take the bidding beyond the four-level in search of a slam. Now, with the introduction of 'Swiss', instead of making the direct jump to game for which his hand is strong enough, responder bids either 4♣ or 4♢ to pin-point his controls. 4♣ shows four-card trump support, two aces, and a singleton, while 4♢ shows four-card trump support, again two aces, but this time no singleton.

♠ K 9 7 4
♡ A 9 7 3
♢ 8
♣ A J 8 6

This hand would qualify for a 4♣ response to either 1♡ or 1♠, but bring the ♣6 up and make it into the ♢6, and it would qualify for a 4♢ response.

Opener can now review his hand in the light of the knowledge that his partner, though not strong enough for a force, has a first-class trump fit for him as well as two aces. If he still does not fancy the idea of even investigating for a slam he merely converts to his original suit, either 4♡ or 4♠ as the case may be. If, however, he views the prospects optimistically, there are various things he can now do.

If the response has been 4♣ and he now wants to know which singleton his partner holds, he bids 4♢. Responder, of course, cannot possibly have a trump singleton as he has already guaranteed four-card trump support. If his singleton is in *diamonds* he rebids four of the *trump* suit, thus being able to show this particular singleton at a conveniently low level. With the singleton in either of the two remaining suits he cue-bids the suit concerned.

Another means of investigation available to opener is to use the logical extension of 'Blackwood', the Acol Direct King Convention. The 4♣ or 4♢ response *already having shown the number of aces held by responder,* opener has no need to ask this question again. His 4 N.T., therefore, by-passes the request to show aces and asks immediately for kings, if any, on the 'Blackwood' scale, (see Chapter 18).

A few words of warning here, which really only underline the need to use foresight in the use of this convention. It is unwise for responder to bid either a 'Swiss' 4♣ or 4♢ on a hand which he is not fully confident should be bid at least to game level, as the implication is strong that responder would be willing to hear opener make a further move towards a slam. Then from opener's side of the table, he must remember that, if the response has been 4♣ and he now wants to follow with 4♢ to ask which singleton is held, the reply may block the 4 N.T. level to ask for kings. Opener will, therefore, have to decide which is the more important, to discover where his partner's singleton lies or whether he has a king in addition to what he has already shown. Note, by the way, that he is unlikely to hold more than one king as two aces, two kings, and four-card trump support with a side-suit singleton could hardly constitute less than a force. The yardstick should be in the region of 13-14 honour plus distributional points.

Example sequences :

	N.	S.	
1.	1♠	—4♣ or	*Showing no interest in further slam investiga-
		4♢	tions.
	4♠*		

2.	1♠	—4♣*	*Showing 4-card trump support, two aces, and
	4♢**	—4♠***	a side-suit singleton.
		or 4♡****	**Asking which side-suit singleton
		or 5♣****	***Showing the diamond singleton
			****Showing the club or heart singleton, whichever is held.

3. 1♡ —4♣   *Asking immediately for responder's kings on
   4 NT*   the 'Blackwood' scale.

4. 1♡ —4♣   *Asking which singleton
   4◇* —4♡**   **Showing the diamond singleton
   4 NT***   ***Asking for kings

5. 1♡ —4♣   *Asking which singleton
   4◇* —5♣**   **Showing the club singleton, which blocks
                   opener's possible 4 N.T. request to ask for
                   kings.

You will note in sequence No: 5, when opener has been prevented from using the 4 N.T. bid to ask for kings, he should have anticipated this possibility and decided which was the more important for him to know, kings or singleton.

FORCING RESPONSES

When a responding hand is so strong that responder is immediately sure of a game and possibly a slam it is not enough to make a simple change-of-suit response, a limit bid, or even a delayed game raise or 'Swiss' bid. Any of these would leave opener in the dark as to the strength held, thus running the risk of the optimum contract being missed. It is necessary in such cases to make a response which will *compel* opener to keep the auction open until at least a game contract has been reached, and this is done by way of a forcing take-out. This is a bid in a new suit at one level higher than is needed for a simple take-out, that is, 1♠—3◇, or 1◇—2♡. These jump bids are *unconditionally forcing to game*.

It goes without saying that opener must not immediately take fright if he holds a minimum for his bid. Playing Acol, responder will be well aware of how weak an opening bid may be, so it is opener's duty to keep the bidding open until at least a game contract has been reached whilst concentrating on telling the truth, the whole truth, and nothing but the truth about his hand. Opener's rebids are fully covered in Chapter 8 so, in the meantime, let us return to responder's forcing take-out.

Obviously there are many types of hand on which responder will need to use a forcing take-out, but these cannot be tied by arbitrary rules and point counts. To say that you must *always* force on 17 points, or *never* force on less than 16 points is only to impose the straight-jacket which Acol seeks to avoid, and although there are guiding indications, the final decision must be left to judgement of the individual situation. The one emphatic rule which can be given without equivocation is *always force on a hand where game is certain and slam is possible*. The delayed game raise explained earlier in this chapter is not a contradiction of this rule as it is used on hands where responder, although determined to play in a game, is not yet sure which way the hand is going and wants to hear opener's rebid before deciding on the best resting place.

The simplest situation in which a forcing response is needed is on a hand with good support for opener's suit coupled with strength in one or more side suits.

♠ Q 8 6 5　　Although containing only 14 honour points, this
♡ K 7　　　　hand adds up to a lot more distributionally if
◇ A K Q 9 6 4　partner opens 1♠. Opener only needs to hold the
♣ 5　　　　　♡A in addition to a decent spade suit to make a
little slam an odds-on certainty, so the correct response is a forcing jump to 3◇. A spade game is as certain as anything can be, and the slam a high probability.

♠ A K Q J 2　　When partner opens 1◇ this hand contains a force
♡ A Q　　　　 of 2♠, at least a game somewhere being certain,
◇ J 9 4　　　 and a slam highly probable. In the actual event
♣ 9 7 3　　　 from which it is taken, opener's left-hand opponent
intervened with 1♡, which even upgrades responder's hand. The 2♠ force allowed time for exploration with no danger of the bidding being dropped below game level, and the sure 6◇ slam was reached.

In the two examples above responder, whilst holding support for his partner's suit, also had a strong side suit which would furnish a happy parking-place for most of opener's losers. But responder can well qualify for a forcing bid without this asset.

♠ Q 5　　　　　17 honour points facing a 1♠ opening bid and at
♡ A K 10 6 5　least a partial fit for spades. Even if the opening
◇ K 10　　　　 bid is the lightest of light variety a game some-
♣ K Q 5 3　　 where is certain and, if stronger, a slam may well
be reached. Force with 3♡ and, if opener merely rebids 3♠, raise to 4♠. He will have got the message and may still be able to make a slam try.

♠ 5　　　　　　Compare this hand, however—the same honour
♡ A K 10 6 5　count, but a complete misfit if partner can do
◇ K Q 10　　　 nothing except repeat his spades. Bid a quiet 2♡
♣ K Q 5 3　　　and await developments—after all, you can well
jump the bidding on the next round, which will still be a force.

The point at issue in the last two examples is the difference a trump fit can make. With a fit, even a partial one, you can see where the hand is likely to be going. Without a fit you may need more time for exploration, especially if you want to be sure of not missing a possible final contract of 3 N.T. On the last hand above, for example, if you respond to 1♠ with 3♡ and opener's rebid is 3♠ you must choose between 3 N.T. or 4♣, either of which could turn out to be wrong.

There will be occasions, of course, when responder must force even without a fit for opener's suit. These will be hands so strong that if your partner can bid at all you intend to reach a slam. But these hands come only once in a blue moon, and you can want to force on much lesser hands, even without any fit with opener. A strong two-suiter is a typical example:

♠ —
♡ K 10 7
♢ A K Q 9 5
♣ A K J 8 4

Partner, needless to say, opens 1♠. As responder a game you must, and intend, to bid, even without a shred of a fit for opener's suit. Force with 3♢ and show your clubs on the next round. Compare, however, the following:]

♠ 9
♡ A K 8 6 3
♢ A K 9 7 5
♣ K 10

When partner opens 1♠—of course!—it is wiser to make a waiting bid of 2♡ and to force on the next round with 4♢ if he merely rebids 2♠. Opener will then be able to read you for a big red two-suiter and no better than a singleton spade.

If he can still only rebid his suit, then you can abandon the bidding, even though reluctantly, at 4♠, at least knowing that your winners

♠ K Q J 10 6 5
♡ 9 5
♢ Q 10 8 3
♣ A

will take care of a number of his losers. However, in the actual event this was opener's hand. Having correctly analysed responder's cards from his bidding, opener raised the 4♢ bid to 6♢ and, as you can see, the only loser was the ♠A.

Now let's take a somewhat different situation. If the bulk of your values lies in one long strong suit you should generally force on the first round, as otherwise you may find yourself in difficulties for an expressive rebid. Your partner, perhaps, opens 1♢ and you hold:

♠ 10 7
♡ A K Q J 7 4
♢ 6 2
♣ A 8 6

You have no real diamond support, but if partner can open at all you are prepared and willing to play in at least 4♡. If you do not force with 2♡ on the first round what are you to do if opener's rebid is 2♢ or 2♣? A jump to 3♡ would be a non-forcing, even if strong, limit bid, which might be passed out, and a direct bid of 4♡ may well mean a missed slam. Your alternative of rebidding 4 N.T. may equally prove disastrous, as you can find yourself playing in 5♡ one off. So make your force at once by bidding 2♡ if he opens 1♣ or 1◇, and 3♡ if he opens 1♠.

♠ 4
♡ A Q J 10 9 6
◇ K 5 4
♣ K 3 2

Here is a responding hand which comes from a multiple pairs event, so comparisons on the final contracts reached were available. Opener in all cases bid 1♣, and responders who bid a mere 1♡ ended in 4♡, while responders who forced immediately with 2♡ ended in 6♡ which was comfortably made.

The lesson of these two examples is that on a mainly single-suited hand with enough values elsewhere to give sure promise of game, force immediately, even without support for partner's suit. You will have noticed that, on such hands, 'shape' is of rather more consequence than high point count, though the yardstick for the latter should be in the region of 13-14 points.

Similarly, with good support for opener's suit and a strong side-suit of your own which will furnish opener with discards, force at once; this does not lose time but, in fact gains it, as it means that you can now explore at leisure for a slam contract, with no fear that the bidding will be allowed to die below game. So with a good fit in a strong hand force at once, but without a fit be careful, as you may well be better off making just a simple change-of-suit response on the first round. To get this important distinction quite clear, compare the following hands, on both of which you must respond to 1♠.

♠ A 9 6 3 2
♡ —
◇ A Q J 10 8 6
♣ K 6

Here you are immediately confident of at least a spade game and, if given time to find out how opener's hand is constituted, you can see that a slam is also highly probable. Force with 3◇.

♠ 6
♡ A Q J 7 5
◇ A Q J 7
♣ K 8 3

A beautiful hand, but consider what may happen if you force by bidding your hearts at the three-level. You cannot then show your diamonds over opener's possible rebid of 3♠ without giving up the chance of playing in 3 N.T., which for all your 17 honour points, may well be all the combined hands are worth. So do not force. Make a waiting response of 2♡ and if opener only rebids 2♠ you can try him with 3◇, a new suit at the three-level which is in itself a one round force. If he can still only repeat spades you can convert to 3 N.T. If opener rebids anything but weakly you can come to life and go slamming.

So far we have only considered hands where responder had a suit of his own in which to force. But it can well happen, particularly when you want to force *because* of a fit for opener's suit, that you will have no real suit in which to make the force. In such cases you may force in a short suit, choosing one, if this is possible, lower in rank than your partner's suit, and in which you have 'tops'. The reason for choosing a lower ranking suit is that should opener have a strong liking for the suit in which you make your force, you will always be able to return his enthusiastic raises in it to his own suit.

♠ A K 8
♡ K J 9 6 5
♢ 9 8
♣ A Q 6

Partner opens 1♡ and you immediately have visions of a slam. You are far too strong for any direct raise in hearts or for a 'Swiss' response, so force with 3♣, *not* 2♠. If opener happens to like spades and you elect to force in that suit you may find it difficult to get him back into hearts, whereas after a force in clubs you will always be able to get your own way.

Let's switch the above hand around, to illustrate the point about having 'tops' in the suit in which you force. This time partner opens 1♢ and you hold:

♠ A K 8
♡ A Q 6
♢ K J 9 6 5
♣ 9 8

If you force with 3♣ you will find later that you will never be able to persuade your partner that this is your weakest suit, and it is a psychological fact that he will always rely on you for a control in that suit. So here you have no choice but to force in a non-existent major. In such circumstances you may do well to consider bidding a direct 4 N.T. Blackwood (or your chosen slam convention) unless your hand is such that you are willing to remove all your partner's enthusiastic raises in the major, including a final slam contract, into No Trumps.

On a balanced hand which *ipso facto* contains at least partial support for opener's suit, you should force on about 16 or more honour points or, later in the auction, you may find it impossible to persuade your partner that you are as strong as you are. Remember that opener will be basing the rest of his bidding on the knowledge that (a) you have the strength to force, or (b) you could only make a simple response.

Although, as we have seen, it is impossible to set rigid standards for a hand on which to force it is a safe rule that you should always force on hands where game is certain and slam is possible. Likely situations are:

a) Responding hands containing good support for opener's suit plus a strong side suit which may be used for discards of losers.

b) Single-suited hands with sufficient outside values, when responder feels sure of at least a game in his own suit and on which he can foresee possible difficulties for an expressive rebid.

c) Hands with 16 or more balanced points which in any case must contain at least partial support for opener's suit.

d) Any hand on which responder knows, for the above or any other reasons, where the hand is going, and is determined to play at least in a game contract and possibly a slam.

Before leaving this section compare the following examples from which you will see that, as well as positive information from responder's bids, there is also negative information to be gleaned from the fact that a particular response was chosen, neither a stronger nor weaker one. A hand which qualifies for a forcing bid is too strong or unsuitable for a 'Swiss' response, a hand qualifying for a 'Swiss' bid has specific holdings not contained in one bid by way of a delayed game raise, and so on.

♠ 9 6
♡ K J 8 7
◇ A 9 8 5
♣ K 10 7

When partner opens 1♡ this hand is fully and accurately bid by a limit bid response of 3♡, showing four-card trump support and 11-12 honour plus distributional points in a hand not strong enough for any other bid.

♠ 9 8
♡ K J 8 7 6
◇ 9
♣ K Q 10 8 6

A pre-emptive raise of 1♡ direct to 4♡ does full justice to this responding hand. Opener will understand that responder has no ambitions towards a slam contract and is combining the pre-emptive value of his bid with the hope that, on 'shape',
ten tricks may be made.

♠ A Q 9 6
♡ K Q 7
◇ 7 5
♣ K 10 7 6

Facing an opening bid of 1♠ this hand is too strong for either a limit bid of 3♠ which might be passed, or a pre-emptive bid of 4♠ which might mean a missed slam. It has not got the first-round controls necessary for a 'Swiss' bid. Respond 2♣
and raise direct to 4♠ on the next round.

♠ A Q 9 6
♡ A J 7
◇ 7 5
♣ K 10 7 6

This is the same hand except that now the 5 points in the heart suit are the ♡ A-J instead of the ♡ K-Q. This gives responder the accurate and descriptive 'Swiss' bid of 4◇, ensuring that a spade game cannot be missed.

♠ K J 10 7
♡ 9
◇ A 8 4
♣ A K 10 9 6

Lastly, when partner opens 1♣ this responding hand is too strong for anything but an immediate force, notifying opener of the strength held as well as the fact that it is *too good* for any weaker bid.

From this you will see that these responding bids are not substitutes for each other, and each has its allotted part to play in an accurate auction.

BIDDING YOUR CARDS TWICE

There is one final and vitally important point which must be made and that is on what is known as bidding your cards twice. You may, of course, have a responding hand so good that no amount of signing-off on your partner's part will deter you from going on in search of a slam. But if you have forced on a lesser hand you should leave it to your partner to make the subsequent running. This applies, of course, whether you are opener or responder and is merely based on the Acol principle of bidding your own cards and not bidding your partner's for him. If you have once forced on a hand which is minimum or even just average for this bid, then you have said your little all except, obviously, for steering the hand into the right final denomination. But an Acol-playing partner will revalue his own hand in the light of the knowledge that *his partner* holds the strength to force and should be capable of assessing whether the combined hands may, or cannot, be worth a slam contract. If he elects to investigate further then you will, of course, back him up. Two examples should make this point clear:

♠ K Q 6
♡ K 10 8 5
◇ A 7
♣ A 10 9 8

If partner opens 1♡ you force immediately with 3♣. If he merely confirms heart length by rebidding 3♡ you raise to 4♡. Opener already knows that you were able to force and then support hearts, which also means that you were too strong for a mere 'Swiss' response. There is nothing in the world to prevent him from going on beyond 4♡ if he has values to spare for his bidding thus far. Strengthen the hand by, say, the inclusion of the ♣K and now *you* are the one with values to spare and could not be blamed for making a further try instead of just raising 3♡ to 4♡.

♠ K Q 6
♡ 9
◇ A Q J 5 3
♣ A 10 9 8

♠ 9 8
♡ A Q J 10 7 6 3
◇ 8 7
♣ J 3

Here is a hand from a pairs event where East-West suffered the indignity of having a quite appalling 6 N.T. contract bid and made against them! With North the dealer the bidding should have gone 1◇ from North and 4♡ from South —finish. In fact this was how it went, North pressing on and on in spite of South's repeated heart bids and his, North's, lack of fit for the suit. East led a spade which was won by West's ♠A. A club switch was taken by North's ♣A and the ♡9 was then led, being overtaken by the ♡10, which held. We need hardly tell you

N.	S.
1◇	1♡
3♣	3♡
3 NT	4♡
4 NT	5◇
6 NT	

that the ♡K fell on the ace on the next round giving declarer seven heart tricks, one club, two spades, and a successful diamond finesse for his last two tricks!

This 'top' for North-South was no thanks to North, who bid his hand not only twice but three times. North at least had the grace subsequently to apologise to his outraged opponents, though it is a pity the two red kings were not reversed, when at least justice would have been seen to be done!

PRE-EMPTIVE RESPONSES

If you will refer back to p. 62 you will remind yourself that it can be advisable to jump direct to game in a long suit as, in fact, South should have done on the hand in the preceding paragraph. The situation is, of course, that opener bids a suit for which responder has no real support, though responder can see that the only hope for the hand, either game or part-score, is to play in his own long suit. Such hands may be bid by way of a jump of *two or more* levels, (not to be confused with the single jump of a strong forcing bid). As well as warning opener of the single-suited character of the hand this jump bid will be highly pre-emptive and may well make life more than difficult for the opposition.

Note that the jump to the four-level cannot be made in clubs or diamonds when partner has opened with 1♡ or 1♠, as either would be a 'Swiss' conventional response—which might well land the partnership in acute disaster!

♠ A J 9 7 6 5 4　　If partner opens 1♣, 1◇, or 1♡, make a pre-
♡ 7 2　　　　　　emptive jump response of 3♠ which will describe
◇ 9 4　　　　　　the hand very adequately. If you strengthen the
♣ 8 3　　　　　　suit to ♠A-Q-J or add another spade it would be
　　　　　　　　　worth the direct game bid of 4♠.

♠ 7 2　　　　　　This is the same hand except that the major suits
♡ A J 9 7 6 5 4　are exchanged. Opposite 1♣ or 1◇ from partner
◇ 9 4　　　　　　make the pre-emptive jump bid of 3♡. If he opens
♣ 8 3　　　　　　1♠, however, you cannot bid 3♡ as this would be
strong and forcing, so the choice is between bidding a direct 4♡ or making a simple change-of-suit bid of 2♡. After that you would continue to repeat the suit until opener gets the message. Which course is best is a matter for judgement at the time, taking into account the vulnerability and even, possibly, the quality of the opposition.

RESPONDING AFTER A PREVIOUS PASS

To round off this chapter some further mention of two points must be made, the difference a previous pass can make to the correct response, and the difference an intervening bid from responder's right-hand opponent can make.

Taking first the case where responder, as first or second hand, has already passed, his simple change-of-suit is no longer forcing.

1♡—1♠
or
No
1♡—1♠

Compare these two sequences, in the first of which responder's change-of-suit is a one-round force, and in the second of which it is no longer forcing and can be passed by opener. Even a two-level response (No—1♡—2♦) loses its forcing character, so a responder who has previously passed must beware of the risk of being left in a simple change-of-suit bid when the hand obviously 'belongs' in opener's suit. The reason for this is the need to guard against the chance that third or fourth-in-hand opening bids are often made on slender values at duplicate, opener intending to pass anything his partner bids. In the following example responder, not having previously

♠ A 10 7
♡ K 9 7
♦ A 9 8 4 3
♣ 7 6

passed, is in no difficulty and merely makes a temporising bid of 2♦. Once he has passed originally, however, he is in a more difficult position, as 2♦ might well be passed by opener and a much better heart contract be missed. On balance it will generally be wiser to raise to 3♡, even lacking the four-card support which this limit bid strictly requires.

Apart from the occasional hand, such as the one above, on which you may find it expedient to break the normal rules for limited responses, the limit bids remain unchanged. If a responding hand contains an honest limit raise of opener's major suit opening to either the two or three-level, that will still be the best response. In the minor suits the emphasis changes somewhat, as responder will no longer want to make a change-of-suit response into a fragile major which may be passed out when there is a good minor suit fit available. As already explained in Chapter 3, therefore, it will generally be wiser to give up the change-of-suit response in favour of a limit bid at the appropriate level.

♠ K J 9 6
♡ Q 7 4
♦ Q J 8 3
♣ 9 5

Here, not previously having passed, you would bid 1♠ in response to any other one-level opening bid. Having once passed, however, bid 1♠ if partner opens 1♣ or 1♡, but raise his 1♦ opening to 3♦.

It is also possible that partner's opening bid will put a very different complexion on a modest responding hand which was not worth an opening bid, so here is a new rule to remember—a jump bid in a new suit by a passed hand is only a *one-round* force, not a game force. It should be based on a fit for opener's suit and a maximum or near maximum pass.

♠ K Q 9
♡ K Q 9 8 6
♢ 10 9 7
♣ J 9

This hand is nearly, but not quite, worth an opening bid. When partner, third or fourth in hand, opens 1♠, responder can bid 3♡, a simple one-round force. Opener can now revalue his hand in the knowledge that responder did *not* use a limit bid of either 2♠ or 3♠. He has, therefore, good, though not four-card spade support and a reasonable heart suit. If this fits well with his own hand, opener can bid 4♠ direct or sign off in 3♠.

RESPONDING AFTER AN INTERVENING SUIT BID

The question of how to reply to opener's bid when there has been a take-out double on responder's right is dealt with fully in Chapter 15, and here we confine ourselves to responder's actions when the intervening bid has been made in a suit.

Firstly, a responding hand containing a suit limit bid in support of the opening bid seldom has to look further afield than this particular raise. The intervention, in fact, makes no difference whatsoever to the values for a limit bid response, and a hand which would have raised opener's 1♠ to 2♠ or 3♠, for example, should do so now.

If responder would have made a No Trump limit bid in reply, then a slight variation comes into the picture as, in addition to the values needed for the response, a bid of No Trumps at any level over an intervening bid must guarantee a good hold on the suit intervened.

♠ K J 6
♡ J 8 4
♢ J 10 8 5
♣ A J 10

With no intervention responder would bid 2 N.T. facing any opening bid. If, however, the opening were 1♢ and next hand came in with 1♡ there is no hold on hearts, and the limit raise to 3♢ should be preferred. If the intervention were 1♠ or 2♣, then once again 2 N.T. becomes an honest reply.

The humble response of 1 N.T., normally little more than a keep-open bid on anything between 5-9 points when no more constructive bid is available also takes on a different character. mere keep-open response, because opener has been given a second When there has been an intervening suit bid, 1 N.T. is no longer a turn to bid. 1 N.T., therefore, becomes a much more positive bid showing, in particular, a stop in the suit intervened and, it also goes without saying, insufficient values or the wrong 'shape' for a penalty double.

♠ K 10 7
♡ 8 5 4
♢ Q 9
♣ J 8 5 4 3

In an uninterrupted sequence you would respond 1 N.T. to partner's opening of 1◇, 1♡, or 1♠. Opposite 1◇ or 1♡, if there is an intervening bid of 1♠ you can still bid 1 N.T. because of the spade stop. If, however, partner opens 1♠ and the intervention is 2◇ or 2♡ you cannot possibly bid 2 N.T., and it is better to raise mildly to 2♠.

♠ K J 7
♡ 8 5 4
♢ Q 7 6
♣ J 8 7 6

On this 7-point hand if partner opens 1♣ responder is not strong enough (remember this?) to bid 1 N.T. The response, therefore, intervention or no intervention, would be 2♣. If the opening bid is 1♡, without intervention responder would bid 1 N.T. With a 1♠ intervention responder could still bid 1 N.T., confirming the spade guard. *But* if opener bids 1◇ and there is an intervention of 1♡, responder's wisest action is to pass.

A responding hand which had intended to make a pre-emptive jump bid in a new suit should do so undeterred—unless by any chance the intervention came in responder's suit, when he would double like a rocket! Nor does an intervening bid make any difference to a responder who had intended to use a 'Swiss' response. In this sequence South's 4♣ is just as 'Swiss' as it would have been without East's intervention. In the case of a responder wanting to force, the intervention may make a difference by using up a bidding level, but this is catered for by the fact that South's 3♣ bid is forcing in any case, and there will seldom if ever be a situation where South, with a strong hand, is at a loss for an expressive bid even when there has been an intervention.

N.	E.	S.	W.
1◇	1♡	3♠)	
		or 4♠)	

N.	E.	S.	W.
1♡	1♠)	4♣	
	or 2♣)		
	or 2◇)		

N.	E.	S.	W.
1♠	—	3♣	
	or		
1♠	2◇	3♣	

This is all really just a matter of common, or bidding, sense, and the fact is that, as with your own intervening bids (Chapter 16) or the use of a double (Chapter 15), the Acol System has no special conventions of its own. When as responder you hold only what one might call a token bid, which you would make just to keep the bidding open for one round to give your partner a second chance, then you can take advantage of the opportunity given by the intervention to pass. On the other hand, you must not allow yourself to be bamboozled out of your own contract by an obstructive intervening bid and must use your own judgement as to the best course of action—not forgetting that any ill-advised intervention may give you the chance to take a juicy penalty by a business double.

A useful bid, and also incidentally, another fairly modern modif
cation, is an immediate cue bid in the suit intervened. This used t

N.	E.	S.	W.
1♡	1♠	2♠	

show a powerful responding hand with goo
trump support for opener coupled with nc
less than second-round control of the su
intervened. Nowadays this immediate overcall is used as a sort c
utility bid, not necessarily a cue bid but still a game force, responde
still being doubtful as to the best final denomination. The origina
meaning of the bid is not barred, and responder's second round bi
will clarify his intentions. In the meantime opener should treat th
bid as a directional asking bid (see Chapter 16), and reply accord
ingly.

a) ♠ A K J
   ♡ A 9
   ◇ J 10 8
   ♣ J 9 8 6 5

b) ♠ A 10 9
   ♡ 9 8 3
   ◇ K Q 10
   ♣ K J 9 8

c) ♠ A 9 8
   ♡ K J 9
   ◇ Q 10 7
   ♣ A Q 7 6

Here are three South hands and in each case North has opene
1◇ which East has overcalled with 1♡. On all three South's bes
bid is 2♡. Taking each in turn, on (a) 2♡ is superior to 2♣ because
if North can be stimulated into bidding 2 N.T., 3 N.T. should be
happy contract. On (b) again, 3 N.T. is likely to be the safest resting
place if North can bid it, failing which there should be a good pla
for 5◇. On (c), where North is highly unlikely to be able to rebi
in No Trumps, South can do this himself unless North's rebid show
a strong hand, when South will be able to embark on exploration fo
higher things.

Competitive bidding such as often develops when the oppositior
intervenes, needs more judgement than straightforward biddin,
between two players in an uninterrupted sequence. Only experienc
and common sense can be your final guide. For instance, when face
with the problem of whether to double an intervening bid or go fo
a No Trump game for your side, vulnerability must be taken int
account. Say your partner has opened 1♠ which is overcalled witl
2♡. This, doubled and two down for 500 points is more thar
adequate compensation at duplicate for a non-vulnerable 3 N.T.
whereas against non-vulnerable opponents you would score onl
300 for the double as against 600 if you bid and made a vulnerable
3 N.T.

For the most part, bid your cards as naturally as possible. If a
normal response is still available make it. If the intervention upset
your normal call then you may have to vary your strategy, as care

ust be taken not to drive the auction too high. When making your
ecision, remember any revaluation of your hand which may be
dicated. For example, if you hold ♣ K-J-x over an intervening
ub call you can mentally upgrade these four points rather than
e-value them as you would have to do had clubs been bid on your
ft.

RESPONDING AFTER AN INTERVENING NO TRUMP BID

irst and foremost, if your right-hand opponent comes in with a
o Trump intervention, find out what it means. This, of course, you
o by asking intervener's partner what he understands by the bid.
andard Acol requires that a 1 N.T. intervening bid should be based
n a strong hand—a minimum of 15 and probably 16 points—
cluding a good stop in the suit opened (see Chapter 16). But
layers do sometimes vary this rule and you may well meet
pponents who will bid a weak No Trump in this position. More
ften than not, and provided you are awake to the fact that the bid
weak, it can be punished as it deserves by a business double.

If the 1 N.T. is based on a strong hand the chances are reasonably
igh that you will have nothing sensible to respond in any case.
fter all, opener and the next hand have certainly accounted for
ore than half the available points already. Specific guidance is
ifficult to give as so much depends on responder's actual holding
nd the vulnerability. A non-vulnerable intervening 1 N.T. doubled
r penalties may well not gain you nearly as much as your own
ulnerable game, though to defeat vulnerable opponents by two
icks, if you can double, is more than adequate compensation for
non-vulnerable game.

In practice the best results will probably be obtained by doubling
hen vulnerable against non-vulnerable opponents on a modest
olding of something between 7-10 points and going forward firmly
wards your own game if holding anything stronger. Thus if you
hoose to double, opener will know that your hand is limited and
an base his own further bidding on that knowledge.

I.	E.	S.	W.	South:	
♠	1 NT	?		♠ 7 5	With N-S vulnerable against
				♡ K 8 2	non-vulnerable opponents
				◇ K J 6	South can double, not only
				♣ Q 10 8 6 3	limiting his hand but show-

ing North that this is the
most likely spot for gaining
plus-score. Reverse the vulnerability and a double is still almost
ertainly the best bet.

N.	E.	S.	W.
1♠	1 NT	?	

♠ J 10
♡ K 10 9 6
◇ Q 7 6
♣ A J 7 4

Here a vulnerable South i
too strong to double a
intervening 1 N.T., particu
larly if the opponents ar
not vulnerable. Bid 2 N.T

showing 11-12 points just as you would do without the intervening
1 N.T. At equal vulnerability double anyway.

In dealing with these situations what you have to try to do is t
judge whether a positive bid as opposed to a double will gain yo
the best result, and each hand can only be judged on its own merits
Don't let yourself be caught napping by expecting a strong han
on your right when it is, in fact, weak.

Finally, if the intervening bid on your right is 2 N.T., *find ou*
whether this is intended as a natural strong bid or as an 'Unusua
No Trump' (see Chapter 16). In standard Acol it will be the con
ventional Unusual No Trump but here again a minority group exist
who use it as a natural bid showing something in the region of 2(
points. These are not true Acol players but make sure you are no
going to be caught napping by not understanding what your op
ponents are doing.

Having discovered that the 2 N.T. bid is conventional, you
actions will depend very much on the particular situation. Fo
instance, if the 2 N.T. bid comes over your partner's opening 1♠
or 1♡ it will be asking for a take-out into a *minor* suit, probably wit
a sacrifice contract in view. Block this if you can by raising you
partner's bid to the highest possible level for which you are qualified
If you yourself have the minors it may pay dividends to keep quie
and then double the opponents' final contract.

As you will have gathered, these are not straightforward situation
which can be governed by hard and fast rules. But Acol is a
common sense system, and if you apply common sense when th
occasion arises you are far more likely to be right than wrong.

) Your partner, North, opens the bidding with 1♣. East does not intervene. What would you, South, bid on the following hands?

   a) ♠ K J 8 6: ♡ A Q 5: ◇ K 7 5 3: ♣ Q 4:
   b) ♠ K 10 8 4: ♡ K Q 7: ◇ A 9 7 6: ♣ A J:
   c) ♠ A 9 7 6: ♡ 7: ◇ K J 10 8: ♣ K J 5 3:
   d) ♣ Q 10 9 8: ♡ A 10 8 6: ◇ A 6 5 2: ♣ 8;
   e) ♠ A 9 6 2: ♡ 6: ◇ A Q 10 9 5: ♣ A Q 8:

.) Your partner, North, opens the bidding with 1♡. With no intervention, what would you bid on the following hands?

   a) ♠ 8: ♡ J 7 6: ◇ A K Q 10 9 7 5: ♣ K 2:
   b) ♠ K 9 3: ♡ Q 9 5: ◇ K Q 10 7: ♣ K Q 4:
   c) ♠ A K J 9 5 2: ♡ Q 9: ◇ A 8 3: ♣ J 9:
   d) ♠ K 7: ♡ Q J 9: ◇ A J 9 5: ♣ K Q 7 4:
   e) ♠ K Q 5: ♡ Q 9 5: ◇ K Q 10: ♣ K Q 4 2:
   f) ♠ 9 2: ♡ 7: ◇ A K Q 9 4: ♣ A K J 9 3:
   g) ♠ A K Q 10 6 4: ♡ 6: ◇ A 8 6 2: ♣ 5 3:
   h) ♠ A 4: ♡ K Q J: ◇ J 9 6 5 4 3: ♣ A Q:
   i) ♠ A 9 5 4: ♡ 10: ◇ A Q 9 8: ♣ A Q J 6:
   j) ♠ 10 9: ♡ A 9 7 6: ◇ A J 9 5: ♣ K Q 8:

) At Love All your partner deals and opens 1♠ and next hand intervenes with 2◇. What should you bid on the following hands?

   a) ♠ J 7: ♡ A Q 10 6 5: ◇ K 6 4 3 2: ♣ 6:
   b) ♠ K 8 6: ♡ K Q 10 7 5: ◇ 7 5 2: ♣ J 8:
   c) ♠ Q 8 6 4: ♡ K 7 5 3: ◇ 9 2: ♣ 7 5 4:
   d) ♠ K Q 10 7: ♡ A Q 9 6: ◇ A: ♣ K J 7 5:
   e) ♠ J 5: ♡ A Q 10 8 4: ◇ 8 7: ♣ K 7 3 2:
   f) ♠ K J 6 4: ♡ A Q 9 2: ◇ 5 3: ♣ 7 5 4:
   g) ♠ Q 9 2: ♡ 9 5: ◇ 7 5 4: ♣ A Q 9 7 5:
   h) ♠ 8: ♡ K J 6 4: ◇ K J 9 8 5: ♣ 7 3 2:
   i) ♠ K 6 3 2: ♡ 10 8 6 4: ◇ 8:. ♣ K 4 3 2:
   j) ♠ 9 7 4: ♡ K 10 9 3: ◇ K J: ♣ A K J 6:
   k) ♠ K 10 7: ♡ 8 7 6: ◇ 7: ♣ A K J 6 5 3:
   l) ♠ Q J 8 4: ♡ K 7 5 4 2: ◇ 5: ♣ A J 4:
   m) ♠ 7 2: ♡ 6 4 2: ◇ A Q 9 5: ♣ A J 7 4:
   n) ♠ J 7 6: ♡ K 10 3: ◇ A Q 4: ♣ Q 9 6 3:

ANSWERS TO REVISION QUIZ ON CHAPTER 7

1) a) 2◇   This is a delayed game raise hand—not quite strong
           enough to force on the first round but intending to put
           partner straight to 4♠ if he merely rebids 2♠. Of
           course, if he takes stronger action, you will be fully
           prepared to join in the fun!

   b) 3◇   Now you must force immediately, as you are far too
           strong for any other action.

   c) 2♣   This time again you delay your raise, although you have
           no intention of stopping out of game. You want to hear
           partner's rebid.

   d) 4♣   This is the conventional bid showing full values for a
           direct raise to 4♠, including two aces and a side suit
           singleton.

   e) 3◇   An immediate force is in order here. Game is certain
           and slam is more than merely possible.

2) a) 3◇   You will be in great difficulties to find a suitable rebid if
           you do not make an immediate force on this hand,
           especially as you have a fit with hearts.

   b) 2◇   This time you do not want to force on the first round.
           You have, in spite of your 15 points, no first round
           controls, so you would like to hear partner's rebid
           before giving a delayed game raise of some sort.

   c) 2♠   As in (a) above, you may be in hopeless difficulties for a
           rebid if you do not force at once.

   d) 3◇   With 16 points and a heart fit, you force in a suit
           ranking below partner's suit and, having two, select the
           better one of the two.

   e) 3♣   Again, with 17 points you really must force, or later you
           will find it impossible to make your partner believe how
           good your hand is. Force in clubs which, though the
           same in point-count, are longer than the diamonds.

   f) 3◇   This is a case of no fit for partner but two suits of your
           own, both so good that you feel sure game must be on
           somewhere between your hand and partner's opening
           bid.

   g) 2♠   Even with no fit at all for partner's hearts, you cannot
           afford not to force with such a good suit plus an outside
           ace.

h) 3◇ 17 points and a good fit for partner's hearts, so you must force, but don't fall into the trap of doing this in clubs. With a six-card suit of your own and, above all, so many of partner's heart honours, is there not a very strong chance that his bid was partly based on diamond honours?

i) 1♠ Definitely a hand on which *not* to force on the first round. You have only a singleton heart and no long suit of your own, so take it slowly—you will get another chance to bid. If partner signs off with 2♡ your best bet will probably be a direct bid of 3 N.T.

j) 4◇ Using the same convention as in 1 (d), you show a hand strong enough for an immediate raise to 4♡, with 4-card trump support, two aces and *no* singleton.

3) a) Double. With 10 points, only a doubleton spade and five of the opponent's suit, you must be on to a good thing. If they try to escape into clubs, partner can possibly double.

b) 2♡ This is the bid you would have made without intervention and you can make it naturally just the same.

c) 2♠ Again this is a natural bid. Your weak hand is just good for a 2♠ Limit Bid with or without the diamond bid.

d) 3◇ The forcing bid which gives you time to explore for the best game contract. If partner has the club ace you will be thinking in terms of the Grand Slam.

e) 2♡ Here again, you would bid 2♡ without the intervening bid and there is no reason to alter your bid.

f) 3♠ A natural Limit Bid which the intervention does nothing to alter.

g) 2♠ On this hand you would just have managed a switch to 2♣ as your response. As, however, the 2◇ call now forces you to the three-level if you want to show your clubs it is wiser to suppress them in favour of a 2♠ raise.

h) Double. No support for partner, 8 points and five diamonds. This should be your best available contract.

i) 2♠ Another natural Limit Bid.

j) 3◇ Either 2♡ or 3♣ would be misleading, as would a raise in spades at this stage, although you want to reach a game.

k) 3♣ This time your club suit is too good to hide and you
        can well afford to hear partner rebid 3♠, which you will
        raise to 4♠, risking that he holds the hearts covered.

l) 2♡ You are too strong for a 3♠ Limit Bid which you fear
        partner might pass, so you temporise with 2♡. If he
        only bids 2♠ over this you make a delayed game raise
        to 4♠.

m) Double. This should be a good bet and is really your only
        possible bid, as you cannot offer No Trumps with
        nothing at all in hearts.

n) 2 NT For all its point count, the hand is too evenly balanced,
        especially with three of partner's suit, to double the 2◇,
        and you make, since you hold a double stop in that
        suit, a natural Limit Bid of 2 N.T.

Chapter 8

Opener's Rebids

OPENER'S SECOND-ROUND LIMIT BIDS

IN Chapter 3 we have already mentioned various opener's rebids from the point of view of his choice when responder has used a limit bid. There is no need to repeat these, so now let's go the next step on our way and examine the different limit bids available to opener himself on the second round.

In the bad old days before approach-forcing methods in general and the Acol System in particular were developed, many rebids were forcing which can now be passed with a clear conscience. In a sequence such as this, for example, North's 2 N.T. could well mean that, whilst recognising that he must keep the bidding open, he had nothing further to say. But when playing Acol, as South's 2♡ is not forcing it is only common sense that North's 2 N.T. is constructive, being bid in a situation in which North is free to pass. If you look at this hand you will see that having opened 1◇, there is nothing North can bid in response to 1♠ except 2◇. But when South makes a second try with 2♡ North, with a partial fit for both partner's suits, not to mention a good stop in the fourth suit, is worth another try. On this occasion responder has produced a second bid in spite of the apparent sign-off rebid from opener, and opener now has the opportunity of showing that his partner's bidding has strengthened his hand. 2 N.T. is a limit bid, and responder is expected to decide the final contract unless, of course, his second rebid is forcing or requires 'preference' correction from North. Thus South might pass 2 N.T., raise to 3 N.T. or rebid one of his majors. If he bid 3♡ North would 'correct' to 3♠.

N.	S.
1◇—	1♠
2◇—	2♡
2 NT	

North:
♠ 8 7 2
♡ Q 8
◇ A K 10 9 8
♣ K Q 4

N.	S.
1♠—	2♡
2 NT	

Another example of the changing face of bidding might be this. In days gone by 2 N.T. could again well mean 'I have nothing further to say'. Nowadays it has a very clear message—an opening hand of 15-17 points—and with this positive information responder is expected to be

able to judge whether to pass or go on to game in No Trumps or a
suit.

You should learn the following table of Opener's No Trump
rebids by heart. Remember, however, that they are calculated on
quite a conservative basis and also that they assume more or less
balanced hands. If you have useful suit lengths or good intermediate
cards such as 9's and 10's, then the requirements can be shaded.
No alibis, please, for failing to bid up 'because I was one short of
the point-count, partner,' when you've got a good solid suit and
an obvious play for game.

1) If responder has replied
to your opening with a
simple change-of-suit at
the one-level (i.e., 1 ◇ —
1 ♠):

Opener's rebid of:
1 N.T. shows 14-16 points
2 N.T. shows 16+ to 18 points
3 N.T. shows 19 points

2) If responder has replied
to your opening with a
simple change-of-suit at
the two-level (i.e., 1 ◇ —
2 ♣):

2 N.T. shows 15-17 points
3 N.T. shows 17-19 points
(Due allowance must be made
for a 'good' or 'bad' hand for
the count).

3) If responder has replied
to your opening of 1 ♡ or
1 ♠ with 1 N.T.:

2 N.T. shows 17-18 points
3 N.T. shows 19 points

All these opener's rebids are limit bids which means that
responder is under no obligation to bid again. This does not mean
that he *must* not bid again, and clearly he should do so if the
announced values in opener's hand make prospects appear bright,
that is, if responder is better than minimum and sees hopes of game.
In the first two cases above, responder's strength is virtually
unknown, except that he is not strong enough to force. In the third
case responder's hand is limited to between 5-9 honour points and
opener's 2 N.T. is invitational. On a minimum hand responder can
pass but, if nearer to his possible maximum, he should elect to bid
the game. On a holding of 19 points opener, of course, takes matters
into his own hands and bids the game direct, as even if his partner
has the minimum of 5 points the combined hands will contain at
least 24 points.

In No. 3 above you will have noticed that only opener's rebids
after a major suit opening are mentioned. If you turn back to the
final paragraph of Chapter 6 you will be reminded that a
1 N.T. response to either 1 ♣ or 1 ◇ requires something better than a
mere 5 points. In responding 1 N.T. to a 1 ♣ opening, for example,

a minimum of 8 points is required, and the values for opener's No Trump rebids can then be lowered. In the sequence 1♣—1 NT—2 NT, responder is known to hold at least 8 points, so opener's invitational 2 N.T. is based on his need for responder to hold 10 points, or a 'good' 9 points to make the game contract worth while. In the same way, opener can bid 3 N.T. direct on 17 or even a good 16 points when he knows responder has at least 8 points.

Opener's No Trump rebids are not confined to the occasions when the response has been a change-of-suit or in No Trumps—they can also be used when responder has given a direct suit raise. For example, you open 1♠ on this hand and responder raises to 2♠.

♠ A Q 10 6
♡ Q J 9
◇ K J 8
♣ K 10 7

You would not feel inclined to pass this without a further try, and the most expressive rebid is 2 N.T., showing your 17-count (two 10's=$\frac{1}{2}$ pt. each) in an evenly-balanced hand. This is clearly invitational, and responder can judge between passing 2 N.T., raising to 3 N.T., converting to 3♠ or bidding 4♠ direct, according to whether his original response were maximum or minimum, suitable for No Trump play or only suitable for a spade contract. By inference, of course, opener's suit is unlikely to be more than a four-card one for, with a known 5-4 fit he would certainly make his further effort by way of a trial bid (see Chapter 10) or a direct jump to 4♠.

Another type of opener's rebid is a jump in his own suit, which is used to show approximately seven playing tricks in the suit concerned, i.e., a 'shape' hand with at least a six-card suit which is a little under strength for an opening Strong Two (see Chapter 11).

♠ A 9
♡ A Q J 10 8 2
◇ K J 3
♣ 9 8

Opener bids 1♡ to which responder makes a simple reply of 1 N.T. or 1♠. Opener has no sensible rebid available other than a repeat of his own heart suit, but the quality of the hand is far too good for a mere 2♡ which is a sign-off and which might well be passed when game is available. The rebid must be 3♡, strong and invitational but not forcing and responder once again can judge whether to pass, raise to 4♡, or take some other action.

♠ A Q 9 8 7
♡ K Q 9
◇ J 7
♣ Q J 4

A simple raise by opener of responder's change-of-suit bid speaks for itself. After the obvious 1♠ opening, if responder bids 2♡ opener should raise to 3♡ which is a non-forcing limit bid denying the strength for anything more. If the response had been 2◇, opener's rebid would be 2 N.T.

The vital basic Acol principle of bidding your own cards and not your partner's cannot be stressed too often. If you hold the values to bid game direct, or to make a forcing bid announcing that game must be reached, don't wait for your partner to do it for you, because he very likely won't.

1♡—1♠
3♠

♠ K 10 8 2
♡ A Q 9 8 5
◇ K 8
♣ Q 6

In this sequence opener's 3♠ rebid is once again non-forcing, but though highly invitational, it denies the values to bid game direct. Here is an example, and if you get the impression that opener, starting with 1♡, should jump to 4♠ if his partner bids a mere 1♠, remember that by his one-level response, responder has not guaranteed more than five or six points and a 'biddable' spade suit, so leave the rest to him. If that is really all he has he will pass a 3♠ bid by you, but with a reasonable hand he will accept the carrot held out to him and bid the game.

There is one other situation which falls into place here, and that is when, as opener, you pick up a hand such as this. Though too

♠ A Q 8 4
♡ A J 5 3
◇ A 6 4
♣ A 8

strong to open 1 N.T., this is a hand eminently suited to play in No Trumps if responder bids either minor. *But* if responder is weakish your combined forces might play much better in one of the major suits—and responder may well have a four-card fit for either. If you open 1♠, the higher of two equal and adjacent suits and responder, because he holds only 7 points, is unable to show a four or five-card heart suit at the two-level, you may miss a perfect heart fit. If you *open* 1♡ you will not miss a heart fit as he will be able to give a direct raise; nor will you miss a spade fit, as responder would be able to show even a four-card spade suit at the one-level. So by opening 1♡ on a spade-heart hand which you hope to play in No Trumps, you gain yourself the best of all possible worlds, that is, the chance to find a fit for either major or to go into No Trumps if the response is 2♣ or 2◇. All this and heaven too, without having to resort to an unnecessary 'prepared' minor suit opening bid.

CHANGE-OF-SUIT REBIDS

In Chapter 2 we examined opener's simple change-of-suit rebids which need be little, if any, stronger than a sign-off rebid at the two-level in opener's original suit. These new suit rebids, you will remember, are strictly non-forcing, and responder may pass, give preference to the first bid suit, or raise or jump raise, as his strength suggests.

a) ♠ A Q 9 7 3   b) ♠ A Q 9 7 3
   ♡ K Q 10 6 4   ♡ 8 7
   ◊ 8 7   ◊ K Q 10 6
   ♣ 6   ♣ A 3

   1♠—2◊   1♠—2♣ or 1♠ —2♡
   2♡   2◊   2 NT

Note that in example (b) the addition of the ♣A was needed to make the hand worth an opening bid at all, since the five-card spade suit in the original 11 point hand does not offer a sound rebid if partner responds 2♡.

Now we come to the stronger hands on which neither a simple second-suit rebid nor a limit bid will do justice to the holding.

♠ K 3
♡ A Q 10 8 4
◊ K Q J 9
♣ A 5

1♡—1♠
3◊

or

1♡—2♣
3◊

Strong though this hand is, it only qualifies for an opening bid of 1♡, but immediately partner responds with any 'free' bid at all, game is in sight. A count-showing No Trump limit bid could result in completely the wrong contract and a simple rebid of 2◊ over a 2♣ response could be passed. In such circumstances Acol uses a jump rebid in a new suit which is *unconditionally forcing to game*. The probabilities are that such a bid will be made on a two-suited, or at least a semi-two-suited hand, but the message is clear—if responder can bid at all, a game contract, and possibly a slam, must be reached.

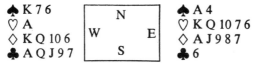

♠ K 7 6   ♠ A 4
♡ A   ♡ K Q 10 7 6
◊ K Q 10 6   W — E   ◊ A J 9 8 7
♣ A Q J 9 7   ♣ 6

The above hand is from actual tournament play. West dealt and opened 1♣ to which East responded 1♡. When West rebid 3◊, showing determination to bid at least a game however weak the 1♡ response, it did not take much imagination on East's part to go 'slamming', and the final contract of 7◊ was reached in comfort.

♠ A Q 10 8 4
♡ K 3
◊ K Q J 9
♣ A 5

This is the same hand as in the previous example except that the major suits have been changed round to illustrate a further point; in this instance after a 1♠ opening any change-of-suit bid by responder must be at the two-level. If the response happens to be 2♣ opener can make his forcing rebid of 3◊ as he did before, but if the response is 2♡ it would be madness to have to crowd the auction by bidding 4♢ in order to ensure another chance to bid. So here another rule comes into the picture namely, a new suit bid at the three-level is *forcing for one round*. Note the difference from example (b) on p. 113, where opener rebid 2 N.T. rather than show strength he did not possess by rebidding 3♢.

This new suit bid at the three-level is a one-round force made in the knowledge that responder's minimum will be 8 points and this, from opener's point of view, makes exploration for the best game contract a good proposition. Compare the two following examples:

a) ♠ A Q 10 7
   ♡ 9 7
   ♢ K Q 10 6
   ♣ K Q 9

1♣—2♡
2 NT*

*Showing the count and evenly-balanced nature of the hand.

b) ♠ A Q 10 7
   ♡ Q 9 7
   ♢ K Q 10 6
   ♣ K 9

1♣—2♡
3♢*

*With the better heart fit, making sure the best game contract will be reached. If responder rebids 3♡ this will be raised to 4♡.

If in this or similar sequences the new suit bid at the three-level is not accepted as forcing, opener can be in serious trouble for a rebid which expresses his strength, at the same time as making sure his partner will keep the bidding open. A jump rebid, which would have to be at the four-level, uses unnecessary bidding space and also cuts out the possibly best 3 N.T. contract. On a hand such as (b) above, for example, the opening bid would have to be 1♢ with a jump to 2♠ over a 1♡ response; otherwise the bidding would be 1♣—2♡—4♢ and the latter would carry quite a different meaning.

REVERSE BIDS

You have already met the term 'reverse' in these pages, and now the time has come to define this more clearly, particularly as the interpretation and implication of a reverse bid is one of the most controversial. Even the experts differ so widely in their views that the English Bridge Union's Convention Card includes a space for an explanation of each partnership's understanding! You will not go far wrong, however, if you remember that the standard definition of an opener's reverse is a bid in a third suit in an uncontested auction which prevents responder from returning to the first suit at the two-level. In other words, a player 'reverses' when his first bid is made in a suit lower-ranking than his second suit *and* when his second bid is made at the two-level.

When a player shows two suits he is offering a choice for trumps,

1♡—1♠
2♢—?

and his partner is expected to show preference. In simple non-forcing sequences this is done by passing the second bid suit, returning opener to his first suit, or raising or jump raising one or other suit according to the strength held. In this

1♡—2♢
2♠

second sequence, where opener has bid hearts before spades, responder cannot avoid going to the three-level to show preference for hearts. To safeguard this the opening bidder must guarantee a strong hand, strong enough to stand a three-level contract, for which reason a genuine reverse should be treated as a one-round force.

A reverse bidding sequence should never be chosen *in order* to show strength, but should be used only when expedient and when the necessary strength is held. It follows from this that the first bid suit is always longer than the second as otherwise, even on a strong

♠ A K J 8
♡ K Q J 9 7
♢ 7
♣ K 10 4

hand, the higher-ranking suit could have been bid first and the lower-ranking shown by a jump bid on the second round. Here, for example, you are strong enough to open 1♡ and rebid 2♠ over a 2♣ or 2♢ response. Make the ♣4 into the ♠4, however, and there is no reason in the world not to open a normal 1♠. Be careful, by the way, not to confuse this situation with the

♠ A Q 8 4
♡ A J 5 3
♢ A 6 4
♣ A 8

type of hand mentioned earlier (reproduced for convenience of reference) where you open 1♡ for quite a different reason. Here you do not intend to rebid in your equal-length spade suit unless to raise a spade response. You are merely hoping to facilitate a spade response, or to go into No Trumps over a club or diamond response or heart raise.

Note that the rebid of a higher-ranking suit at the *one*-level does

1♢—1♡
1♠

not constitute a reverse, as it may merely be taking the opportunity to show a second suit—probably a four-card major when you have rightly elected to open a six-card minor as in this example. Had partner's response been 2♣ instead of 1♡, you would have rebid 2♢ and not bid 2♠.

♠ A Q 9 7
♡ J 8
♢ A J 10 9 7 4
♣ 7

1♣—1 NT
2♠

Since the normal order of bidding a hand with two *black* suits of equal length is to bid the clubs first, a rebid of 2♠ over a 1 N.T. response to 1♣ is not a reverse in the accepted strength-showing sense. It shows the second suit in a hand which opener does not fancy for a No Trump

1♠—1 NT   contract. Note in this connection that, except in the
2♣   case of a 1 N.T. response to 1♠, it is impossible for
    BUT   opener to show a secondary club suit except at the
1♠—2◇   three-level. The clubs will be shorter than the spades
3♣   or the club opening would have been chosen, and the
       new suit bid at the three-level is a one-round force

often known as a 'high reverse', with spades guaranteed longer
than clubs (i.e., at least 5-4) in a strong hand. Compare these next

Compare: three sequences to clarify. In the first, opener's 2◇
1♠—2♣   rebid merely shows an opening hand with two possible
2◇   trump suits. In the second opener's 'high reverse'

1♠—2♡   of 3♣ or 3◇ is forcing, showing a strong hand with
3♣ (or 3◇)   at least a five-card spade suit, and in the third
       opener uses a jump rebid to show his strength, as
1♠—2♣   responder's 2♣ bid has left the two-level free.
3◇

1♡—2♣   Compare also these two sequences. In the first,
2♠   with moderate and possibly quite considerable
   and   strength held by responder, opener's 2♠ rebid is
1◇—1 NT   a strength-showing reverse. In the second, responder's
2♠   strength is limited to a *maximum* of 9 points, for
       which reason most players do not regard opener's

rebid over a No Trump response as a forcing reverse, but merely
as an attempt to find a better spot to play the hand.

Care must also be taken to distinguish between a true 'reverse'

N.	E.	S.	W.
1♣	1♠	2◇	—
2♡			

and a mere two-level rebid when this occurs
in a contested auction. In this first sequence
East's intervention forced South to show
his diamonds at the two-level and North,
therefore, to bid hearts at the two-level when

1◇	2♣	2♡	—
2♠			

doubtless he had intended to bid 1♡ over a
1◇ response. In the second, had East not

intervened with 2♣, South would have been able to bid 1♡ and
North to rebid 1♠.

1♡—2♡   To avoid subsequent confusion there is one other
2♠   sequence to be mentioned here. When you come to
       Chapter 10 you will find that opener's rebid of 2♠
is a trial bid, made after hearts have been agreed as trumps. It
is, in fact, a one-round force, but not necessarily carrying the same
implications as a normal 'reverse'.

Finally, to end this section, compare the two following hands.
When selecting your opening bid on the first you face the problem

of either opening 1♡ and rebidding the rather straggly heart suit
over a 2♣ or 2◇ response (thus never showing
the spades) or alternatively of making the untruth-
ful opening of 1♠ which risks being given preference to spades when you rebid in hearts. Either way
you have to tell a lie because to open 1♡ and rebid
2♠, a forcing reverse, is unthinkable. Of the two
choices it is probably wiser to open 1♠. On this
second hand, however, you can well afford to open
1♡ and show from your subsequent bidding that
this suit is the longer. Note also that when
responder bids 2◇ over 1♡, the use of the forcing
reverse of 2♠ is valuable in the extreme. If he cannot trust responder to regard it as forcing, opener is in great difficulties for an appropriate rebid. Over a 2♣ response he could have jumped to 3 N.T.
to make certain of reaching a game, but this is impossible over 2◇,
though clearly a game must be bid somewhere.

♠ A J 8 7
♡ A Q 8 5 3
◇ K 6 4
♣ 5

and

♠ A Q 8 7
♡ A K J 9 4
◇ K Q 6
♣ 5

REBIDS WHEN RESPONDER HAS FORCED

Basically, when opener's partner makes a forcing response, opener's
rebids follow the same pattern except that they are, unavoidably,
made at a higher level. In the first example sequence
the rebid of 2◇ is merely showing a second possible
trump suit. But if responder forces, as in the next
example, then opener's 3◇ rebid is doing no more
than show his second suit at the forced higher three-
level. In fact, if opener has a second biddable suit he
must take this earliest possible moment to show it.

1♠—2♣
2◇
or
1♠—3♣
3◇

If the opening is based on a single-suited hand
opener's three-level rebid is neutral, confirming length,
that is, a rebiddable suit, and denying a second biddable
suit. The subsequent bidding will show whether or not opener
is minimum.

1♠—3♣
3♠

In the case of the No Trump rebids when responder has forced,
a rebid at the lowest available level indicates a minimum hand with
no additional values. For example, having opened
1♣ intending to rebid 1 N.T. on this hand, if
responder forces with a two-level bid in a new suit,
opener's rebid is 2 N.T. which shows that he had
intended to rebid 1 N.T. over a simple response.
Add, say, the ◇Q, and opener would still have started with 1♣

♠ Q 10 6
♡ K J 4
◇ A 8 2
♣ A J 5 2

intending to rebid 2 N.T. over a simple one-level response, but

1♣—2♠
3 NT

now, if responder forces, opener must jump one step to show his added values and make it clear that he had intended a 2 N.T. jump rebid over a normal response.

There is one conventional rebid which falls into place here and that is a jump bid in opener's own suit when a forcing situation is in being, as it is when responder has jump-bid a new suit. In this case opener should jump-bid his own suit if it happens to be long and self-supporting.

♠ Q 7
♡ Q 9 5
◇ 6
♣ A K Q J 9 6 5

You would, of course, open 1♣ on this hand and, in the normal course of events, repeat clubs. If responder forces with a two-level bid in any other suit the correct opener's rebid becomes 4♣, guaranteeing the long and solid trump suit, self-supporting and, with any reasonable luck, containing no losers.

Let us end this section with one final example which carries the

♠ Q 7
♡ Q 9 5
◇ 6
♣ A K 9 8 7 6 5

bidding one stage further. You will have opened 1♣ on this hand which, except for the club suit itself, is exactly the same as the previous one. If responder makes a one-level reply you would repeat clubs. If he forces with, for instance, 2♠, you rebid 3♣ to confirm suit length. Now responder follows with 3♡—what do you bid next? If your reaction is to repeat clubs again, forget it. You have already made a truthful opening bid and rebid so now the least you can do, holding Q-7 in one of your partner's suits and Q-9-5 in the other, is to tell him of his luck. Raise 3♡ to 4♡.

You will by now have realised how important it is always to try to select as your rebid one which adequately expresses the strength of your hand. If making a limit bid, bid to the full strength of the holding. If a game or slam is in sight make a forcing bid which responder cannot pass. Try never to sign off if you hold better than a light opener, and never make a simple change-of-suit rebid when you are strong enough for something better.

CHOICE OF BID — SHOWING SHAPE

Before going into the question of showing the shape of your hand we would refer you back to the section on 'Choice of Bid' at the end of Chapter 2. It is not necessary to repeat it here but we suggest that you should revise it before going on.

Most rules can never be hard and fast. They are inevitably over lapping and somewhat conflicting, and there will be many occasion on which you will have to judge for yourself which should prevail. It is only fair to say that much bidding becomes a matter of choice— one can bid a particular suit in the firm conviction that partner will respond in a particular one of the remaining three, only to have him upset all your plans and careful 'preparation' by responding quite differently. The Acol System, however, does not advocate the over-use of the principle of preparedness, or anticipation of partner's likely bids, which may have the effect of bidding his cards for him, and the Acol player must learn to use his discretion. As far as is consistent with commonsense the Acol player should follow the rules set out on p. 32, whilst bearing in mind the need for a satisfactory rebid.

Remember always two important Acol principles:

1) Make the most natural bid available in the circumstances existing at the time, and

2) In bidding two suits you are asking partner to show his preference for one or the other and you must, if you can do so without giving a false impression of your hand, tell him which of the two you prefer.

Hands with two biddable suits of equal length normally come quite simply within the rules for natural bidding, the exception being spades and clubs, when clubs should be bid first. Two-suited hands, when the suits are of different length, require rather different treatment if you are to be sure of giving partner the right information.

A suit is not re-biddable unless it is of at least five-card length. If, therefore, you bid your longest suit first (p. 32, Rule 1) and then bid and re-bid in another suit, the second suit must be rebiddable, i.e., of five-card length, and the first bid suit is, therefore, likely to be at least as long if not longer.

1♡—2◇
2♠—3◇
3♠—?

Here you will recognise opener's 2♠ rebid as a 'reverse' —a bid out of the natural order—and by virtue of the fact that the showing of two suits asks partner to show his preference, the strength to allow for being given preference at the three-level is implied. In this case, however, when responder repeats his diamonds instead of giving preference, opener's next bid, a repeat of spades, clearly shows that his spades are rebiddable, i.e., a five-card suit, and his only reason for bidding out of the natural order—spades before hearts—must be that his hearts are even longer. Opener must, therefore, be at least 6-5 in hearts and spades.

Your general rule, therefore, with two good biddable suits of unequal length is to bid the longer suit first and then bid *and rebid* the shorter, but only provided that the shorter one is itself at least a five-card suit. Here is an example hand which might well apply to the bidding sequence above.

♠ A Q J 9 7
♡ A Q 10 7 6 5
◇ 7
♣ 8

Although not particularly high in honour points, this hand is distributionally powerful, even if not quite good enough for an opening Strong Two. Open 1♡ and then bid and rebid the spades. Change the holding by reducing the heart suit to five and you would open 1♠ in the normal way, after which you can bid and rebid hearts.

♠ A K J 9
♡ K Q J 10 8
◇ K 9 6
♣ 5

Here you would open 1♡ and, being strong enough to 'reverse', would bid 2♠ over responder's 2♣ or 2◇, but your *second* rebid should be in hearts.

An exception to this, already touched on briefly earlier in this chapter, is when holding a 6-4 two-suiter. In such cases you should bid *and repeat* your six-card suit before showing the shorter *unless* the four-card suit is a major which can be shown at the one-level.

♠ A Q 8 6
♡ 7 6
◇ A Q 10 8 6 4
♣ 5

So on this hand open 1◇ and, if responder bids 1♡, make the cost-nothing rebid of 1♠. If, however, his response is 2♣ you should rebid 2◇, not 2♠.

There is one other exception to the rule about bidding and rebidding a six-card suit before showing a four-card one, and that's when the four-card suit is heavily topped by honours.

♠ 7
♡ A J 9 7 5 3
◇ A K J 10
♣ A 5

Here you have almost a 2♡ opener, but not quite. Bid 1♡ and if partner responds 1♠ or 2♣ rebid 3◇, which is the only way you can do justice to this hand. If partner now bids 3 N.T., show your 6-4 pattern by taking out into 4♡. Lastly, you may already have noticed that you may have to 'bend' the rules if you pick up a weak two-suiter with adjacent suits, and when the shorter suit ranks above the longer one.

♠ 7 2
♡ A J 9 7 6
◇ A 10 8 6 5 3
♣ —

If you open 1◇ you will be faced with 'reversing' (reserved, as you know, for much stronger hands) to show your hearts over a black-suit response. The lesser evil is to open 1♡ leaving yourself a comfortable rebid of 2◇. The only risk you run is a responder's 'preference' return to hearts which you do not actually prefer.

4-4-4-1 HAND PATTERNS

The opening bid on hands of 4-4-4-1 pattern poses a problem of its own though Acol, as usual, provides a simple and logical solution. For many years the rule was simple—on hands with three biddable suits, open one of the suit below the singleton. This meant that with a singleton spade you bid 1♡, with a singleton heart you bid 1◇, with a singleton diamond you bid 1♣ and, regarding the suits as forming a circle, with a singleton club you bid 1♠. This rule did not prove entirely satisfactory, and Acol has modified it as follows:!

> With hands of 4-4-4-1 pattern containing three biddable suits open the suit below the singleton *except* when the singleton is in clubs, when open 1♡.

The first thing to note here is the use of the word 'biddable' as sometimes one of the three suits is so weak that it can be regarded as of value only if partner bids it. Such hands should be treated as two-suiters to be bid according to the natural rules, and not as three-suiters at all. For example, when deciding

♠ 8
♡ 9 7 5 4
◇ A K 5 4
♣ A Q 8 3

what to bid on this 13-point hand, disregard the hearts and bid the hand as a diamond-club two-suiter. Open 1◇ and rebid 2♣ if responder bids 1♠. But if he bids 1♡ come to life and bid 3♡.

Going back to the rule itself, the need for the exception will be clear if you examine the following examples where opener's singleton is a club:

Opener's Hand: Responding Hands:

♠ A J 5 4   a) ♠ 8 3   b) ♠ 8 3   c) ♠ 8 3
♡ K Q 8 3   ♡ J 10 7 6   ♡ J 5   ♡ A 5 4 2
◇ A Q 9 5   ◇ K 4   ◇ K 10 6 3   ◇ K 4 3
♣ 2   ♣ K Q 9 7 5   ♣ K 9 7 5 4   ♣ A 5 4 3

Consider opener's hand opposite the three different responding hands shown. If opener bids 1♠, technically the 'suit below the singleton', holding Hand (a) responder will bid 2♣. Opener will be on a guess as to whether to rebid in hearts or diamonds and if he chooses diamonds responder can do no more than 'correct' to 2♠ and the perfect heart fit will be missed. If, in Responding Hand (a), you switch the two red suits, and make declarer 'guess' his rebid as 2♡, the diamond fit will be missed. Holding Hand (b), responder would doubtless reply 1 N.T. to 1♠—and now what? Once again opener's rebid is just a guess, and if he picks hearts instead of diamonds the fit will be missed. On Hand (c) responder will almost certainly elect to bid 2 N.T. over 1♠, and for the third time opener will be on a guess, though the heart fit stares the partnership in the face if it can be found.

All this difficulty can be avoided if, when the singleton is in clubs, the opening bid is 1♡. If responder has a reasonable spade suit he will surely bid it himself. If he responds 2♣, therefore, you can rebid 2♢, confident that the better fitting of the two red suits will be agreed for the final contract. If responder bids 1♠ or 2♢ when you open 1♡ you have effectively eliminated all problems as to your rebid, and over a No Trump response you can bid diamonds, knowing that the spade fit has not materialised. The risk of missing a heart contract, of course, does not arise, as you have bid the suit yourself.

Before going on it is worth pointing out, perhaps, that a 4-4-4-1 hand is somewhat devoid of 'playing strength' until a trump fit has been located. Declarer can well face disaster with only a four-card trump suit if he is forced early on to ruff his short suit. For this reason it is seldom wise to open on a 4-4-4-1 hand with a weak point count, and 13 honour points should generally be regarded as the minimum requirement—remember that there are *no* distributional points to be added unless a prospective trump suit is of five-card length or more.

REVISION QUIZ ON CHAPTER 8

1) You open 1♡ to which your partner responds 1♠. What is your rebid?

   a) ♠Q 10: ♡A K 9 4 3: ◊K 9 6: ♣Q J 4:

   b) ♠J 4: ♡A K Q 5 4: ◊K 9 5: ♣K J 4:

   c) ♠J 4: ♡A K Q 9 8: ◊Q J 9: ♣A Q 4:

   d) ♠10 5: ♡A K J 10 7 4: ◊A 5: ♣K 9 2:

   e) ♠Q 3: ♡A Q J 9 4 3: ◊10 9 5: ♣K 3:

   f) ♠Q 9: ♡A Q J 10 8 5 4: ◊A 4 2: ♣5:

2) You open 1♡ to which your partner responds 2◊. What is your rebid?

   a) ♠9 3: ♡K J 9 6 4 2: ◊K 4: ♣A J 6:

   b) ♠K 10 3: ♡A K 10 5 4: ◊Q 3: ♣A 4 2:

   c) ♠A J 5: ♡K Q 10 9 6: ◊Q J: ♣K Q 10:

   d) ♠8: ♡K Q J 10 7 6 4: ◊Q J 3: ♣A J:

   e) ♠10 6: ♡A K J 4 2: ◊J 9 4 2: ♣A J:

   f) ♠K Q 9 4: ♡A J 10 9 6: ◊A 4: ♣K 3:

3) In the bidding sequences shown, what should North (opener) rebid on the following hands?

	N. S.
a) ♠J 3: ♡K Q 9 7: ◊A K 8 5 2: ♣Q 3:	1◊—1♠ ?
b) ♠J 3: ♡K Q 9 7: ◊A K 8 5 2: ♣Q 3:	1◊—2♣ ?
c) ♠A K 7 5 3: ♡Q 6: ◊J 9: ♣K Q 8 3:	1♠—2◊ ?
d) ♠A K 7 5 3: ♡Q 6: ◊K 9: ♣K Q 8 3:	1♠—2◊ ?
e) ♠K 7: ♡A J 9 8 6 5: ◊A J 6: ♣Q 7:	1♡—1♠ ?
f) ♠K 7: ♡A J 9 8 6 5: ◊A J 6: ♣Q 7:	1♡—2♣ ?
g) ♠A Q J 9 4: ♡K 9: ◊A J 10 9: ♣Q 6:	1♠—2♡ ?

4) As dealer you open the bidding with 1♡ and your partner forces with 3◇. What would you rebid on the following hands?

    a) ♠ K 7: ♡ A Q 10 9 4: ◇ Q J 4: ♣ A 4 2:
    b) ♠ K 7 4: ♡ A Q J 10 9: ◇ Q 10: ♣ A J 5:
    c) ♠ A Q 10 4: ♡ K Q 10 9 7: ◇ K 4: ♣ A 6:
    d) ♠ 9 5: ♡ A K Q 10 7: ◇ A 3: ♣ K Q 10 4:
    e) ♠ A J 10: ♡ K Q 10 7: ◇ A 8: ♣ Q 10 5 3:
    f) ♠ 7: ♡ A K Q J 10 4: ◇ A 6: ♣ 9 7 5 3:
    g) ♠ 7 5 3: ♡ K J 10 9 6 5: ◇ Q 8: ♣ A 3:

5) What would you open on the following hands, and why?

    a) ♠ K 10 9 4: ♡ 7: ◇ A Q J 9: ♣ K Q J 3:
    b) ♠ A Q 8 6: ♡ K Q 10 5: ◇ 4: ♣ Q 10 9 3:
    c) ♠ A J 8 6: ♡ K Q 10 5: ◇ K 10 9 3: ♣ 4:
    d) ♠ A K 10 6: ♡ 8 6 4 2: ◇ A Q 9 3: ♣ A:
    e) ♠ K Q 10 6: ♡ A Q 9 6: ◇ 9 7 6 5: ♣ A:

6) Assuming no opposition interference and a simple suit take-out by responder, how would you plan the bidding of these hands, as opener?

    a) ♠ 9: ♡ A Q 10 9 3: ◇ A Q J 9 6 4: ♣ 6:
    b) ♠ 4 3: ♡ —: ◇ A J 10 9 6 4: ♣ K Q 10 9 5:
    c) ♠ 6 2: ♡ A J 9 6 4 3: ◇ A K Q 10: ♣ A:
    d) ♠ A J 10 9 4 2: ♡ K 9 3 2: ◇ K 5: ♣ J:
    e) ♠ K Q 10 9 6: ♡ 6 3: ◇ A: ♣ A J 5 4 3:
    f) ♠ K Q 9 6 4 3: ♡ —: ◇ 4: ♣ K Q 10 9 6 3:
    g) ♠ A K Q 5 4: ♡ K 10 9 7 4 3 2: ◇ —: ♣ A:
    h) ♠ Q J 9 4: ♡ A K 10 9 5: ◇ 6 3: ♣ K J:

ANSWERS TO REVISION QUIZ ON CHAPTER 8

1) a) 1 NT You do not want to sign off in 2♡ and you have something in every suit as well as the right point count.

   b) 2 NT Again, your point count justifies this bid in preference to any other.

   c) 3 NT You take it into your own hands and bid game direct. Even with an absolute minimum from partner you have 24 points between you.

   d) 3♡ Too strong for a sign-off, not strong enough for a game bid, and unsuitable for a No Trump bid. Announce your long strong trump suit in this way.

   e) 2♡ Just our old friend, the sign-off after a typical Acol Light Opener.

   f) 4♡ This time you can hardly do less than have a try for game, and from your point of view it must be in hearts.

2) a) 2♡ The simple sign-off once more—there is no other bid.

   b) 2 NT No need to sign off here with 16 points.

   c) 3 NT Partner should have at least 8 points to bid at the two-level, so you should have 26 between you and you have a stop in every suit.

   d) 3♡ Exactly the same story as in (d) in No: 1 above.

   e) 3◇ A simple raise of partner's suit, showing him a fit. Not forcing.

   f) 2♠ This is a major suit 'reverse', a one-round force, which makes sure you will have the best chance to reach the right game contract.

3) a) 1 NT Showing the count, and all the hand is worth until South can show he is able to bid again.

   b) 2♡ The same hand, but note the difference when South can respond at the two-level. North's holding is now worth a forcing 'reverse'.

   c) 2 NT Another count-showing bid, avoiding a rebid of 2♠. All the hand is worth.

   d) 3♣ The same hand except for the ◇K, and it is now worth the one-round force of a new suit at the three-level.

   e) 2♡ This bid has something in reserve if South can bid again, but remember that he may have a very weak hand for a response at the one-level.

   f) 3♡ Once South can show ability to respond at the two-level, North is strong enough for a jump rebid (non-forcing but highly invitational) of 3♡.

g) 3◇ North is in an impossible position if South cannot be trusted to treat a new suit bid at the three-level as forcing. South's reply should clarify his hand leaving North free to judge the best final contract.

4) a) 4◇ With 16 points opposite your partner's force, you are far too strong to make a neutral rebid and there is no reason to suppress your diamond fit. If partner has forced on a short minor he will be telling you so by returning to hearts.

 b) 3♡ This time your hearts are stronger and your diamond support weaker. Make a waiting rebid, and see what happens next.

 c) 3♠ You have an enormous hand of your own, on which you are quite strong enough to 'reverse'. Do not panic because you only have K-4 of partner's diamond bid— he very probably means you to play in a heart slam anyway!

 d) 4♣ Take this first opportunity to show your second suit, which you had every intention of bidding whether partner forced or not.

 e) 3 NT Over a simple change-of-suit to 2◇ you would have shown your 'shape' and count by bidding 2 N.T., so now the forced higher level carries the same significance.

 f) 4♡ The Acol conventional bid in a forcing situation, which shows a long and solid suit with no losers, needing little or no support.

 g) 3♡ You had a near minimum opener in the first place, so all you can do is confirm that at least you have heart length.

5) a) 1◇ A normal 'suit below the singleton' with three biddable suits.

 b) 1♣ This is another of the same—the suit below the singleton.

 c) 1♡ This is the exception—three biddable suits and the singleton in clubs.

 d) 1◇ This may facilitate a 1♡ response on a 4-card suit, and you are strong enough to bid 2♠ over a 2♣ response.

 e) 1♠ This hand must be regarded as a two-suiter in spades and hearts. Bid the higher ranking first and follow with hearts unless you are able to support a diamond bid from partner.

6) a) Open 1♦, which is the longer of the two suits, and then bid
   and *repeat* hearts. This will tell partner that your longer
   suit is diamonds and that as your hearts are rebiddable
   (at least five) your diamonds must be at least six.

   b) Open 1♦ and show clubs on the next round. On the third
   round (if any) rebid the clubs.

   c) Open 1♥ and show the diamonds on the next round with a
   jump force, e.g., 1♥—1♠—3♦. If partner retreats into
   3 N.T., show your 'shape' by taking out into 4♥.

   d) Open 1♠ and repeat 2♠ on the next round—a simple sign-off
   bid, unless partner bids hearts, which you will raise
   to 3♥.

   e) Open 1♣ and rebid 1♠. This is the exception to the rule of
   bidding the higher ranking of two equal suits.

   f) Open 1♣ again. The same rule holds good even if they are
   both now six-card suits.

   g) Open 1♥, the longer suit, and make a "reverse" into spades
   on the next round. Repeat spades to show they are
   rebiddable (five) and that hearts, therefore, are longer.

   h) Open 1♥. Support if partner bids spades, otherwise rebid
   2 N.T. over 2♣ or 2♦—only a slight overbid.

Chapter 9

Responder's Rebids

ALL bids are important, of course, but one of the most important is responder's rebid. At this stage opener will have made his opening bid and rebid in reply to the initial response, and responder should by now have a very good idea as to whether the combined holdings are going to be worth a slam contract, a game, or a mere part-score.

Apart from passing opener's rebid, which responder is always at liberty to do if it is not forcing and he has nothing more constructive to say, responder's own rebid should aim at clarifying his first bid if this is necessary. By this we mean that if, for instance, the first response were a limit bid either in a suit or in No Trumps, then no question of a rebid arises unless it is to 'correct' (or show preference) or if opener makes a forcing rebid. In the latter case, of course, responder must find a sensible and expressive reply to the force. If responder himself made a forcing change-of-suit response at his first turn, his next bid should aim at showing opener which way things are going.

In previous chapters we have already mentioned various responder's rebids as, for example, when opener's own rebid may affect responder's view of his hand (Chapter 7, delayed game raise and second-round force), and the time has now come to gather all these responder's second-round bids together into one chapter for easy reference. The simplest way of doing this will be with a number of comparative examples, arranged in groups. Remember that all these hands had the necessary qualifications for an initial response to an opening bid, and now responder must find the best means of clarifying his original response and helping the partnership towards the correct final contract.

Minimum or Sign-Off Rebids:

N.	S.	South:	
1♡—1 NT		♠ 10 8 7	When no forcing situation is in being, the
2♡—No		♡ 9 7 3	simplest and most emphatic responder's
		◇ A 9 4	sign-off bid is a pass. Here South can have
		♣ K 6 3 2	nothing further to add to his original

1 N.T. limit bid so, with no obligation to bid further, he takes his opportunity to say 'No Bid'.

N. S.	*South:*	
1♡—1♠	♠ A 10 8 7	In this case South shows no greater
2♡—No	♡ 9 7 3	values by his one-level bid of 1♠ than
	◇ A 9 4	he did by bidding 1 N.T. in the pre-
	♣ 6 3 2	vious example. He again makes the only reasonable second-round bid of a pass.

On yet other occasions responder, with an equally weak hand, will be under an obligation to rebid, even though his partner has not forced. This will be when opener's rebid has been made in a second suit and responder is required to show his *preference* for one or the other.

N. S.	*South:*	
1♡—1♠	♠ K J 9 6	Here South's bid of 2♡ is a simple
2◇—2♡	♡ 10 8 4	*preference* showing no additional values
	◇ 10 9	but preference—which does *not* consti-
	♣ K 7 6 2	tute a raise—for North's first suit.

1♡—1♠	♠ K J 9 6	Exchange South's red suit holdings, and
2◇—No	♡ 10 9	he would show his preference for his
	◇ 10 8 4	partner's second suit by passing. In
	♣ K 7 6 2	this next example, holding three of both his partner's suits, South should give
1♡—1♠	♠ K J 9 6	preference to the first suit on the assump-
2◇—2♡	♡ 10 8 4	tion that this is at least as long as, if
	◇ 10 9 2	not longer than, the second.
	♣ K 7 6	

It makes no difference if South's original response is a limit bid of 1 N.T.—he should still show weak preference for one or other of North's suits by, in the first sequence, putting him quietly back to 2♡ or, in the second, passing 2♣.

1♡—1 NT	♠ K J 9
2◇—2♡	♡ 10 8 4
OR	◇ 10 9 2
1♡—1 NT	♣ K 7 6 2
2♣—No	

On a different type of hand, one with little outside its own long trump suit, responder can make an equally emphatic sign-off by repeating his own suit at the lowest available level, more than once if need be:

N.	S.	South:
1♡	—1♠	♠ Q 10 9 6 5 4
2◇	—2♠	♡ 7 3
		◇ K 8
		♣ 9 4 2

With no real fit for either of North's suits, South signs off in 2♠ which, as he was at liberty to pass North's non-forcing 2◇ rebid, shows a minimum hand with a rebiddable spade suit.

1♡	—1♠	ditto
1 NT	—2♠	
	OR	
1♡	—1♠	
2 NT	—3♠	

In both these two sequences, South holding the same hand, North's own rebid was a limit bid so South's only obligation is to 'correct', if he thinks this wise, to give his view of the best final contract. North, of course, will accept South's view as final and will not bid again.

N.	S.	South:
1♡	—1♠	♠ Q 10 9 6 5 4
2♡	—2♠	♡ 7
		◇ K 8 3
		♣ 9 4 2

Here South, by his lowest available level of rebid in his suit shows a rebiddable suit, no alternative to offer, and not even tolerance for North's suit.

N.	S.	South:
1♡	—1♠	♠ Q 10 9 6 5 4
2◇	—No	♡ 7 3
		◇ K 8 3 2
		♣ 9

Compare this example, only different in distribution from the one above. It's not good enough for a *raise* in North's second suit, but with the excellent fit for diamonds there is now no need for South to do anything but sign off by passing.

N.	S.	South:
1♡	—1♠	♠ Q 10 9 6 5 4
2◇	—2♡	♡ 9 7
		◇ 9
		♣ K 8 3 2

Again only a slight change in South's hand, but here his wisest course is a simple preference bid of 2♡, just as much signing off as his previous pass. Note, by the way, that if South's heart and club suits had been exchanged, he would have raised 1♡ to 2♡ in the first place.

N.	S.	South:
1♡	—1♠	♠ Q 10 9 6 5 4
2◇	—2♠	♡ 9 7
2 NT	—3♠	◇ 9 3
		♣ K 8 3

South's series of rebids in his own suit, in spite of all North's efforts constitute a determined sign-off, at the same time driving it home that his only real asset is his rebiddable spade suit.

N.	S.	South:
♠—2♠	♠ Q J 5 4	
◇—3◇	♡ 7 3	
	◇ 5 3 2	
	♣ K 10 7 3	

South's original 2♠ was a limit bid and North's 3◇ a trial bid (see Chapter 10), a one-round force. South shows that he has nothing extra to his first raise by a sign-off bid of 3♠.

Stronger Rebids:

Next we come to stronger responding hands—ones on which either because of, or in spite of, opener's rebid, responder's hand is worth another try. He no longer wishes to sign off but to make a constructive bid in the hope of reaching a game contract. Under this heading we can group second-round limit bids either in responder's own or in his partner's suit, strong preference bids amounting to a raise, and the delayed game raise. Details of the latter were covered in Chapter 7, so here we merely include a few examples to keep the picture complete.

N.	S.	South:
♡—1♠	♠ A Q J 8 7	
♣—2 NT	♡ 10 2	
	◇ K J 4	
	♣ J 8 3	

South's hand is strong enough for an immediate 2 N.T., though clearly his best first response is 1♠. However, when North shows clubs as his second string, South makes a further effort, showing his count and diamond stop by a rebid of 2 N.T.

N.	S.	South:
♣—1♠	♠ K Q 10 7	
♣—3 NT	♡ A J 4	
	◇ K J 9 2	
	♣ 6 3	

Here South has the values for an immediate 3 N.T., but rightly makes the possibly far more constructive first-round response of 1♠. When all North can do is to repeat his clubs, South bids the No Trump game direct.

N.	S.	South:
♣—1◇	♠ A J 9 3	
♠—3♠	♡ 7 6	
	◇ K 10 9 6 4	
	♣ Q 8	

South correctly bids his longest suit on the first round, and when North rebids 1♠ game in that suit looks highly probable. The 3♠ rebid is highly invitational but not forcing and North will do his best to bid the game. Had North opened 1♠ instead of 1♣, South would have raised to 3♠ immediately instead of showing the diamonds.

N.	S.	South:
1♡	—1♠	♠ A Q J 8 5
2♣	—3♡	♡ K J 7
		◇ 9 8 2
		♣ J 7

South's 3♡ rebid is a jump prefer-ence, or raise in hearts, though does *not* show four-card heart sup-port. This can be inferred because with four hearts South would either have made a direct limit raise in the suit or, if rather stronger, have used a delayed game raise to 4♡ on the second round. He is, therefore, strongly inviting, though not unconditionally demanding, a game contract from North.

N.	S.	South:
1♣	—1♡	♠ 10 9
1♠	—3♣	♡ A J 10 7
		◇ 7 5
		♣ Q J 9 8 6

It is clearly more constructive for South to respond 1♡ than to raise clubs on the first round so he makes what is in effect a waiting bid. North's rebid shows a black two-suiter and South now gives jump preference—a raise—in clubs. Though highly invitational, North may elect to pass, though he could go on in clubs or convert to 3 N.T.

N.	S.	South:
1♡	—1♠	♠ A Q J 7
2♡	—4♡	♡ K 10 7 5
		◇ K J 8
		♣ 9 2

Here we have the delayed game raise in action, South being too strong for a limit bid in hearts and not quite strong enough to force on the first round. If North had made a strong opener's rebid South would have been able to explore for a possible heart slam. Meanwhile his waiting bid of 1♠ allows him to hear North's rebid before making up his mind as to the best final contract.

N.	S.	South:
1♡	—1♠	♠ A Q J 9 8 7
2♣	—3♠	♡ 10 2
OR		◇ K 9 4
1♡	—1♠	♣ Q 8
1 NT	—3♠	

South's jump rebid in his own suit is another highly invitational though non-forcing bid which North should be very reluctant to pass. South clearly holds a strong suit in a hand which he doesn't fancy for No Trumps and North should try to assist towards the game contract for which South is clearly angling.

N.	S.	South:
1◇	—1♡	♠ 8
1 NT	—3◇	♡ A Q 7 5 3
		◇ K J 6 4
		♣ 9 8 7

Similarly here, North should be unwilling to pass the 3◇ rebid, as South could well hold something like the example hand, which makes it difficult for him to find the one rebid which will make sure the right game is reached.

N.	S.
1♡	—1♠
1 NT	—2 NT
3♡	
or	
3♠	

South:
♠ A J 10 5
♡ 7 5 3
◇ K 9 6 4
♣ 9 8 7

Note in passing that it is only common sense to regard North's *third* bid as forcing, especially if a 12-14 point opening No Trump is being used, in which case North can be expected to hold 15-16 points for his 1 N.T. rebid. These, added to the points held by South, should make a game, though whether the safest spot will be 3 N.T., 4♡ or 4♠ remains to be decided.

Strong Rebids—Forcing:

It is not always necessary for responder to force on the first round to make sure of reaching a game contract, and there are several situations where he can make use of a forcing, as distinct from even a highly invitational, rebid. A new suit bid at the three-level or a 'responder's reverse', for example, are one-round forces by means of which he can make sure of another turn to bid. A jump bid in a new suit is a game force, as too is a rebid which either by-passes or removes another game contract for one below game-level. Responder's reverses require special clarification, and we will take these first.

RESPONDER'S REVERSES

A 'reverse', as explained in Chapter 8, is the bid of a lower-ranking suit before a higher one. Responder as well as opener can reverse, though the bids carry a somewhat different significance. Like an opener's reverse, a responder's reverse is generally regarded as a one-round force, and may well be an attempt on responder's part

N.	S.
1♡	—2♣
2♡	—2♠

to reach a No Trump game contract, though the chance that he holds a two-suiter is by no means excluded. Responder's first bid suit should be at least of five-card length, and by virtue of the fact that opener may have to raise the bidding level to three to show preference, the reversing hand should contain greater strength than would be needed for a simple rebid in a new suit. Compare these next two sequences.

N.	S.
1◇	—1♠
2◇	—2♡

South
♠ A J 9 7 2
♡ K Q 10 6 4
◇ 8 7
♣ 9

In the first South bids his suits in normal order, inviting North's preference for spades or hearts over North's repeat of his own suit (or if North had rebid 1 N.T.), as even a mild fit for either of South's suits is likely to produce a better result.

N.	S.	*South*
1◊	—1♡	♠ A Q J 9
2◊	—2♠	♡ A J 10 9 6
or		◊ Q 7
1◊	—1♡	♣ 7 5
1 NT	—2♠	

In the second case, however, South is strong enough to bid his five-card suit first and to 'reverse' into 2♠ over North's rebid. By this he implies that his heart suit is longer than his spades—at least five cards, that he is good enough to stand preference to 3♡, and also that he is himself unable to bid No Trumps—clearly for lack of a club stop.

As long as the reverse bid is treated as a one-round force there is no danger in using it in this way, and the only final result is likely to be the best contract. Opener should take the rebid as an invitation to 3 N.T. if he holds the fourth suit covered, and should not give a wildly enthusiastic raise to game in the reverse-bid suit in case responder has only used the bid for purposes of a force on a three-card holding.

Note that if *opener's* rebid is made in a second suit the entire character of responder's rebid can change. It can become a 'fourth-suit-forcing' bid and not merely a reverse (see p. 137). Compare the following sequences to get the situation clear :

1◊—1♠ 2◊—2♡	1◊—1♡ 2◊—2♠	1◊—1♡ 2♣—2♠	1♡—1♠ 2◊—3♣	1♡—1♠ 2◊—3♣
Non-forcing, showing a second biddable suit and asking for preference.	A responder's reverse —a one-round force probably in search of a No Trump game.	Fourth-suit-forcing, a one-round force *not* guaranteeing a rebid.	New suit at the three-level, a one-round force.	Fourth-suit-forcing at the three-level, a one-round force guaranteeing at least one further bid.

N.	S.	*South:*
1◊	—1♡	♠ A K 7
2◊	—2♠	♡ K J 8 7 3
		◊ J 8 4
		♣ 8 6

If responder's second-round 'reverse' were not forcing he would not dare to bid 2♠ here. What he's actually trying to do is to find out whether North can guard clubs for a No Trump contract. North, of course, will be entitled to place his partner with a five-card heart suit and put him back to that at the three-level if appropriate. For this

N.	S.	*South:*
1◊	—1♠	♠ A K 7 4
2◊	—2♡	♡ K J 8 7
		◊ J 8 4
		♣ 8 6

reason, if you change the distribution as here, South should respond 1♠ in the first place, *not* the lower-ranking 1♡, which gives him a straightforward rebid of 2♡ if North merely rebids 2◊.

N.	S.	South:
1◇	—1♡	♠ 8 6
2◇	—3♣	♡ A Q 8 7 5
		◇ J 6
		♣ A K 7 4

There's absolutely no need to 'shoot' 3 N.T. once it is also clearly understood that responder's new suit bid at the three-level is a one-round force. North should treat this as angling for 3 N.T. which he will bid if he can provide a spade guard. Lacking this, he will make the most expressive rebid that he can.

OTHER FORCING RESPONDER'S REBIDS

Before going on to consider the fourth-suit-forcing convention in more detail, let's take a look at other situations where the fourth bid, as in the previous example, becomes forcing for at least one round.

N.	S.	South:
1◇	—1♡	♠ 8
1 NT	—3◇	♡ A Q 7 5 3
		◇ K J 6 4
		♣ 9 8 7

N.	S.	South:
1♡	—1♠	♠ K Q J 7 4
1 NT	—3♡	♡ A J 8
		◇ 7 5 3
		♣ Q 10

N.	S.	South:
1♣	—1♠	♠ K Q J 9 7
1 NT	—3♡	♡ A J 9 6 4
		◇ 7 3
		♣ Q

We had a look at this one on p. 132. When the opening bid has been in a major suit opener should be even *more* unwilling to pass the jump rebid. Compare this next example where South can be in real trouble unless he is sure his partner will take his 3♡ rebid as forcing. South could raise to 3 N.T. which his count justifies, but this would be 'shooting' when a major suit game may be far safer.

Following opener's 1 N.T. rebid responder's jump in a new suit is unconditionally forcing for one round though it does *not* promise a further bid. In other words, though North must reply, if all he can do is give simple preference to 3♠, South may use his judgement and either pass or bid on to game. As ever, North should aim at rebidding his hand to the full and if, after South's strong suggestion of a two-suiter, he does not fancy his chances in 3 N.T., he should try to bid either 4♡ or 4♠.

N.	S.	South:
1♡	—1♠	♠ A K Q 9
2 NT	—3♡	♡ J 10 9
or		◇ 9 3
1♣	—1♠	♣ K 10 8 4
2 NT	—3♣	

When opener's rebid has been 2 N.T., responder's return to his partner's suit at the three-level is unconditionally forcing. It offers opener the choice between going on in his first bid suit, rebidding 3 N.T. or perhaps showing delayed support for responder's suit. By inference, when the opening bid has been in a major suit, four-card trump support is denied, and the bid also suggests a possible weakness—in this example diamonds—which opener will have to cover if bidding the game in No Trumps. If South held four-card support for opener's major he would either have used a limit bid as his first-round response, or a delayed game raise if stronger over the 2 N.T. limit bid.

N. S.	South:
1◇ —1♡	♠ 7 4
2 NT—3♣	♡ A K Q 7 2
	◇ 10
	♣ A Q 10 9 3

In addition to a return to opener's suit after the 2 N.T. rebid, responder's three-level rebid in a new suit is also a one-round force. Clearly if South, with a hand such as this, knows that 3♣ may be passed,
he may be in trouble. But if he knows that North will take it as a one-round force, South can show his two-suiter without by-passing the 3 N.T. level.

N. S.	South:
1♠—2◇	♠ J 6
3♠—4◇	♡ Q 9
	◇ A K J 10 8 4
	♣ Q 6 2

South's rebid of 4◇ is what is called an inferential force. As he was at liberty to pass North's 3♠ limit bid, which he would have done on a weaker hand, his rebid, even though this is made in his own suit, shows added values, and is a request to
North to bid the best game contract. The rebid of 4◇ also infers at least a partial spade fit, as North's most likely rebid is 4♠ which South can be expected to tolerate.

N. S.	South:
1♠—2◇	♠ 7
2♠—4♣	♡ A 7
	◇ K Q 10 8 6
	♣ A Q 10 9 7

South's jump rebid in a new suit, even though not made until the second round, is still unconditionally forcing. As it by-passes the possible 3 N.T. level it requires North to bid what he considers will be the best
suit game contract in the light of his knowledge of South's obvious two-suiter.

N. S.	South:
1♡ —2◇	♠ —
3 NT—4♣	♡ 7
	◇ K Q J 7 6 4
	♣ K Q J 10 7 3

A less likely hand for a No Trump game contract it would be hard to find. When South takes out 3 N.T. into a suit contract below game level he shows his two suiter and asks for North's preference at game level.

N. S.	*South:*	
1♡—2◇	♠ 10 8 7	This is the 'new suit at the three-level' discussed previously. With
2♡—3♣	♡ Q 6	almost certainly the values for
	◇ K J 10 7 4	game between the combined hands,
	♣ A Q J	yet unable himself to rebid in No

Trumps because of the lack of spade guard, South makes a forcing rebid which invites North to rebid in No Trumps if he can stop the spades. As we saw previously, however, South might be two-suited, but this he can show on the next round, having assured himself of a chance to bid again.

FOURTH SUIT FORCING

The conventional use of a bid in the fourth suit is not an essential part of the Acol System, but it is so widely used nowadays, and so extremely useful when the occasions for it crop up that it deserves a section to itself. It is not a new convention being, in fact, as old as the Baron System from which it originally came—a system which was a good deal more in vogue in the 1940s than it is today.

The modern technique is to use a bid in the fourth suit as an unconditional one-round force—it is something of an extension of the Directional Asking Bids explained in Chapter 16 which you

N. S.	
1♡—1♠	will come to presently. In this sequence, for example, South's rebid of 2◇ is in the fourth suit and is, therefore,
2♣—2◇	forcing.

Fourth-suit-forcing must never be used just because you cannot think of anything else to say. It is a forward-going and constructive bid to be used when the hand contains no honest and natural rebid yet, on the combined values, responder feels that game should be 'on' provided the best final contract is found. Most particularly it can be used when responder suspects that the best final denomination will be No Trumps provided partner can produce at least a partial stop in the fourth, as yet unbid, suit. Note that, in a sequence such as the above, if South himself held a good stop in diamonds he could make his rebid in No Trumps. A bid in the fourth suit, therefore, does *not* show a good holding in that suit, but *asks whether partner can do anything about it.*

When replying to a fourth-suit-forcing bid, remember that your partner is seeking a game contract, and will be anxious for you to clarify your hand, if possible even further than your original rebid has done. If you can guard the fourth suit, then give priority to a bid in No Trumps at the appropriate level, that is, according to your strength. Don't bid a mere 2 N.T. if, for example, you hold something like 16 points and a good stop in the fourth suit. If you

cannot oblige with a bid in No Trumps, then perhaps you can
show some support for your partner's suit, either at the lowest
available level or by a jump bid if strong enough. Otherwise repeat
your own choice of trump suit.

The player who makes the conventional fourth-suit bid should
confine himself to using it only when holding a minimum of Q-x
or J-x-x in it, that is to say, holding a partial guard himself which a
partial guard in his partner's hand will 'boost' into a stop in the
suit. Otherwise the partnership may well find itself in the ignominious position of playing in a highly scientific 3 N.T. with no
more than Q-x of the fourth suit in one hand and J-x in the other!

As with so many conventions, different players use fourth-suit-
forcing in different ways but, except for the ranks of the experts who
in any case need no text book, the following examples should
give you a sound working knowledge of how to use it. The
examples are based on a simple version which fits in well with the
rest of the system, being founded on common sense!

N.	S.	South:
1♠	2♣	♠ K 8 6
2◇	2♡	♡ Q 9
		◇ K 10 5
		♣ A K 10 7 4

South's first response is routine but
clearly, when North rebids 2◇, he
has no sound natural rebid although
he wants to play in game. South,
therefore, uses the fourth-suit-forcing
conventional rebid, asking North
whether he can supply a guard of any sort in hearts so that the
partnership can play in 3 N.T.

N.	S.	South:
1♠	2♣	♠ J 7
2◇	3 NT	♡ A J 10 7
		◇ 7 4
		♣ A K 10 7 4

Compare this next example where
South himself holds an excellent
heart stop and so rebids 3 N.T. (the
value of his hand). It would be pointless for South to rebid in hearts—
the partnership would merely be bid-
ding against each other, one holding spades and diamonds, and the
other clubs and hearts.

N.	S.	South:
1♣	1◇	♠ Q 8
1♡	1♠	♡ A J 5
		◇ A 10 9 6 3
		♣ J 9 4

Here again South's first response
is routine but he has no sound natural
rebid. A raise in clubs or hearts
might either be passed when game
is 'cold', or could prove disastrously
wrong; the alternative of a rebid of
2 N.T., the count which the hand is worth, could be equally
disastrous if no sure stop in spades is held. The answer is to use a
fourth-suit-forcing bid of 1♠ *asking* for help in this department,
not showing it. As these simple fourth-suit bids are forcing for one

round only, the auction can be allowed to develop to game or dropped short of it, according to North's next bid.

N.	S.	South:
1♣—1◇		♠ Q 10 7
1♡—1 NT		♡ 8 6 2
		◇ A Q 8 7 3
		♣ J 6

Here are two more comparative examples. On the first South has just the values to keep the bidding open for another round by a simple rebid of 1 N.T. On the second, quite a different situation arises, as game is probably available if the right fit is found. A fourth-suit-forcing rebid of 1♠ will allow North to clarify his hand—if he rebids in hearts South will raise to 4♡. If he rebids in No Trumps, South will raise to 3 N.T.

N.	S.	South:
1♣—1◇		♠ J 10 9
1♡—1♠		♡ K 8 6
		◇ A Q 8 7 3
		♣ A 6

N.	S.	South:
1♣—1◇		♠ 9 7 4
1♠—2 NT		♡ K J 8
		◇ A Q 10 7 6
		♣ Q 7

To underline the point just once more before going on to other aspects of the convention, don't use it when, as here, the hand contains a sound natural rebid. 2 N.T. *shows* the count and heart stop, whereas 2♡ would *ask*.

N.	S.	South:
1◇ —1♠		♠ A Q 10 7 4
2♣ —2♡		♡ A J 10 9 8
2 NT—4♡		◇ Q 2
		♣ 7

Here South has a genuine strong two-suiter in the majors, and you might think that, using this convention, he would be in difficulties. What he does, however, is to make his natural first-round response of 1♠ and then to rebid what North will undoubtedly take as a fourth-suit-forcing 2♡. If North confirms a stop (which here equals a fit) in hearts by bidding 2 N.T., South can take out into 4♡, showing his two-suited hand. If North merely rebids one of his minors at the three-level, again South can take out into hearts to show a two-suiter, but only at the three-level, asking for preference between his two suits. Compare this next example, however, which is not strong enough to bid in this way. South

N.	S.	South:
1◇—1♠		♠ K Q 9 7 5
2♣—2◇		♡ Q 10 7 5 4
		◇ J 8
		♣ 6

cannot indicate game ambitions by a fourth-suit-forcing bid of 2♡ and a subsequent conversion to 3♡, as North would be entitled to expect a much stronger hand than South actually holds. Probably his safest course, therefore, is to give simple preference to 2◇.

N.	S.	*South:*
1♥	—2♣	♠ Q 3
2♦	—2♠	♥ 8 7
		♦ 9 6
		♣ A K Q J 10 7 6

If as South you 'shoot' 3 N.T. on the second round, it will serve you right if your opponents run off the first six tricks on the marked spade lead. We all know you may be lucky and get away with it, but that won't make it good bidding! The better course is to *ask* North if he can assist towards a spade guard by making your 2♠ call. This will ensure that you won't get into 3 N.T. without at least one combined stop in the suit. Lacking this, your side can play in clubs.

So far we have looked only at bids in the fourth suit at the two-level, which are used as a one-round force. Note that they *do not* guarantee another bid on the next round, and the auction may be dropped after partner's response, with no further effort to reach game if that seems the wisest course. There are, however, two other situations which must be mentioned.

First, a bid in the fourth suit at the three-level promises at least one further bid. In this first example South is a little strong and 'shapely' for a second-round rebid of

N.	S.	*South:*
1♥	—1♠	♠ K J 10 8 5
2♦	—3♣	♥ A 8
		♦ 9 5
		♣ A Q 10 9

1♥	—1♠	ditto
2♣	—3♦	

3 N.T., so makes use of a fourth-suit-forcing bid of 3♣ as being the best means of exploring for the safest game contract.

Secondly we come to a *jump* bid in the fourth suit, as in this last example. You will note that South holds exactly the same hand as before but that North's rebid is 2♣, not 2♦ as previously. A lesser hand than South has here could, as we have already seen, be bid by way of a two-level fourth suit (2♦) rebid. One method in current use employs this *jump* rebid in the fourth suit as a mild slam invitation with opener's second suit agreed as trumps, and North may now start cue-bidding if his hand suggests that South's invitation should be accepted. Failing this, he should make his own most natural rebid.

Before leaving 'Fourth Suit Forcing', let's have a look at a few examples from the other side of the table. The example hands now are North's and he is selecting his rebid when his partner has used a forcing bid in the fourth suit.

N.	S.	North:
1♠	—2♣	♠ K Q 7 5 4
2◇	—2♡	♡ K 10 8
2 NT		◇ A J 10 7
		♣ 4

Although somewhat minimum for his opening bid, North has no reason to refuse the information that he *has* a guard in hearts and should, therefore, respond to the fourth-suit bid with 2 N.T.

N.	S.	North:
1♠	—2♣	♠ K Q J 5 4
2◇	—2♡	♡ K 10 8
3 NT		◇ A J 10 7
		♣ 4

North's hand here is just a little stronger—the quality of the spade suit is better. Remembering that South, by his fourth-suit bid of 2♡ is suggesting a game contract, North should bid 3 N.T., not a mere 2 N.T.

N.	S.	North:
1♠—2◇		♠ K Q 10 9 5
2♡—3♣		♡ A Q 9 8 6
3◇		◇ J 10 7
		♣ —

The fourth-suit bid at the three-level is forcing and also promises at least one further bid. Clearly North can't confirm a club stop for a No Trump contract so, having bid his hand accurately, he should show some support for South's diamond suit by bidding 3◇.

N.	S.	North:
1♠—2◇		♠ K Q 10 9 5
2♡—3♣		♡ A Q 9 8 6
4◇		◇ A 10 7
		♣ —

This time North, facing a partner who is strong enough to show game ambitions, is himself too good for a mere 3◇. He should bid 4◇ which by-passes the 3 N.T. level and allows South to select the best suit game contract, 4♡, 4♠, or 5◇. Remember South has promised a further bid, so 4◇ will not be passed.

N.	S.	North:
1◇—1♡		♠ A J 10 7
1♠—2♣		♡ 6
3♣		◇ A K J 6
		♣ Q J 10 8

North has opened one of the suit below the singleton. Now here is a new rule to add to your armoury of responses to a fourth-suit bid. With four card support, and provided this does not by-pass the 3 N.T. level, prefer a single raise in the fourth suit. South's 2♣ may not—and probably is not—showing a genuine suit, but as the partnership is headed for a game contract anyway, there is no harm in showing distribution at this point. This bid is, of course, particularly revealing, as South will be able to see that North holds a 4-4-4-1 distribution, if not even 5-4-4-0.

N.	S.	North:
1♠	—2◇	♠ A K J 8
2♡	—3♣	♡ A K J 7
3 NT		◇ 6
		♣ 9 6 5 3

Here, even though on a 4-4-4-1 hand, North correctly opened 1♠, treating the hand as a major two-suiter and the clubs as of interest only in support if they are bid opposite. The three-level fourth-suit bid, promising at least one other bid, also finds four-card support *but* a raise in clubs would cut out the 3 N.T. level. North should, therefore, rebid 3 N.T. and South, if he should remove 3 N.T. to 4♣ showing a two-suiter, will know from the assurance of a stop in clubs given by the 3 N.T. response, that he will find at least some club support facing him.

N.	S.	North:
1♠	—2♣	♠ A K Q 9 8
2◇	—2♡	♡ 10 9
3♠		◇ A 9 7 6
		♣ Q 10

Clearly North connot confirm a heart stop when South makes his fourth-suit enquiry of 2♡; nor, with only a doubleton, does he want to return South to 3♣ at this point. A mere 2♠ bid, denying a heart guard or club support would fall far short of doing justice to this hand, and North's best bet is a jump rebid of 3♠, leaving it up to South to decide on the best game contract.

REVISION QUIZ ON CHAPTER 9

1)   N.   S.   What should South rebid in each case?
   1♠—2◇   a) ♠9 4: ♡A 7 3: ◇K Q 10 9 6: ♣K Q 5:
   2♡—?   b) ♠K 9 4: ♡A 7 3: ◇K Q 10 9 6: ♣Q 5:
           c) ♠Q 6: ♡9 4 3: ◇K Q J 7 2: ♣7 5 3:
           d) ♠9 4 3: ♡Q 6: ◇K Q J 7 2: ♣7 5 3:

2)   N.   S.   What should South rebid in each case?
   1◇—1♡   a) ♠K J 9: ♡Q J 10 7: ◇J 9: ♣A 9 7 3:
   2◇—?   b) ♠K J 9: ♡Q J 10 7 6: ◇J 9: ♣10 9 6:
           c) ♠K J 9: ♡Q J 10 7 6 4: ◇9: ♣10 9 6:
           d) ♠K J 9: ♡Q J 10 7: ◇J 9: ♣A J 9 6:

3)   N.   S.   What should South rebid in each case?
   1♡—1♠   a) ♠K J 9 7 6: ♡K J 8: ◇A 7: ♣7 5 4:
   2◇—?   b) ♠K J 9 7: ♡K J 8: ◇J 7: ♣K 10 9 8:
           c) ♠K J 9 7: ♡A J 8: ◇K 10 9 8: ♣Q 4:
           d) ♠K J 9 7 6: ♡A J 8: ◇K 10 9: ♣6 4:
           e) ♠K J 9 7: ♡A J 8 4: ◇K Q 2: ♣6 4:

4)   On each of the four hands below, what should South rebid in the three following sequences?

N. S.	N. S.	N. S.
(i) 1♠—2◇	(ii) 1♡—2◇	(iii) 1♡—2◇
2 NT—?	3♣—?	2♠—?

   a) ♠Q 10 9: ♡K 6: ◇A Q J 9 4: ♣J 9 4:
   b) ♠Q 9: ♡7 6: ◇A J 10 9 4 2: ♣10 9 4:
   c) ♠10 9: ♡K 6: ◇A Q J 9 4: ♣Q 10 4 3:
   d) ♠10 9: ♡10 6 3: ◇A Q J 9 4: ♣J 9 4:

5)   On the two hands below, what should South rebid in the sequences shown?

S. N.	S. N.	S. N.
(i) 1♡—1♠	(ii) 1♡—1♠	(iii) 1♡—2♠
1 NT—2♡	1 NT—3♡	2 NT—3♡
?	?	?

South holds:
   ♠Q 4:, ♡A J 7 6: ◇K J 9 6: ♣K J 3:

(b) S. N.	S. N.	S. N.
(i) 1♡—1♠	(ii) 1♡—1♠	(iii) 1♡—2♣
2◇—3♣	2◇—4♣	2◇—2♠

South holds:
   ♠Q 4: ♡A K Q J 7: ◇K Q 9 6 2: ♣3:

ANSWERS TO REVISION QUIZ ON CHAPTER 9

1) a) 3 NT A second-round limit bid, showing the count and the good stop in clubs.

   b) 3♣ A fourth-suit-forcing request to North to show whether he can help with a 'boost' to South's ♣ Q-5, in which case 3 N.T. will probably be the best contract. If not, North will rebid a major and South will raise to game in it.

   c) No With nothing extra at all to the original response, South passes to show preference for North's second suit.

   d) 2♠ This is (c) with the major suits exchanged. South gives a preference bid of 2♠—not a raise in spades.

2) a) 2 NT North's weak rebid must not deter South from making another try to reach a game contract.

   b) No Nothing extra to show, and no better denomination to suggest.

   c) 2♡ South is sure that a two-level contract in his suit cannot be worse than one of 2◇.

   d) 3 NT Even after the weak rebid by North, South has the values to go to game. He has good stops in the other three suits.

3) a) 3♡ A jump preference bid from which North will understand that, though not having four-card heart support, South has good support for hearts as well as extra to his original response.

   b) 2 NT With a good hold on clubs, a 2 N.T. bid at this stage will pave the way to the best contract. Although North can pass 2 N.T. (a limit bid) he will not do so if he has anything extra to his bidding thus far.

   c) 3♣ A fourth-suit-forcing bid, designed to discover whether North has any help towards a club stop for No Trumps.

   d) 3♡ A *raise* in hearts, as compared with the mere preference bid of 2♡.

   e) 4♡ This is, of course, a delayed game raise, as South was too strong for a raise to 3♡ or jump to 4♡ in the first place.

4) a) 3♠   A forcing rebid (return to opener's major suit after his
(i)   2 N.T. rebid) asking North to choose between a final
            contract of 3 N.T. and 4♠.

   b) 3◇   A weak sign-off in South's own long suit, as he sees no
          future for a No Trump contract and has poor support
          for spades.

   c) 3 NT North has shown a minimum of 15 points which, added
          to South's, brings the total well over the 25-26 required
          for game.

   d) No   Compare this with (b) above, where South was able to
          take out into his own long suit. Here he has no reason
          to suppose that any other contract will be better—or
          worse—than 2 N.T.

(ii) a) 3 NT South has the same hand as in the four questions above,
          but his partner's forcing rebid (a new suit at the three
          level) can make all the difference to his answers. North
          has said that as South can bid at the two-level, he now
          has clear hopes for game, and South must try to clarify
          his previous response.

   b) 3◇   Being forced to speak again, South's best action is to
          confirm that his only real asset is a long rebiddable
          diamond suit.

   c) 4♣   At this stage South cannot be sure whether North is
          actually prepared to play in clubs, or whether he is
          using it just as a force. No harm, however, can come
          from confirming that South has no need to sign off
          weakly and that he can support clubs.

   d) 3♡   This is a simple preference for partner's first suit, in
          reply to the forcing rebid.

(iii) a) 3♣ North's rebid is a *forcing* 'reverse', to which there is no
          reason why South should not himself respond with
          another forcing bid—a fourth-suit-forcing 3♣. If North
          has any club assistance, No Trumps may well turn out
          to be the best final denomination.

   b) 3◇   Again forced to rebid, South's best course here is to
          deny reasonable support for spades or the values to
          give preference to 3♡, by rebidding his only real asset.

   c) 2 NT Compare this with (a) above, in which South was seeking
          help for a club stop. Here he has it himself, which he
          shows by his response to the forcing reverse.

d) 3♡   With his diamonds not worth rebidding at the three-level and with insufficient strength to suggest a No Trump contract, South does the only thing open to him, which is to put North back to his first-bid suit which, by his reverse bid, he has announced himself able to stand.

5) a) i) Pass.   North's bid is a simple weak preference for playing in hearts rather than No Trumps. If he had four-card heart support he would have shown it by a limit bid on the first round.

  ii) 3 NT   This time North's rebid is a strongly invitational one and South can afford to accept the invitation. However, as he has only a four-card heart suit, he prefers 3 N.T. to 4♡.

  iii) 3 NT   Here North's 3♡ is unconditionally forcing, even if he had not made a game force on the first round. Not really wanting to play in 4♡ without four-card support, South returns to 3 N.T.

b) i) 3◇   North's fourth-suit-forcing bid of 3♣ is asking whether South can stop the suit for a No Trump contract which obviously he cannot do. North, therefore, repeats his diamonds to show that the suit is rebiddable.

  ii) 4♡   North's jump rebid in the fourth suit is a mild slam try which agrees South's second suit, diamonds, as trumps. With no other feature in his hand worth showing, South rebids hearts to show his strong suit.

  iii) 2 NT   South responds to North's question by a bid in No Trumps which confirms a partial spade guard.

Chapter 10

Trial Bids and Cue Bids

THE reason for grouping Trial and Cue Bids together in one chapter is, as Iain Macleod said in his fine book *Bridge Is An Easy Game*, that all Cue Bids are Trial Bids. Even if not all Trial Bids are Cue Bids, both are exploratory, and it is this which links them conveniently together. Trial bids are normally used when seeking a game contract which appears to depend on a 'fit'. They ask for information but do not necessarily give it except in a negative sense. Cue bids are also trial bids in that they seek information about the best final contract, usually when a possible slam is in question, but they also *give* information, as they confirm first-round control of the cue-bid suit. Needless to say, both are unconditionally forcing for one round.

TRIAL BIDS IN THE MAJOR SUITS

Using less scientific methods in the old days, if you had a good opening bid to which partner's response was a simple raise to the two-level, and if you felt that your hand did not quite justify a direct jump to game, you would have bid a tentative three of your suit with the idea of testing the strength of responder's raise. If maximum he would bid the fourth—if minimum he would pass. This method was, of course, completely hit-and-miss, in no way taking into account the all-important question of 'fit'. Everyone knows that two powerful hands facing each other can come to grief on the rocks of a distributional misfit, while it is not uncommon for the most cheeky of 'sacrifice' contracts to be successful because their slender resources happen to fit like peas in a pod.

Just very occasionally, when your partner raises your opening one-bid to the two-level, your only concern will be whether the raise is based on a maximum or minimum, in which case the old 'test' raise to three would be in order (1♡—2♡—3♡—partner, can you give me the fourth?) but far more often the use of a trial bid instead of the 3♡ bid will replace guesswork with other bids asking a specific question. Responder may reply negatively, positively, or sometimes by 'passing the buck'. His hand is already known to be weak, a single raise of opener's suit being the least encouraging response available. Opener himself was not strong enough to start with anything better than a one-bid, even if a fairly good one, so now it remains to be discovered whether responder's very limited goodies are in the right place or not.

Trial bids were so christened by Iain Macleod who helped to develop them, and they are now an integral part of the Acol System. To carry the use of these bids to the full extent set out in his chapter on the subject is not everybody's choice, and in any case such precise shades of meaning require close partnership understanding, which is somewhat beyond the scope of this book. Here you are learning to use the Acol System with any reasonable Acol-playing partner without coming to grief. We shall, therefore, confine ourselves to the basic use of Trial Bids, which is to discover whether that vitally essential 'fit' is present on doubtful game hands. Remember that a trial bid is purely exploratory and gives no specific information other than the somewhat negative inference that opener does not feel strong enough to bid game direct without more than minimum assistance, and that the probable point of weakness is the suit in which the trial bid is made.

The classic situation for the use of a simple trial bid is when opener's bid of 1♡ or 1♠ has been raised to the two-level by responder. If he fancies his chances opener should bid the game direct at this point, but if doubtful he can make a trial bid, selecting the side-suit *in which some help would be welcome*. In this sequence 3♣ is a trial bid in the suit which is North's most likely danger-spot. From the mere fact that he does not pass the 2♡ response, North is shown to be better than minimum, though he has already been warned as to the weakness of South's hand. Responder in turn should reply as follows:

N.   S.
1♡—2♡
3♣— ?

1) On a minimum hand for his raise, wherever his values, he should convert to opener's suit at the lowest possible level, (3♡).

2) On a maximum hand for his raise, again wherever his values, he should bid direct to game (4♡).

3) If doubtful he should let his holding in the trial-bid suit decide, so here, with 'help' in clubs, he should bid 4♡, but lacking such help he would sign off in 3♡.
    done without raising the bidding level. In this last case, if

4) One other alternative is to 'pass the buck' if this can be responder's values are in diamonds he can deny help with clubs by bidding 3◇, though if the trial bid had been 3◇

he could *not* 'pass the buck' by bidding 4♣ unless he is willing to force opener to 4♡ in any case.

Returning to No. 3 above, it is important to understand what constitutes 'help' in a side-suit. A void or singleton coupled with four-card trump support would clearly be invaluable, and even a doubleton should be considered adequate, as it will control the suit for not more than two losers. In the honour card line, the ace, or the guarded king or queen are likely to be helpful, though knaves and tens are seldom of much use.

The use of these exploratory trial bids, *telling* responder where help is most likely to be needed, avoids the need to bid game 'blind' on ill-fitting hands, and is precise instead of general. Let us look at some responding hands, all worth no more than a raise of opener's 1♠ to 2♠. You will see how difficult it would be for responder to judge the right course of action if opener rebid a 'test' 3♠, and how different it is if, instead, opener makes a trial bid of 3♣.

(a) ♠ Q 7 5 3
    ♡ J 4 3 2
    ◇ K 8 6 3
    ♣ 5

Bid 4♠ direct with four-card trump support and a club singleton.

(b) ♠ K 8 4 2
    ♡ 6 4
    ◇ 10 8 6
    ♣ A J 5 4

Here the ♣A is sure to be invaluable and responder can bid 4♠ without further ado.

(c) ♠ A 7 6 4
    ♡ K 8 3 2
    ◇ 8 6
    ♣ 7 5 3

With no help in clubs and no added values to the original raise, sign off in 3♠.

(d) ♠ Q 10 8 2
    ♡ J 7
    ◇ K J 10 6
    ♣ 7 5 2

No help in clubs but you had a *good* raise to 2♠, so now 'pass the buck' by showing the diamond holding—3◇.

(e) ♠ Q J 6 5
    ♡ K Q 6
    ◇ J 10 9
    ♣ 7 5 2

No help in clubs but again you had a maximum raise to 2♠ and in this case you can bid 4♠ direct.

To make the situation even more clear, compare a typical 1♠ opening with just two variations of a hand on which responder would bid 2♠. Although weak on honour points, opener is distributionally strong and must fear missing a game if the two hands fit well.

♠ K Q J 7 6 2   Responder: ♠ A 8 5 4   OR ♠ A 8 5 4
♡ 8   ♡ J 6 3   ♡ Q J 6 3
◇ K 7 2   ◇ Q J 6 3   ◇ J 6 3
♣ A 10 9   ♣ 7 2   ♣ 7 2

The game is almost certain to be made if responder holds the first of the two hands, and almost equally certain to go down if he holds the second. Note that responder's count and shape are exactly the same in both cases and if the bidding went 1♠—2♠—3♠, responder would be absolutely at sea as to whether to pass or raise. Using trial bids opener selects diamonds as his most likely danger-spot. On the first responder's hand the reply is an immediate 4♠. On the second, the heart holding is not really worth a 'pass the buck' bid and responder should sign off in 3♠.

There is one other important point to be made about responding to a trial bid after a major suit opening, and this concerns a trial bid in the *second* major suit for which responder has four-card support. Opener, in addition to the major he has already bid, may hold a second four-card major and, if there is a 4-4 fit for this, the original suit may well furnish a parking place for losers. The rule, therefore, is that with a four-card fit for the major suit trial-bid by opener, and if willing to play at game level in any case, responder should raise the second major. Here is the example responding

♠ A 8 5 4   hand quoted above when opener's trial bid was
♡ Q J 6 3   3◇. If the trial bid is 3♡, responder is willing for
◇ J 6 3   the hand to be played in either 4♡ or 4♠. He
♣ 7 2   should raise to 4♡, showing the four-card suit
and opener can either pass or convert to 4♠.

Similarly, if opener makes a trial bid of 2♠ after a 1♡—2♡ sequence, it is quite possible that his hand is 5-4 in hearts and spades, and no harm can come from responder raising to 3♠ with a four-card fit, provided he is willing for his partner to play at the four-level in either suit. It does not really matter *why* opener is making this 'reverse' bid—which responder must treat strictly as a trial bid—it is merely up to responder to give the appropriate answer.

Thus by the use of trial bids we can frequently *explore* rather than guess, which is much more satisfactory, but there is one other point you should not forget. If opener is strong enough to bid his game direct without making a trial bid he should do so. A denial by responder that he does not hold the 'help' requested may well tip off the opposition as to their best line of defence. From this it should be plain that you should never make a trial bid unless you are strong enough to stand at least a three-level contract if responder signs off and your weakest suit is attacked first. You should also stick to the Acol principle of bidding what you think you can make, and if this is a game, bid it without further ado.

TRIAL BIDS IN THE MINOR SUITS

In the minor suits the use of trial bids at the two-level is rare. A minor suit game contract is a very high one to hope to reach in the face of responder's simple raise from the one-level to two. Though one must just allow for the possibility, a far more likely resting-place will be either a part-score or a game contract in No Trumps.

♠ A 6 5
♡ 8
♢ A 10 9
♣ K Q J 9 8 6

Responder has raised your 1♣ opening to 2♣. It will not take more than the ♣A to make that suit good for six tricks and if responder can stop hearts . . . ? So make a trial bid of 2♢, not asking for help in diamonds after the minor suit opening, but asking responder to show any reasonable stop he may have in hearts or spades. If he shows a hold on spades by bidding 2♠ you cannot do more than convert to clubs, but if he bids 2♡ you have a good chance of running nine tricks in No Trumps when the outcome of a 5♣ contract must be highly doubtful. With no help by way of a major suit stop which he can show, responder will convert to 3♣. Note the important difference from a trial bid following a major suit opening and raise—after the minor suit opening, the emphasis is on discovering whether or not responder can help with a guard in *another* suit with a no trump contract in view.

♠ 8
♡ K 8 7
♢ J 8 7 4
♣ A 8 6 3 2

1♣—2♣
2♡—4♣

On a very unbalanced hand such as this responder can reply to the trial bid with a jump rebid in opener's minor which cannot be misunderstood. The original 2♣ raise is already so limiting that the subsequent jump can only mean long trump support, a shortage making the hand unsuitable for no trumps, and willingness to suggest a possible minor suit game contract in the knowledge that, if opener were not better than minimum, he would not have been able to make a trial bid.

CUE BIDS AND RETURN CUE BIDS

The point at which the exploratory trial bids give way to the wholly informatory cue bids is when the opening bid has been raised to the three-level, or at any time when the trump suit has been agreed, either directly or inferentially, and obvious explorations for a slam are getting under way. With a weak response such as a single raise, giving information to responder is hardly likely to be important, but if responder is good enough to have given a double raise or any other strong response, he may well be the one capable of judging whether a slam contract is likely to be a good proposition.

A cue bid is never made whilst the trump suit is in doubt. In

1) 1♡—3♡

sequences such as these three, there is no doubt at all but that hearts are agreed as trumps.

2) 1♡—3♣
　3♢—3♡

A cue bid shows first round control of the suit and also suggests interest in a higher contract than the mere game immediately available. In sequence No. 4, for example, the 4♣ bid, when opener could bid a direct 4♠, shows either the ace or a void in clubs. Following this responder can show either the diamond or heart ace (or a void in either) at the four-level without jeopardising the game contract if the control shown is not the one opener hopes to hear about.

3) 1♡—2♢—3♢*-No
　3♡

*cf. Directional
Asking Bids,
Chapter 16.

4) 1♠—3♠
　4♣

♠ A K J 6 4
♡ K Q 9
♢ 8 7
♣ A Q 5

Suppose you've opened 1♠ on this hand and partner has raised to 3♠. Responder may have a wide variety of holdings for his bid but the one essential for a slam will be control of the diamond suit. So opener cue bids 4♣ and responder can now make a return cue bid or take any other action indicated by his hand. Let's have a look at three possible responding hands bearing in mind that the accepted rule for cue bidding is that the lowest-ranking control should be shown first.

(a) ♠ Q 9 8 3　　(b) ♠ Q 9 8 3　　(c) ♠ Q 9 8 3 2
　　♡ A J 8　　　　　♡ 6 3　　　　　　♡ K 10 7 4
　　♢ 6 3　　　　　　♢ A J 8　　　　　♢ K J 9 2
　　♣ K 10 6 3　　　♣ K 10 6 3　　　♣ —

Assuming that the bidding has started with 1♠—3♠, on hand (a) if opener next cue bids either 4♣ or 4♢ responder can bid 4♡. On hand (b) he can respond to a cue bid of 4♣ with 4♢ and on hand (c) if the cue bid is 4♣ he will know that this is duplication of values with his own void and will sign off in 4♠. Note also that in the case of (a), if opener cue bids 4♣ the return cue bid of 4♡ *denies* the diamond control, or this would have been shown first.

1) Responder, holding nothing in reserve for his initial three-level bid, must not make any response to a cue bid that drives the contract above game level.

2) With better than a minimum he should reply, if he can, with a return cue bid or take any other sensible action.

3) If doubtful, but provided the bid does not raise the level of the contract, he should make a return cue bid if he can. Change the opening hand a bit, which will make this clear:

♠ A K J 6 4
♡ A Q 5
♢ K Q 9
♣ 8 7

Now, if opener wishes to make a cue bid, it must be 4♡ so that any return cue bid must be at the five-level. With a bare minimum for his 3♠ raise, responder should not cue bid 5♣ or 5♢, but should sign off in 4♠. Judgement, of course, comes into the picture here. Presumably opener is interested in a slam or he would not be risking the five-level contract.

♠ Q 9 8 3 2
♡ A 8
♢ A 9 8
♣ 9 8 6

Having responded to 1♠ with 3♠ on this hand, if opener next cue-bids 4♣ bid 4♢. This, being the lower-ranking of the two aces, doesn't deny holding the higher-ranking ♡A, whereas a return cue bid of 4♡ would deny holding the ♢A.

♠ J 8 6
♡ Q 9 8 3
♢ A 8 2
♣ K J 8

(a) 1♡—3♡   (b) 1♡—3♡   (c) 1♡—3♡
    4♣—4♢   3♠—4♢   4♢—4♡

Both (a) and (b) are cost-nothing return cue bids which don't push the contract above game level, though in (b) responder *denies* holding first-round control of clubs. In (c) responder has nothing else to show and in any case, his ♢A appears to be duplication of values. Compare this

♠ A 8 2
♡ Q 9 8 3
♢ J 8 6
♣ K J 8

next hand, which is exactly the same except that the spade and diamond holdings are exchanged. Here, with the bare requirements for his 1♡—3♡ raise, responder should not make a return cue bid of 4♠ over opener's 4♣ or 4♢, and should merely return to 4♡. Substitute the ♣Q for the ♣J, and now the hand is maximum for the 3♡ raise, and the ♠A can be shown over 4♣ or 4♢, even though it pushes the level of a heart contract up to five.

Cue bids can be made by either member of the partnership. Here's just one example to make the situation clear. Made by responder, of course, a cue bid will almost certainly become justified because opener's rebid has strengthened responder's hand.

♠ Q 4   1♣—1♡
♡ K J 10 7 5   3♡—4◇
◇ A 10 9 4
♣ A 6

With every intention of going at least to 4♡, responder realises that he holds a much better hand than he need do for his bidding thus far, and also that the 3♡ rebid has strengthened his holding still further. His 4◇ cue bid will inform opener of this and may well pave the way to a slam contract.

You will see from this that it is often possible to pinpoint whether a specific control is held or not and, thereafter, to bid or stay out of a slam without ever having recourse to a slam convention at all. The 5◇ 'one ace' reply to a 'Blackwood' 4 N.T. for instance may leave you in the dark as to *which* one ace, when very possibly this information could have been obtained by way of cue bidding.

Cue bids can be carried to much greater lengths than given above, showing second round controls as well, but you will not need these expert refinements until you reach the rarified heights of high-level tournament bridge.

REVISION QUIZ ON CHAPTER 10

1) Your partner raises your opening 1♠ to 2♠. What do you bid next?

    a) ♠ A Q 9 7 4: ♡ K Q 10 5: ◇ 9 8 2: ♣ A:

    b) ♠ A Q 9 7 4: ♡ K J 9 6: ◇ A 4: ♣ A 3:

    c) ♠ K J 9 4 3 2: ♡ A 9 6: ◇ Q 7 2: ♣ 6:

    d) ♠ A Q 10 7 4 3: ♡ K J: ◇ J 10 9: ♣ A 5:

    e) ♠ Q J 9 7 4 3: ♡ A: ◇ A K J: ♣ 7 5 2:

    f) ♠ K Q 10 9 7 5: ♡ 9 8 4 3: ◇ K 4: ♣ A:

2) Your partner raises your opening 1◇ to 2◇. What do you bid next?

    a) ♠ Q 10 4: ♡ A 5: ◇ K Q 10 8 4: ♣ A Q 6:

    b) ♠ Q 4: ♡ K 3: ◇ A K J 9 4 3: ♣ A 10 4:

    c) ♠ J 5: ♡ A Q: ◇ K J 10 8 6 4: ♣ K Q 10:

    d) ♠ A Q 6: ♡ Q 10 4: ◇ K Q 10 8 4: ♣ A 5:

    e) ♠ K J 9: ♡ 6 3: ◇ A K Q 7 4 3: ♣ K J:

    f) ♠ K J 10: ♡ A Q 9: ◇ K Q 10 8 4: ♣ 7 5:

3) As responder in the following sequences, what is your second round bid?

    a) 1♡ —2♡ ♠ Q 9 8 7: ♡ J 9 7 6: ◇ 8: ♣ Q 9 6 5:
        3◇— ?

    b) 1♠ —2♠ ♠ K J 9 8: ♡ 8 7: ◇ K 7 6: ♣ 8 6 5 3:
        3♣— ?

    c) 1♡ —2♡ ♠ Q J 8 7: ♡ K 10 9 8: ◇ 8: ♣ 8 6 5 3:
        2♠— ?

    d) 1♠ —2♠ ♠ Q 9 8 7: ♡ 9 6 5: ◇ K J 9: ♣ 9 8 7:
        3♡— ?

    e) 1♡ —2♡ ♠ 9 8 7: ♡ Q 9 8 7: ◇ K J 9: ♣ 9 6 5:
        2♠— ?

    f) 1♡ —2♡ ♠ 9: ♡ K J 9 8: ◇ K 8 4 3: ♣ 10 9 6 5:
        2♠— ?

4) You open 1♠ to which partner responds 3♠. What do you bid next?

    a) ♠ A Q 10 7 4 3: ♡ A Q 6 3: ◇ K Q 6: ♣ —:

    b) ♠ K Q 10 9 4: ♡ 9 5: ◇ A Q 10: ♣ A K 4:

    c) ♠ A Q 9 5 4: ♡ 10 9 7 6: ◇ A 6: ♣ A 7:

    d) ♠ A J 9 7 4 3: ♡ 6 5 2: ◇ 4: ♣ K J 5:

ANSWERS TO REVISION QUIZ ON CHAPTER 10

1) a) 3♢ A Trial Bid saying that your main weakness appears to be in diamonds and asking if the 2♠ raise contained any help in it.

   b) 4♠ A direct game bid with no need for a Trial Bid on the way.

   c) No. If partner can only raise to 2♠ you do not want to be in a game contract.

   d) 3♢ A Trial Bid, again in the suit in which you would like some assistance.

   e) 3♣ If partner's single raise contains both top spade honours he won't have any club help but you will still have a good play for game if he raises direct to 4♠ on his trump holding.

   f) 3♡ Heart assistance, either in honours, a short suit, or a four-card fit, would be vital to a game contract.

2) a) 3♣ If partner has the ♢A and responds by showing a spade stop, you have a good chance for 3 N.T.

   b) 3♣ If partner can show a spade stop, and with the lead coming up to you, you again have a good chance of 3 N.T., failing which, 4♢ should be pretty safe.

   c) 2♡ Here again you are interested in a spade stop.

   d) 2♠ This tells partner that you are strong and suggests that he might try 2 N.T. if he has any 'plus' to his 2♢ raise, or show whatever stop he has on the way up.

   e) 2♠ You are pretty certain of six diamond tricks, but must hear about a heart stop before you try No Trumps.

   f) 2♡ If partner offers you a spade stop you know clubs will be wide open and will revert to 3♢.

3) a) 3♡ You have the barest minimum for your bid in spite of the diamond singleton.

   b) 3♢ You cannot help with clubs, but it costs nothing to show the diamond guard.

   c) 3♠ Not being minimum for the 2♡ raise, you can afford to raise 2♠ to 3♠.

   d) 3♠ A minimum raise, only three hearts, and no alternative but to sign off.

   e) 3♡ The same story, so sign off again.

   f) 4♡ With distribution, your hand is good for your original raise, so whether opener has a four-card spade suit or wants help in the suit, you can oblige. Bid 4♡—do not sign off.

4) a) 4♣   A Cue Bid, showing first round control by virtue of the
           void. If partner can show the ◇A it will be lovely, but
           the ♣A will be duplication of values.

   b) 4♣   You must know whether partner can control the hearts
           before getting yourself above the game level.

   c) 4♠   You do not even *want* to investigate slams here. Settle
           for the game contract direct.

   d) No. An Acol Light Opener answered by a Limit Bid which
           is not forcing, so on your very minimum hand you accept
           the opportunity to pass.

VOID-SHOWING WITH BLACKWOOD

There are various licensed methods of combining void-showing
with the responses to a 'Blackwood' 4 N.T., but the most usual way
is to make the required response, but jumping one level to do so if
the hand also contains a void.

West	West	East
♠ K J 8 2		1♠
♡ A 9 6 5 4	2♡	3◇
◇ Q 7 6 4	4♠	4NT
♣ —	6◇	?

Facing a 1♠ opening West's hand is worth a delayed game
sequence, so he bids 2♡. East makes a strong rebid, a 'high reverse'
and now West shows his values by a jump to 4♠. When East bids
4 N.T., Blackwood, West shows his one ace and one void by bidding
6◇, not merely 5◇. The rest is up to East.

Chapter 11

Strong Two Opening Bids and Responses

THE Acol Opening Strong Two Bids and responses are no less fundamentally important to the system than the bids which have formed the theme of the previous chapters. They are an integral part of the system and are carefully dovetailed with the bids required for both lesser and stronger hands. There has grown up, of recent years, something of a vogue for 'weak twos in the majors'. This may be all very well for experts who can understand and handle the full implications of the various changes involved, though it is often a rather pathetic sight to see ordinary Club players happily announcing 'weak twos' without having any clear idea of the other changes and modifications that this involves. It is *not* just as simple, for example, as saying that any Acol Strong Two will be opened with a conventional 2◇ with a 2♡ negative—the whole further sequence will also be changed, and many of the 'weak two' bidders don't appear to realise that they should also learn a system of responses and raises to the weak two bids themselves! One very clear fact emerges, and that is that the system will no longer truly be Acol, and you will not find it possible to sit down and play with any assurance of success with an unaccustomed partner who wants to use such variations. So here are the invaluable straightforward Acol Strong Two Opening Bids and responses, without which no Acol player's armoury is complete.

As you already know and will learn in detail in Chapter 12, the Two Club opening bid in Acol is a cypher bid, the system's conventional way of announcing a hand of great power. The club suit, therefore, is not available for Strong Two openings. Opening bids of 2♠, 2♡ or 2◇ are Strong Twos. and these openings are reserved for hands of power and quality which don't qualify for a 2♣ opening. If you remember that a hand should always be opened with the *strongest* bid for which it qualifies, you will realise that a Strong Two is something of an in-between bid on a hand *too good* for a one-level bid and not quite good enough for 2♣.

Opening Strong Twos are unconditionally forcing for one round. and may be used on hands promising high hopes of game with the most slender assistance from responder. The weakness response. which is employed to ensure that opener has a further opportunity to bid, is 2 N.T.

Opening Strong Twos are *not* glorified one-bids, and hands which require time for the development of the bidding are better opened at the one-level. Strong Twos are reserved for hands of a *type*, and not for hands of any specific point count. They should be used only when opener sees prospects of a game in his hand with minimum support, and when he can afford the luxury of skipping one round of bidding in order to show this.

You don't count honour points for an opening Strong Two—you count playing strength, or playing tricks, and the suitable hands fall into three classes:

1) Prospective game hands with one long and powerful suit with eight playing tricks at the suit bid.

2) Powerful two-suiters so good that, played in the suit which fits responder's hand best, eight tricks or more are likely to develop. In this case the opening Two, being a one-round force, gives opener a certain chance to show both suits.

3) Class 3 is the most difficult to judge, covering hands which, because of their shape or actual content appear to fall between the upper limits of a one-bid and the lower limits of a 2♣ bid. The yardstick to apply is the urgency of opener's need for a reply from responder, even if he has less than the very slender holding of 5 or 6 points which he would need to reply to a one-bid.

Before we get down to examining hands, let us get clear what a playing trick is. It is an expected trick if the holder or his partner is declarer, an attacking trick or winner as distinct from a defensive winner. As for counting the tricks in a strong suit, you are entitled to allow for a reasonable break of the outstanding cards. Thus a seven-card suit headed by the four top honours may be counted as seven playing tricks whereas, if headed by the A-K only, it should be counted as six playing tricks, in the reasonable expectation of losing one trick in the suit. Eight cards headed by A-Q-J can be counted as seven playing tricks, and such tops at the head of a seven-card suit as six playing tricks. Not only the suit itself counts, of course, but outside high cards as well. Thus a solid seven-card suit plus an outside ace counts as eight playing tricks.

OPENER'S REBIDS

Before going on to examples let us just run over the rules for opener's rebids.

First and foremost, if responder makes a positive bid to an opening Strong Two, the sequence becomes *forcing to game*, so here we will confine ourselves to the occasions when responder replies with the negative 2 N.T.

2♡—2 NT
3♡
    The simple three-level rebid is *not* forcing, and responder may now pass. He will not, however, do so if he can possibly help it, as a hand which can guarantee eight playing tricks doesn't need much to make ten. As a corollary to this, if opener thinks he has a play for game without assistance, he must bid it himself and not risk responder's pass.

2♡—2 NT
3◇
    Another *non-forcing* sequence, that is, a simple rebid in a second suit. If extremely weak responder may pass 3◇ or give preference to 3♡ (*not* constituting a raise). With some help to offer he should, of course, bid 4◇ or 4♡. (But see p. 164).

2♣—2 NT
4♡
    The jump to game level is *not* forcing but merely shows a powerful two-suiter and the wish to play either in 4♡ or 4♣. Responder may pass 4♡ or give preference to 4♣.

2♣—2 NT
4◇
    Forcing—a jump bid below game level. Responder must choose between converting to 4♣ or raising to 5◇.

2♡—2 NT
3♣
    Forcing—a reverse rebid. Responder must choose between raising to 4♣ or giving preference to 4♡ in the knowledge that opener's first bid suit will be longer than the second—or there would have been no reason not to bid them in the natural order.

Now we'll have a look at some examples of the different types of Strong Two opening bids.

CLASS 1—SINGLE-SUITED HANDS

Class 1 hands, which are based on one long strong suit, might be

♠ A K Q J 8 6
♡ 8
◇ A 10 9
♣ A 6 4

♠ —
♡ K 5 4
◇ A Q J 9 7 6 4 2
♣ A 5

something like any of these examples. In the first, the six solid spades plus two outside aces make up eight playing tricks so open 2♠. In the second you are entitled to count seven playing tricks in diamonds which, with the ♣A and guarded ♡K make up a good eight playing tricks, making the hand worth a 2◇ opening. In the third example, though the eight tricks are not quite so cast-iron, you would be un

♠ K Q 7   lucky indeed if the holding did not yield eight
♡ A K J 10 8 7 2   tricks played with hearts as trumps.
♢ K 6   If you look at these three hands you will see
♣ 8   that they present great problems if opened with
             a mere one-bid, as there is no rebid which
will do justice to the holdings. A jump to the three-level, though
strong, might be passed out and a game missed, and a direct jump to
game level might equally well mean a missed slam. So announce
your strength by an opening bid of two of your long suit, and give
your partner the chance to judge the value of even meagre support.

Before we leave these Class 1 hands, there is one other point
which may usefully be made clear. The specific requirement for this
bid is a hand with eight playing tricks at the suit bid, and a hand
with eight trumps to the four top honours, even with nothing whatsoever outside, fulfils this requirement. Such a hand not only may,
but should, be opened with a Strong Two, particularly third-in-hand
after two passes, if only on account of the pre-emptive value of the
bid. The opening bidder is unlikely to get into any trouble as, if
his partner's hand is completely worthless, the bidding can be
allowed to die at the three-level. Even if not one single trick
develops from dummy opener is not likely to be more than one
down while, very possibly, having obstructed a fourth-hand opening
bid which might have led to the opponents' game contract, when
opener might well have felt compelled to 'sacrifice' at a much
higher level.

As for opener's rebid, following a negative response a simple
rebid at the three-level can be passed out, so if opener wants to
make certain of playing in game he must bid it direct.

CLASS 2—POWERFUL TWO-SUITERS

With this class of Strong Two the eight playing tricks may not be
immediately apparent, but the strength and 'shape' will be such that,
if a fit with responder's hand is found, at least eight tricks are likely
to develop, and possibly more. The Strong Two opening bid ensures
a chance to show both suits and also, if strong enough, to make
certain that a game contract is reached.

♠ A K Q J 8   If you open a mere 1♠ on this hand partner may
♡ A Q J 10 9   pass, though with as little as a three-card fit for one
♢ 7 4   or other of your suits you have a good chance of
♣ 5   making game. Open 2♠ and rebid 3♡ over
             2 N.T.

♠ A Q J 9 7 2 Here you want to play in game in whichever
♡ A K 10 7 6 3 of your suits responder can tolerate, let alone
◇ — support! Open 2♠ and rebid 4♡, asking for
♣ 6 his preference.

♠ 8 No problems here—open 2♡ and if all responder
♡ K Q J 10 9 6 can do is bid 2 N.T., rebid 3♣ to get preference
◇ A from partner. Strengthen it a little, say by making
♣ A Q 10 9 8 the hearts ♡ A K J 10 9 6, and you should open
 2♡ and rebid 4♣, forcing to 4♡ or 5♣.

♠ A K J 8 6 Open 2◇ on this hand and 'reverse' into 3♠ over
♡ 8 responder's 2 N.T. You are strong enough to
◇ A K J 9 5 4 stand either a raise to 4♠ or preference to 4◇,
♣ 2 when it wouldn't be much of a gamble to go on
 to 5◇.

A powerful two-suiter qualifying for a Strong Two when one of the two suits is clubs presents no special problems, as the higher-ranking can be shown first, followed by a rebid in clubs. When, however, the hand is a Class 1 single-suiter in clubs, the choice may lie between opening 1♣ and forcing on the next round—if any—or devaluing an opening 2♣ bid slightly. Compare the two following hands :

♠ A No problem here—open 2◇ and rebid 3♣,
♡ — which gives a very accurate picture of the hand.
◇ K Q 10 9 6 5 With the second example, if the suit were any-
♣ A J 10 5 3 2 thing but clubs there would be no problem,
 a Strong Two opening in the suit concerned.
 As it is, you must choose between opening 1♣
♠ A 3 —and risk being passed out at that contract—
♡ — or opening 2♣ for which you are technically
◇ K J 8 under strength. The latter is the better choice
♣ A K J 10 6 5 3 2 but responder, when rebidding after the se-
quence 2♣—2◇—3♣, as you will see in the next chapter, should just bear in mind that the opening bid may not be quite up to standard.

CLASS 3—POWERFUL HANDS NOT QUALIFYING FOR ANOTHER OPENING

These hands are, as we have already said, the most difficult to judge. If they were not exceptionally strong they could be opened with a one-bid but they are too good for this. They generally contain something in the region of 20 honour points and, because of their shape or actual content, are unsuitable for either a 2 N.T or a 2♣ opening bid. They fall into a number of distributional classes and are opened as Strong Twos only because there is a danger that they may be passed out when game is on with even less than minimum support from partner.

♠ A J 9 3 2
♡ A K J 4
◇ 8
♣ A Q J

Here, with 20 points, you can see that the remaining 20 points in the pack may be so divided that, if you open 1♠, the hand could be passed out, whereas if responder happens to have a 4-card fit for hearts you have every chance of making the ten tricks for a game, let alone a useful part-score—for remember after 2♠—2 NT—3♡ the bidding can die at that point.

♠ 6
♡ A Q 9 2
◇ A K Q 7 4
♣ K Q 3

♠ K J 10 8 5 2
♡ 8
◇ A K 4
♣ A K 7

♠ A 10 7 5 4 3
♡ A K J 3
◇ A Q J
♣ —

On none of these three hands do you want the bidding to die below game-level if responder has 'the smell of an oil rag'. Tell him this by opening with a Strong Two, in each case in your longest suit. Remember it is not just for the sake of the sound of it that you make this bid, but to let your partner know that your hand needs very little assistance from him to make game. You don't demand a slam contract, or even, for that matter, a game contract, but you do make it clear that you have a powerful distributional hand needing less support than an ordinary run-of-the-mill hand would do to produce a game.

To sum up, opening Strong Two bids are reserved for hands of character. They may be single or two-suited or just obviously too good for a one-bid. This does not mean that they are glorified one-bids but hands which, while unrelated to point count or quick tricks, give prospects of game with minimum support from partner, and on which opener can afford to skip one level of bidding in order to tell his partner this.

RESPONDING TO STRONG TWO OPENING BIDS

The responses to Strong Two opening bids fall into two main classes, negative and positive, and the latter sub-divide into new suit responses, direct suit raises, and 3 N.T. responses. We will take them in that order.

Negative response: A Strong Two opening is forcing for one round and the negative response, denying the values set out in the categories below, is 2 N.T. Broadly speaking a hand will not qualify for a positive response unless it contains at least one honour trick and, according to the particular circumstances, it may need more. But remember that responder is not at liberty to take it upon himself

♠ 8 2
♡ J 8 6 5 4
◇ J 9 8 6 4
♣ 8

to pass a Strong Two opening however bleak his hand may appear. Here, for example, if partner opens 2♠ responder must bid 2 N.T., as the hand could prove a gold mine if opener is two-suited in spades and one of the red suits.

♠ 8 7
♡ Q 7 2
◇ 10 7 5 2
♣ 9 8 5 4

Respond 2 N.T. to any Strong Two opening. Pass next time after the sequence 2♠—2 NT—3♠, but if opener's rebid were 3♡, raise to 4♡.

♠ Q J 7 5 4
♡ 10 9 6
◇ Q 8 4
♣ 7 2

Respond 2 N.T. to any opening Strong Two, including 2♣. If opener rebids 3♠ raise to 4♠. If the sequence should be 2♠—2 NT—3♡ give jump preference to 4♠.

♠ 8 5
♡ K 10 9
◇ 10 9 8 5
♣ Q J 8 3

If partner opens 2♠ respond 2 N.T. If he rebids 3♠ bid 3 N.T. on distributed strength. If instead he rebids in a second suit, raise that suit.

From the above you will have realised that even reasonable trump support combined with other rather slender values should be bid first as 2 N:T. as a corollary to which, of course, the positive responses carry somewhat specific messages. But even after the original negative reply, responder can often help, by way of a judicious rebid, to steer the final contract into 3 N.T.

2♠—2 NT
3◇

In this sequence, for example, where opener has shown a strong spade-diamond two-suiter, to hear that responder holds a heart suit is hardly likely to be of much interest. Any bid of 3♡ by responder at this point should, therefore, be read as offering a heart *stop* rather than a playable suit. If opener can rebid 3 N.T. with this knowledge it may well be better than going on in one of his suits. Responder should not show a 'stop' in this way if it drives the contract beyond the 3 N.T. level, which means that here he could not bid 4♣. Furthermore responder should not bid in this way if his hand is otherwise so weak that he cannot stand opener's return to one of his two suits at the forced higher level, in this case 3♠ or 4◇.

Change-of-suit response: The first rule for *any* positive response is that the bidding must thereafter continue until at least a game contract has been reached. With that fact firmly in mind remember too that, as at the lower level of an opening one-bid, a change-of suit response can be made on somewhat less than if the level of the bidding has to be raised. Thus $2\heartsuit$—$2\spadesuit$ or $2\diamondsuit$—$2\heartsuit$ require less than $2\heartsuit$—$3\diamondsuit$ or $2\diamondsuit$—$3\clubsuit$, just as $1\spadesuit$ requires less over $1\heartsuit$ than $2\clubsuit$ does.

$\spadesuit$ 8 3
$\heartsuit$ K Q 10 8 6 3
$\diamondsuit$ 9
$\clubsuit$ 10 9 8 6

A change-of-suit response on one honour trick and a biddable suit is correct on a hand such as this provided the level of the bidding is not raised, that is to say, bid $2\heartsuit$ over an opening $2\diamondsuit$, but 2 N.T. over an opening $2\spadesuit$. With $1\frac{1}{2}$ honour tricks —say the $\clubsuit$K in place of the $\clubsuit$10—you should respond $3\heartsuit$ over an opening $2\spadesuit$.

Bearing in mind also that whether opener is single- or two-suited, news of a long weak suit facing him is not likely to be of interest, so it is better to avoid giving a change-of-suit response in a suit lacking 'tops'. Find some other response if you can. This, once you have got the idea, may well be an immediate raise in opener's suit. But before we go on to these, there is one other new suit response to be covered. This is a responder's *jump* bid which shows a solid self-supporting trump suit with no losers. It should be as good as six to the four top honours or seven to the A-K-Q, the message of the bid being that the suit requires no support from opener.

$\spadesuit$ 5 3
$\heartsuit$ A K Q J 9 8
$\diamondsuit$ Q 3
$\clubsuit$ 9 4 2

If partner opens $2\diamondsuit$ respond $3\heartsuit$ and, if he opens $2\spadesuit$, respond $4\heartsuit$. It is not unknown for a partnership to reach a successful Grand Slam contract facing a void in the trump suit in such a case. But obviously judgement here must be used. For example, if partner opens $2\diamondsuit$, respond $3\heartsuit$, but if he opens $2\spadesuit$ to respond $4\heartsuit$, which might be passed out, would be madness. This hand should play in either $6\spadesuit$ or $7\spadesuit$, according to the number

$\spadesuit$ Q 10 8 6
$\heartsuit$ A K Q J 9 8
$\diamondsuit$ 3
$\clubsuit$ 9 4

of aces held by opener, as the heart suit will absorb all his losers, and the best immediate response is likely to be a 'Blackwood' 4 N.T.!

Direct suit raises: Two basic rules are important here:

1) *A single raise* of opener's trump suit is a constructive and unlimited bid. It shows a responding hand containing trump support *and at least one ace or void*.

2) *A double raise* ($2\heartsuit$—$4\heartsuit$, $2\diamondsuit$—$4\diamondsuit$) shows good trump support, something in the region of 9-10 honour points, and *no ace or void*.

It follows, of course, that a single raise may be stronger than the double jump, and it leaves the maximum bidding space for slam investigations by means of cue bids or your chosen slam convention. The double jump, on the other hand, notifies opener at once that though responder has a reasonably good supporting hand he has *no first round controls*. Any thought of 'slamming' must, therefore, depend on opener himself having at least three first round controls.

♠ Q J 9 5
♡ K 9 7 2
◇ K 8 7 6
♣ 5

If partner opens 2♠, 2♡, or 2◇, raise at once to four of that suit, showing good trump support, about 9-10 honour points and *no* first-round controls. Move the ♣5 up to being the ◇5, leaving a club void, and the correct response to any opening two-bid would be a single raise.

You don't need four-card support for a trump suit which is good enough to be opened at the two-level, and normally J-x-x should be considered adequate. Remember too that if opener has any ideas of 'slamming', the agreement of his suit as trumps is likely to be the most welcome news he can hear. In most instances, therefore, and particularly when the opening Strong Two is in one of the majors, a direct trump raise, if available, will be the best choice.

♠ J 9 6
♡ A 9 7 5 4
◇ 7 4
♣ K J 7

If partner opens 2◇ bid 2♡, but if he opens 2♠ it is better to raise to 3♠ than to make a change-of-suit response to 3♡.

♠ K 10 8
♡ 8 6 2
◇ J 8 7
♣ A 10 5 3

In this next example the choice is slightly more difficult if the opening bid is 2♡, and probably the best response is a waiting bid of 3♣, knowing that you can put opener back to his hearts, or raise his 3♡ rebid to 4♡, with a clear conscience. If he opens either 2◇ or 2♠ give a direct single raise.

♠ Q 8 7
♡ A J 10 7
◇ 6 2
♣ K J 7 5

Respond 2♡ to partner's opening 2◇ bid, but raise either a 2♡ or 2♠ opening to three of that suit. Exchange the ♡A for the ♡K, and this brings us to another point which must be made, the interpretation of a 'biddable suit'.

Over an opening bid at the one-level a one-level response in a new suit (1◇—1♡ or 1♡—1♠) shows no better values than would be needed to bid 1 N.T. in this position. It shows, in fact, at least the values to bid 1 N.T. with, in addition, a biddable suit. If partner

♠ Q 8 7
♡ K J 10 7
◇ 6 2
♣ K J 7 5

opened 1◇, on this hand you would not hesitate to bid 1♡ and, in the same way, you can bid 2♡ over a 2◇ opening, guaranteeing no more than the values for a positive response and a 'biddable' heart suit. Over an opening 1♠ you would hardly bid 2♡, and would probably temporise with 2♣.

To bid at the three-level, either 3♣ or 3♡ over an opening 2♠ would be unwise as, although the hand contains 10 honour points, it does not contain the requisite 1½ honour tricks. Raise 2♠ to 4♠, showing excellent trump support and no first round control.

Three no trump response: There is still another conventional response to an opening Strong Two, and that is a jump to 3 N.T. This shows approximately 10-12 honour points (the equivalent of the 2 N.T. limit bid facing a one-level opening) and again *no ace or void,* i.e., no first round controls. The inference, of course, is also strong that the hand does not contain adequate support for the trump suit, or a direct raise could have been given in preference to 3 N.T.

♠ Q 6 5	If partner opens 2♡ respond 3 N.T., but if he
♡ 7 6	opens either 2♢ or 2♠, raise to four of that suit.
♢ K 10 8 3	In either case the response denies any first-round
♣ K Q 5 2	controls.

♠ 9 5	If partner opens 2♢ respond 2♡, showing the
♡ K 9 6 5	biddable major suit in preference to jumping to
♢ K Q 7	4♢. If he opens 2♡ raise to 4♡. If he opens 2♠
♣ K 9 8 2	bid 3 N.T.

Finally a word about both cue bidding and the use of the Acol Direct King Convention (for details of which see Chapter 18) in conjunction with a response to an opening Strong Two when an ace has been specifically denied. In 2♡—4♡, for example, when responder is known to hold no first-round control, i.e., no ace or void, responder will by-pass showing aces in response to 4 N.T. from opener, and will show kings. Similarly in responding to a cue bid (2♡—4♡—5♣) a return cue bid of, perhaps, 5♢, would show either the king or a singleton, that is, second round control, not an ace or void, which has already been denied.

REVISION QUIZ ON CHAPTER 11

1)   What opening bid would you make on the following hands?

     a) ♠ A K Q 9 6 4 3: ♡ A 10 4: ◇ 6 5: ♣ 3:
     b) ♠ 9 6: ♡ A K Q 10 6 4: ◇ J 10 9: ♣ A K:
     c) ♠ A J 9 6 4 3: ♡ A K 8: ◇ K J 9: ♣ 5:
     d) ♠ 7: ♡ A K J 9 6: ◇ A Q 10 8 4: ♣ A 4:
     e) ♠ K Q 10: ♡ K 9: ◇ 4: ♣ A K Q 7 5 4 3:
     f) ♠ A K 3: ♡ A K Q 9 6 2: ◇ Q 2: ♣ 10 4:
     g) ♠ Q J 4: ♡ K Q J 10 6 4: ◇ A K J: ♣ 4:
     h) ♠ 8: ♡ 7: ◇ A K Q J 9 7 4: ♣ A 10 9 6:
     i) ♠ A Q 4: ♡ K J 9 6 4 3: ◇ K 8: ♣ A 4:
     j) ♠ 9: ♡ A Q J: ◇ K 10 4: ♣ A K Q J 10 9:
     k) ♠ A Q 9 6 4: ♡ A J 10 8 4: ◇ —: ♣ A Q 6:

2)   Your partner opens 2♣. What is your response on the following hands?

     a) ♠ K 9 4 3: ♡ Q 7 3: ◇ J 9 8 2: ♣ Q 4:
     b) ♠ K 9 2: ♡ A 7 4: ◇ Q 7 3: ♣ 10 9 4 2:
     c) ♠ 4 2: ♡ Q 10 9 6 4 3: ◇ 8 3: ♣ J 9 6:
     d) ♠ 4: ♡ K 9: ◇ Q 10 9 6 5 4 3: ♣ 8 7 6:
     e) ♠ A 4 3: ♡ K 3 2: ◇ Q 10 9 6 5 4: ♣ 7:
     f) ♠ Q 10: ♡ Q J 4 3: ◇ K 9 2: ♣ Q 6 3 2:

3)   You open 2♣ and partner responds 2 N.T. What is your rebid on these hands?

     a) ♠ A K Q 10 9 8: ♡ A K 4: ◇ 6 3: ♣ 5 4:
     b) ♠ A Q J 9 8 4 3: ♡ A 10 5: ◇ A 8 4: ♣ —:
     c) ♠ A K Q 10 6: ♡ A K Q 9 5: ◇ Q 4: ♣ J:
     d) ♠ A J 10 9 8 6: ♡ K J 10 9 7 4: ◇ —: ♣ A:

4)   You hold:

     ♠ 7 6:   ♡ 10 9 8:   ◇ Q 10 7 6:   ♣ 9 7 6 3:

Your partner deals and opens 2♡, to which you correctly respond 2 N.T. What do you rebid if he next bids:

     a) 3♡   (b) 3◇   (c) 4◇   (d) 3♠ ?

ANSWERS TO REVISION QUIZ ON CHAPTER 11

1) a) 2♠   This hand contains exactly eight playing tricks at spades.

   b) 2♡   With these six hearts the hand just qualifies for a two bid. It is too strong for a one bid.

   c) 1♠   This hand does not qualify under any of the three classes and must be opened 1♠.

   d) 2♡   This is the two-suiter type where you want to be certain of a chance to show the diamonds.

   e) 1♣   This hand is not quite good enough for a 'devalued' 2♣.

   f) 2♡   Eight playing tricks at hearts should be safe.

   g) 1♡   You can only count seven playing tricks here.

   h) 2♢   There are definitely eight playing tricks in diamonds.

   i) 1♡   This hand is just a normal strong 1♡ opener.

   j) 2♣   This is worth stretching to a 2♣ opening.

   k) 2♠   You must be sure of a chance to show the hearts in case partner does not like spades.

2) a) 4♠   A double jump, showing good trump support and no ace or void.

   b) 3♠   Here you have an ace as well as trump support.

   c) 2 NT An obvious negative response.

   d) 2 NT This too is a negative response in spite of the seven-card diamond suit. Bid this on the next round if expedient.

   e) 3♠   Though your diamond suit is biddable, trump agreement is far more likely to help opener.

   f) 3 NT Evenly balanced—10 points—no ace.

3) a) 3♠   With just your eight playing tricks make the minimum rebid.

   b) 4♠   This time you want to try for game however little partner has, so bid it direct in case he passes 3♠.

   c) 4♡   Bid your second suit at game level.

   d) 3♡   Here again, offer your second suit. Partner may pass, bid 3♠ or raise either suit to game.

4) a) Pass If partner has eight (or even nine!) playing tricks in hearts, your hand is hardly calculated to produce another. His simple rebid is *not* forcing.

b) Pass Here again, the simple rebid in a new suit is not forcing, and you prefer diamonds to hearts, which you show by passing.

c) 4♡ You have now no option but to bid again, as the jump rebid in a new suit below game level is forcing. You are, however, entitled to use your judgement in a case like this. The ♡ 10-9-8 is good support for a suit bid at the two-level and 4♡ may be easier to make than 5◇. Exchange your major suit holdings, however, and you should raise to 5◇.

d) 4♡ Here again you have no option, as the 3♣ 'reverse' is forcing to game. Give preference to 4♡ but, if your major suit holdings were reversed, you would show your preference by raising to 4♠.

Chapter 12

Two Club Opening Bids and Responses

THERE are two groups of hands which qualify for the strongest of all Acol opening bids, Two Clubs, and broadly speaking the division is between hands which are fitted for a suit contract, and the extremely powerful No Trump type hands. The latter will be covered in Chapter 13, and here we shall confine ourselves to the unevenly balanced hands where the intended rebid will be in a suit, not in No Trumps.

All 2♣ opening bids have one thing in common—they announce a powerful hand containing at least five quick tricks, distributionally of game-going strength with little or no support from partner.

An opening 2♣ bid is what is called 'forcing to 2 N.T.', that is to say, the cypher bid of 2♣, which bears no relation to the club holding, is unconditionally forcing for one round and forcing to game except in the sole instance of opener rebidding 2 N.T. (see Chapter 13). One does not count honour points for this opening bid unless it is clear from the start that the intended rebid will be in No Trumps. One counts quick, or honour, tricks and playing strength. Five arid quick tricks with no 'shape' would not qualify for better than a one-bid, because it would not be good enough to *demand*

♠ A 6 5
♡ A 7 5
◇ A K 8 6
♣ A 4 3

a game contract. Here, for example, it would be madness to open 2♣ and force your partner to keep the bidding open to game as, if he has a blank hand, you might well end up with just the five tricks you started with! Open 1◇ and await developments. If responder can't speak at all you're well out of it, but if he can, you will then be able to force a game contract.

The negative reply, which responder *must* give, is 2◇, and his second negative, if he is under an obligation to bid again and has nothing helpful to say, is 2 N.T. We shall be going into the requirements for these and the positive responses shortly, but meanwhile let's have a look at some examples of hands which qualify for a 2♣ opening and a forcing-to-game suit rebid.

♠ A K Q 10 8
♡ A K 6
◇ K Q
♣ A 9 4

A power-house of a hand with which you want to reach a game contract however weak partner's hand. Open 2♣ and rebid 2♠, showing your suit. You *might* go down in 4♠ but with any luck responder might supply the ♠ J-x-x or the ♡ Q, or even a favourable trump break and responder holding a well-placed ♣ Q would be all you needed.

♠ K Q 10 9
♡ A K J 7 3
◇ A 6
♣ A 7

Another powerful game-going hand. Open 2♣ and rebid 2♡ over responder's probable 2◇. If he now bids 2 N.T., try 3♠—you will end in 3 N.T., 4♡ or 4♠, and you won't need a lot of luck to make the contract.

♠ K 6
♡ —
◇ A K J 9
♣ A K Q 9 7 6 3

As mentioned in Chapter 11, it is sometimes necessary to devalue an opening 2♣ bid when the predominating suit is clubs. Here clearly no other opening will do justice to the hand. When you rebid 3♣ your partner will know that you may be a trifle under strength so will not insist on a slam contract in the firm belief that you *must* have five quick tricks. There are two points to learn here, the first being that the fact that opener rebids in a suit, even if clubs, makes the sequence forcing to game.

The second important point is that this strongest of all opening bids is not made merely for the pleasure of hearing the words, but to tell partner loudly and clearly that you hold a hand of game-going strength with, in addition, five honour tricks. This allows responder to judge the value of his own hand which, even with apparently a more than meagre point count, may well become the one capable of suggesting a slam. You will meet one or two examples on these lines when you come to Chapter 17 on quantitative bids. Meanwhile, there is one other opener's rebid to be covered.

OPENER'S JUMP REBID

A jump rebid in a suit made by a player who has opened 2♣ and received a 2◇ response is conventional. It asks responder to cue-bid any ace he may hold in spite of his negative. Obviously if responder held two aces he would have a positive response in the first place, so he can only have one ace at best. In the original version of

2♣—2◇
3♡

this convention the jump rebid, in addition to asking responder to cue-bid any ace held, promised a solid and self-supporting trump suit. It is not, however, a situation in which responder is likely to need such information, the 2♣ bidder being the one in charge and the one best capable of judging the final contract when he has discovered for certain

whether or not responder holds an ace. The negative response,
denying any ace, is 3 N.T. Here's an example

♠ A K Q
♡ K Q J
♢ K Q J 10
♣ A K Q

2♣—2♢
3♣— ?

where the convention can prove valuable. Opener
has no outstanding suit, yet if responder has either
red ace the contract should be 6 N.T. Without an
ace it may as well be played quietly at the three-
level. The bidding, then, would go like this, and if
responder bids 4♢ or 4♡, opener would follow
with 6 N.T. If he bids 3 N.T., opener would pass.

♠ A
♡ A K Q J 9 8 3
♢ K Q
♣ K Q 10

Here's another obvious 2♣ opening. If responder bids 2♢, rebid 3♡. If he cue-bids 4♣ or 4♢
you can go straight to 6♡. If he denies an ace
with 3 N.T., take out into 4♡, at which level
you might just as well play if you can't get

to a slam—unexpected ruffs or bad trump breaks have ruined many
a high-level contract reached in an effort to find out whether some
specific card is there.

♠ K Q J 10 6 5
♡ A K 7
♢ 6
♣ A K Q

Here again, if responder has either the ♠A or
♢A the final contract will be 6♠. Missing both
it might as well be 4♠, not the five-level which is
forced on you if you have to use a 'Blackwood'
4 N.T. to be sure both aces are missing.

Another valuable, though admittedly rare, use for the bid is when
opener holds all four aces himself and knows that he will have to
follow a 'Blackwood' 4 NT—5♣ with 5 N.T. to discover vital
kings. Responder might, after all, have two kings and still only be
able to bid 2♢ opposite the opening 2♣. Here's an actual deal
which cropped up recently:

♠ A K Q J 9 7 6
♡ A Q 7
♢ A 9
♣ A

♠ 10
♡ K 9 4
♢ 10 8 6 5
♣ K 9 7 4 3

The bidding:

W. E.
2♣ 2♢
3♠ 3 NT
4 NT 5♡
7♠

3♠, of course, got the obvious denial of 3 N.T.,
and then 4 N.T. asked for kings—the Acol Direct
King Convention which comes into force when the
number of aces held by responder is already known
for certain. Which two kings can matter, of course,
but opener took a chance on one of them being
the ♡ K—which it was—and the other, whichever
it was, giving a parking place for the ♢9. Thus the bidding could

have been dropped at the five-level if responder had been kingless as well as aceless.

To sum up the requirements for an opening 2♣ bid of this type, then, the hand should contain five quick tricks, except when the predominating suit is clubs, when it may be slightly under strength. In addition, it should be of powerful playing strength, capable of scoring a game with little or no assistance from partner. If the hand does not conform to these standards you may be able to use a Strong Two opening bid or, failing that, settle for a one-bid. Any time you can look at your hand and see that, if partner can't even respond to a one-bid, you have no hope of making game, then you haven't got a 2♣ opening. Remember also that a hand should always be opened with the strongest bid for which it qualifies, so that if you use a Strong Two opening responder will know that you couldn't bid 2♣ and likewise, if you make a one-level opening, however strong your rebid, initially you could not open with a Strong Two or 2♣.

RESPONDING TO TWO CLUB OPENING BIDS

Authorities differ as to the requirements for a 'positive' response to an opening 2♣ bid, but we do not recommend that this should be dropped too low. If you get into the habit of giving a positive response on 'tram tickets' you are likely to find that opener insists on hoisting the contract too high in the conviction that a slam must be available and it is, therefore, wiser to stick to certain minimum standards.

As with all bidding, judgement can enter the picture, but your general rule is that a hand with less than the following qualifies for a 2♢ 'negative' on the first round of bidding:

1) Any one ace and any one king, not necessarily in combination.

2) One honour trick and a reasonably good biddable suit which can be shown at the two-level.

3) One and a half honour tricks and a reasonably good biddable suit if it must be shown at the three-level (2♣—3♣ or 2♣—3♢).

4) Any 8 or 9 point hand, according to the 'quality' of the points.

With less than the above, respond 2♢, and bid more strongly if you can on the next round. If under an obligation to keep the bidding open to game when opener makes a suit rebid, the second negative of 2 N.T. may be used on hands where it is really impossible to produce anything more constructive.

You will note from the above that a first-round response of 2 N.T. is positive, and this may be used when the hand contains no biddable suit. A four-card major is always 'biddable', that is to say, at the one-level you would clearly bid 1♠ in response to 1♡ on Q-x-x-x and an outside ace, though if the suit were transposed to hearts you could not show it over an opening 1♠, and would have to bid 1 N.T. So at the forcing level of a 2♣ opening, it is correct, provided the requirements for a positive response are held, to show a four-card major in preference to bidding 2 N.T. In practice, however, it is unwise to do this unless the suit is worth suggesting as trumps— at least one high honour backed by better than 'little x's', and K-J-x-x should be regarded as the minimum. To show a biddable suit at the three-level, that is, in either of the minors (2♣—2◇ is the negative), it should be at least a five-card suit.

♠ Q 7 2
♡ 10 8 4
◇ K Q 10 8 6
♣ J 3

Respond 2◇ to an opening 2♣, as the hand is not worth a 'positive' bid of 3◇. Exchange the diamond suit with one of the majors, and it is worth a two-level positive bid of either 2♡ or 2♠.

In other words, you judge that the three-level bid is too time-consuming, whereas the two-level bid, if the suit were a major, may save time. Exchange the ◇K for the ◇A, and even though the hand contains only 8 honour points, it is too good to bid even as a first-round negative, and becomes worth 3◇. There would be no question about it, of course, if the suit were a major.

♠ Q 7 2
♡ K 8 4
◇ Q 10 8 6
♣ J 3 2

Compare this 8-point hand—the same honour cards but differently divided, and no longer worth any positive response. Bid 2◇ on the first round. Top it up by making one of the queens into a king and, with no biddable suit, it is worth a positive response of 2 N.T.

RESPONDER'S SECOND NEGATIVE

Once having bid 2◇ to deny a positive response, responder can, of course, bid constructively if his hand is worth it. Except for the one instance when opener rebids 2 N.T., responder is under an absolute obligation to keep the bidding open to game and, with literally nothing worth showing, he rebids 2 N.T. This bid virtually speaks for itself, and common sense will tell you that there are numerous occasions when there will be a more constructive bid available. There are, in fact, two conventional rebids which fall into place here. Remember that both follow the original 2◇ negative response.

RESPONDER'S DOUBLE RAISE OF OPENER'S SUIT

When opener makes his rebid in a suit, a double raise by responder follows the same lines that it did when the opening bid was a Strong Two (p. 165) except that, facing the extra values contained in a 2♣ opening, the double raise can be made more lightly. As before, it

2♣—2◇   proclaims a reasonably good supporting hand with
2♡—4♡   adequate trump support, some scattered honour
           strength and *no ace or void*. As the 2◇ negative has

shown less than 9 honour points (or 8 well-distributed points) opener can expect a maximum of 8 points and possibly less. Also, in the same way that over a Strong Two responder could show 10-12 aceless points by a bid of 3 N.T. (p. 167), so now he can show 6-8 points by a rebid of 3 N.T., always provided, of course, that he is unable to make any possibly more constructive bid such as a raise of opener's suit. Two examples should suffice:

♠ Q 8 6 4   After 2♣—2◇, raise opener's 2♡ or 2♠ rebid to
♡ Q 7 3 2   the four-level. If his rebid is 3♣, bid 3 N.T. The
◇ K 9 8   direct raise having *denied* an ace or void, if
♣ 5 4   opener now bids 4 N.T. he is using the Acol
               Direct King Convention, by-passing the request for
               aces (see Chapter 18).

♠ 8 3   After 2♣—2◇—2♠ bid 3 N.T. to show the
♡ Q 6 5 4   scattered strength and no ace or void. After 2♣—
◇ K 9 8   2◇—2♡, raise to 4♡. Again 4 N.T. from opener
♣ Q 9 8 3   would be asking for kings on the 'Blackwood' scale.

RESPONDER'S SUIT JUMP REBID

A jump rebid in a new suit on the second round following responder's original 2◇ negative shows a long solid self-supporting trump suit *missing* the ace. A solid suit headed by the ace would, of course, have constituted a positive response in the first place, and any outside values would almost certainly have brought the hand into a 'positive' category anyway. Thus opener can expect virtually nothing outside the suit named, but the information that his

♠ 7 4   partner's suit will stand up on its own may be
♡ K Q J 10 8 6   invaluable. Here, for example, the hand is best
◇ 9 8 7   bid by way of an initial 2◇ bid with a 4♡
♣ 8 5   rebid over opener's 2♠ or 3◇.

To round off this chapter, here are some example hands to give you guidance.

♠ 8
♡ 9 6 5 2
◇ 8 7 3 2
♣ 9 7 6 5

Bid 2◇ in response to 2♣ and use the second negative of 2 N.T. whatever opener rebids. However, if the sequence should go 2♣—2◇—2♡—2 NT—3 NT, convert to 4♡. Opener will not be misled into expecting strength you haven't got, but will understand that you prefer a suit contract to No Trumps.

♠ Q 7 2
♡ J 7
◇ 10 9 8 4
♣ 10 9 7 6

Bid 2◇ and 2 N.T. on the second round. But thereafter, give preference if appropriate, e.g., 2♣—2◇—2♠—2 NT—3◇—4◇, or 2♣—2◇—2♠—2 NT—3♡—3♠.

♠ K 9 7
♡ 9 6 5 2
◇ K 10 7
♣ Q J 9

A positive response with no biddable suit, so bid 2 N.T. in reply to 2♣, showing 8-9 honour points. If opener rebids 3♡ raise to 4♡. You have not yet denied an ace, so his 4 N.T. must get a 5♣ 'Blackwood' reply.

♠ 9 6
♡ K J 9
◇ A 10 9 7 5
♣ 6 4 3

Even though it is space-consuming, you must give a positive response of 3◇ on this hand, or subsequently you may find it impossible to catch up. Exchange your suit for one of the majors, and you don't even mind having to bid it at the two-level!

♠ Q 9 7 2
♡ 8
◇ K 8 6 4
♣ Q 7 5 3

Bid 2◇ in response to 2♣ and raise any suit bid other than 2♡ to four. Over 2♡, bid 3 N.T., as you are just too good for a second negative.

♠ 9 8
♡ 9 8 7 6
◇ K Q 7
♣ Q J 8 4

Bid 2◇ initially. Raise opener's rebid of 2♡ to 4♡, or his 3♣ or 3◇ to 4♣ or 4◇. If his rebid is 2♠, bid 3 N.T.

♠ Q 10 8 7 6 3
♡ 7
◇ 8 6 2
♣ 8 5 3

Bid 2◇ initially and then bid and repeat spades until a game contract is reached.

♠ K Q 10 8 7
♡ 8 2
◇ Q 7 6
♣ 9 7 3

Had your suit been clubs or diamonds you could not have risked a three-level positive response. As it is you can bid 2♠ and then judge your further bidding according to opener's rebids.

♠ K Q J 10 8 6   Compare this final hand, however, which is better
♡ 8 2   expressed by a 2◇ response followed by a jump
◇ 7 6   bid in spades to show the solid suit missing the
♣ 9 7 3   ace. Add even an outside queen, and it would be
                  worth a 'positive' 2♠ anyway.

REVISION QUIZ ON CHAPTER 12

1) What opening bid would you make on the following hands:

a) ♠ A K J 9 6: ♡ A 10 4: ◇ K Q 10: ♣ A 4:
b) ♠ A K: ♡ K Q 9 4: ◇ A K Q 9 6: ♣ 8 3:
c) ♠ A K 9 6 3 2: ♡ A 4: ◇ 5: ♣ A J 6 2:
d) ♠ K 3 2: ♡ —: ◇ A K 10 9 6: ♣ A Q 8 3 2:
e) ♠ A 5: ♡ K Q 10 9 5: ◇ A K 4: ♣ K Q 10:
f) ♠ A Q 9 4: ♡ A Q 10 5: ◇ A: ♣ A J 6 3:.

2) You open 2♣ and partner responds 2◇. What is your rebid?

a) ♠ A K J 9 6: ♡ A 10: ◇ K Q 10: ♣ A Q 2:
b) ♠ A 5: ♡ A K 10 9 5: ◇ A K 4: ♣ K Q 10:
c) ♠ A 9: ♡ K Q 9 4: ◇ A K Q 9 6: ♣ A 3:
d) ♠ A K: ♡ A K Q J 9 6 3: ◇ A K 9: ♣ 8:
e) ♠ A J 9 6: ♡ A 10 8 6: ◇ A K: ♣ A K 3:

3) Your partner opens 2♣. What is your response on the following hands?

a) ♠ 8 6 3: ♡ K 10 6 4: ◇ K 9 6 3: ♣ 4 3:
b) ♠ 8 3 2:' ♡ 9 6 4: ◇ A K J 9 5: ♣ J 7:
c) ♠ J 10 9 8 6 3: ♡ A 4 3: ◇ K 10 3: ♣ 6:
d) ♠ K 10 5: ♡ Q 10 4: ◇ J 10 7 4: ♣ Q J 2:
e) ♠ Q 10 9 6 3 2: ♡ Q 3 2: ◇ 4: ♣ J 3 2:
f) ♠ K J 5 4: ♡ Q 10 4: ◇ J 10 7: ♣ Q J 2:

4) Your partner opens 2♣ to which you respond 2◇. Partner now rebids 2♡. What is your rebid?

a) ♠ 9 5: ♡ Q 10 6: ◇ K 9 5 4 3: ♣ Q 9 6:
b) ♠ Q 4: ♡ Q 10 5 4: ◇ K 10 3: ♣ 10 9 4 3:
c) ♠ K 10 9 5 3: ♡ K 4: ◇ 10 9 2: ♣ J 8 4:
d) ♠ Q 5 3: ♡ 10 5 2: ◇ 9 8 4 3: ♣ J 10 6:
e) ♠ —: ♡ Q 9 6: ◇ A 9 8 4 2: ♣ 10 9 6 4 3:

ANSWERS TO REVISION QUIZ ON CHAPTER 12

1) a) 2♣ With five quick tricks and enormous playing strength this is the only opening possible.

   b) 2♣ Again, you have five quick tricks and do not want to find yourself left in anything less than a game contract.

   c) 1♠ Only 4½ quick tricks and not quite an opening Two bid, so start with 1♠.

   d) 1◇ Only 4 quick tricks and clearly not a Two Bid.

   e) 2♣ There's no doubt about this one—a perfect 2♣ bid.

   f) 1♣ The hand has five quick tricks but precious little playing strength so you don't want to force a game contract if partner is very weak. Open with a simple one bid in the suit below the singleton.

2) a) 2♠ You certainly want to play in a game contract, and your good suit is spades.

   b) 2♡ The same story, except that your suit is hearts.

   c) 3◇ Show your long suit before the shorter hearts and await developments.

   d) 3♡ This is a case for the jump rebid, asking partner to cue-bid if he holds the missing ♣A. If he bids 3 N.T. just remove to 4♡.

   e) 2 NT Show your balanced 'shape' as well as the limited strength—even if the limit is a high one!

3) a) 2◇ You have none of the requirements for a positive response on the first round.

   b) 3◇ 2◇ would be 'negative' and you have the 'positive' requirement of an ace and a king, plus a biddable suit.

   c) 2♠ Another positive response but make it in your long suit.

   d) 2 NT With nine points and no biddable suit, you must make the positive response of 2 N.T.

   e) 2◇ The negative response first, and then show your spade suit on the next round.

   f) 2♠ You have the requirements, with 10 points, for a positive response, and it is more economical in bidding space to show your biddable 4-card spade suit than it would be to bid 2 N.T.

4) a) 3♡   With trump support as good as Q 10 6 it is better to give the direct raise than to show your rather miserable diamond suit.

   b) 4♡   The direct raise to game is indicated here as you have particularly good trump support, eight points, and no ace or void.

   c) 2♠   As you cannot give immediate trump support, the best you can do is show your five-card suit.

   d) 2 NT Partner's heart bid does nothing to raise your enthusiasm for this hand. A second negative, honouring your obligation to keep the bidding open to game, is the best you can do.

   e) 3♡   You have heart support, so raise opener's suit, which is sounder than introducing your diamonds—hardly likely to be of interest.

Chapter 13

Two No Trump or Stronger Opening Bids and Responses

WE come next to the big No Trump hands, that is, the ones beyond the scope of the 12-14 and 15-17 points already discussed in Chapters 4 and 5.

Hands suitable for a 2 N.T. opening bid contain 20-22 points, and if even stronger than this are opened with 2♣ followed by the appropriate No Trump rebid. The latter are included in this same group because the same fit-finding and other conventional sequences are used with either, though these differ from the sequences which follow a simple 1 N.T. opening bid.

As we have already learned, playing 'weak throughout' an evenly-balanced 12-14 points can be opened with a bid of 1 N.T. Playing 'variable', the count is increased to 15-17 points if vulnerable, and 'strong throughout' means 15-17 (or even, amongst some die-hards, 16-18 points) whatever the score. We've also considered even stronger hands, up to 19 points, which will probably be bid via a suit opening and the appropriate No Trump rebid (Chapter 8). Both 3 N.T. and 4 N.T. opening bids are used conventionally in the Acol System, 3 N.T. as a pre-emptive bid (Chapter 14) and 4 N.T. for a slam investigation (Chapter 18). But at this point we turn our attention to 2 N.T. opening bids and the associated responses.

TWO NO TRUMP OPENING BIDS

An opening bid of 2 N.T. may be made on an evenly-balanced hand of 20-22 honour points. There is no question of vulnerability involved, and the same distributional limits as in the case of 1 N.T. opening bids apply. There is no law against making the bid on a hand which contains a five-card suit and, indeed, this can often prove an excellent opening, ensuring that the hand will have the lead coming up to, rather than through it. Nor is there a law against having one suit as weak as Q-x, though obviously this is very risky, and one would normally try to find some other opening in the hope of discovering whether responder can cover the weakness. The following hands are typical of a 2 N.T. opening bid:

♠ A K 9
♡ K 8 6 5
♢ K 10 3
♣ A K 5
20 points

♠ K J 10
♡ A Q 8 2
♢ K 6
♣ A Q J 7
20½ points

♠ A Q 9
♡ K J 7 4
♢ K Q 5
♣ A Q 5
21 points

♠ A J 4 2
♡ A J 8
♢ A Q 4
♣ A Q 4
22 points

♠ K J 10
♡ A Q 6
♢ K 5
♣ A Q J 8 7

The fact that, if played in No Trumps, the lead will come up to this hand, and not through it, makes a 2 N.T. opening both correct and tactically acceptable, and even if you switch suits, making the clubs into spades or hearts, 2 N.T. is still the best opening. The hand may, of course, well end up played in a suit contract if responder prefers it, which he will have ample opportunity to show.

RESPONDING TO 2 N.T. OPENING BIDS

A 2 N.T. opening is a limit bid, even if a very powerful one, and in common with all other limit bids it is not forcing, though it does not need much intelligence to realise that, facing a known minimum of 20 points, not very much will be needed from responder to make the game contract a good bet. Any king, queen, or even knave, is likely to fill a gap, and responder should raise 2 N.T. to 3 N.T. on as little as 5 honour points, or even on 4 points if the hand contains good intermediates or a five-card suit.

There is no immediate weak take-out of a 2 N.T. opening bid, as there is over a 1 N.T. opening, so responder cannot bid three of a suit hoping to be left to play in it. The only complete sign-off is a pass.

We shall be discussing the various different responses in turn but, in the meantime, you will not by now be surprised to learn that responder's 3♣ is conventional—and so also is 3♢.

Taking first responses in the major suits, there is an important distinction between a three-level bid, that is, 2 NT—3♡ or 3♠ and a four-level bid, 2 NT—4♡ or 4♠. Remembering that opener is not at liberty to pass the three-level bid, responder shows a biddable suit in which he would prefer to play if opener has a good fit. Responder can, therefore, stand a raise to the four-level and will use his own judgement if opener rebids 3 N.T., showing that responder's suit is his own weakest. He may pass a 3 N.T. rebid or take out into four of his suit if he thinks the hand quite unsuitable for No Trump play.

A direct jump to four of a major is *a mild slam try* in a hand which must be played in the suit named.

Different players interpret these two sequences in exactly the opposite way, bidding to the four-level as a shut-out of any advance by opener, but if you think about it you will realise that, used as suggested above, responder may well find life easier. Wanting to make a mild slam try he can say so at once, whereas if he must first bid at the three-level and then find another suitable forward-going bid over opener's 3 N.T. rebid or raise to game in the suit, he may be in difficulties. Using the four-level bid as a mild slam try he knows that opener can pass or take him up on it, according to his hand.

Before we go on to the conventional responses, let's have some examples.

♠ Q 5 4
♡ 8 6 4
◇ J 9 8
♣ Q 8 6 4

This hand is quite as evenly-balanced as opener's hand can be and, therefore, suitable for play in No Trumps. Raise to 3 N.T. Cut out your ♣Q and the wisest course is to pass the opening bid, as opener would need to hold his absolute maximum to have any reasonable chance of making game.

♠ 5 4 3
♡ 6 4
◇ K J 9 8 4
♣ 9 7 6

Raise 2 N.T. to 3 N.T. *Don't* bid 3◇ which would be conventional (see p. 187) but remember that, facing a 2 N.T. opening, your five-card suit could well produce five-tricks—opener will have the ◇A or ◇Q, if not both.

♠ K 9 8 6 5
♡ 6
◇ Q 7 6 4
♣ 8 6 3

With the heart singleton you feel this hand *might* play better in spades than in No Trumps. Respond 3♠, but pass if opener rebids 3 N.T.

♠ Q J 9 8 7 5 4 2
♡ 9
◇ 8 6
♣ 9 7

Bid 3♠ over 2 N.T. and take out a 3 N.T. rebid into 4♠. In fact continue repeating spades until opener realises that the suit is your only asset and that you have no slam ambitions. (Note, by the way, that the length of the suit makes this hand too good to bid by way of a 'Flint' 3◇, as described on p. 187).

♠ K Q 10 9 8 6 4
♡ K 8 7
◇ —
♣ 8 6 5

Now you are good enough to suggest mild slam interest by bidding a direct 4♠. Partner may pass or take you up on it. He might now make, for example, an advance cue-bid (Chapter 4, p. 61) of 5♣, a pointless action unless he is in favour of trying for a *spade* slam, to which you would respond with 5◇, showing the first-round control.

♠ Q 7 5   This hand is too good to suggest *mild* slam
♡ A K 9 7 6 2   interest by bidding a direct 4♡. Facing a partner
◇ J 6   with a known minimum of 20 points, not more
♣ 8 3   than three of which can be in hearts, this res-
                   ponding hand must be worth a slam contract.
Bid 3♡ and, whether opener rebids 3 N.T. or 4♡, it's up to you
to make another try. Your best bet will be a conventional 4 N.T.,
conventional, not quantitative, because opener knows from your
3♡ bid that you prefer a suit to No Trumps.

NO TRUMP HANDS OPENED WITH 2♣

Well-balanced hands even stronger than these 2 N.T. openings are
bid via the cypher bid of 2♣. Responder will not, of course, know
whether opener intends a suit rebid, as in Chapter 12, or whether
his partner has a No Trump powerhouse, but he makes his normal
response, either negative or positive, and awaits developments.
23-24 points in a balanced hand should be opened with 2♣ and
rebid 2 N.T., and even greater strength, that is, 25 points or more,
can be rebid as 3 N.T. Although you count points, not quick tricks,
when you are considering the bidding of these very powerful No
Trump type hands, you will find it difficult to achieve one worth
the 2♣ opening that doesn't also contain five quick tricks.

The sequences already discussed, as well as the ones to come,
can all be used in exactly the same way over the 2♣ opening and
2 N.T. rebid as over the 2 N.T. opening itself, with only the minor
difference that in the case of the 2♣ opening the greater point-count
is announced and the values for the responses can consequently be
lowered. In fact what we are actually dealing with here is a weak
(20-22 points) 2 N.T. opening and a strong 23-24 points 2 N.T.
opening, and where responder may pass 2 N.T. on 3 honour points,
he should raise when the sequence has started with 2♣. The 2 N.T.
rebid is not forcing, as it is clear that even 23-24 points facing a
well-balanced Yarborough will not produce game! When the rebid
is 3 N.T., game has already been reached, and responder need take
no further action unless he thinks the combined hands better fitted
for a suit contract.

♠ 9 8 6   If the bidding has gone 2♣—2◇—2 NT, then pass.
♡ 9 8 6 5   Your one point is not likely to help even 23-24
◇ J 9 5   points to make a game. Exchange the ♠9 for the
♣ 7 4 3   ♠Q, and you should raise to 3 N.T.

♠ 8 7
♡ 8 5 3
◇ J 9 8 6
♣ K 9 6 5

In the same sequence, raise 2 N.T. to 3 N.T., as even these meagre points must make opener up to more than 26 and, above all, they may furnish entries with which he may be enabled to take one or more essential finesses in his own hand.

♠ 8
♡ K 10 9 8 7 5
◇ 4 3 2
♣ 8 7 5

After 2♣—2◇—2 NT bid 3♡ and convert opener's rebid of 3 N.T. to 4♡, a more probably successful spot than 3 N.T. Opener will recognise the long suit and values just below those needed for a positive response in the first place. Top it up by the addition of, say, the ◇A, and it becomes worth the slam try of 4♡ over 2 N.T.

THREE CLUBS IN RESPONSE TO TWO NO TRUMPS (CONVENTIONAL)

We come next to the important conventional 3♣ response, and remember that this carries exactly the same meaning when the sequence has started with 2♣—2◇ as it does over an opening 2 N.T. except that, once again, responder knows of opener's greater strength and must use his judgement accordingly.

You will almost always hear this convention called 'Stayman over 2 N.T.', but this is quite incorrect. The convention, in fact, owes its inception to the Baron System, with which it was used as long ago as the early 1940s.

Once again the purpose of the bid is to discover a possible 4-4 trump fit, and opener is required to respond by showing his four-card suits in ascending order, that is, the lower-ranking first. If his only four-card suit is clubs, he rebids 3 N.T. With two he bids the lower-ranking first unless one of the two is clubs. This is the hand quoted as an example in the first 'Baron' book:

♠ K J x
♡ Q J 10 x
◇ A K J
♣ A Q x

The bidding in the two rooms was:

N.	S.	and	N.	S.	
2 NT	3♣		2 NT	3♣	(The Baron
4♠	6♠		3♡	3♠	sequence)
			3 NT	5♡	
			6♡		

```
        N
  W          E
        S
```

♠ A Q x x x
♡ K x x x
◇ x x
♣ x x

Played by North, the heart slam cannot be defeated except by a 4-1 trump break plus a wrong guess as to which minor suit to finesse. Played by South it cannot be made as East had both the ♣K and ◇Q. The 6♠ contract was in any case an inferior one and, particularly played by South, had no possible chance of success.

As we've already said, this 3♣ bid can be used in exactly the same way when the sequence has started with 2♣—2◊—2 NT, in which case responder needs about 2 points less when considering a slam try.

With these very big hands, however, one is not normally so much concerned with going down as with finding the best possible resting place for either a game or slam, and this 'Baron' method particularly facilitates the difficult-to-reach minor suit contracts. Before coming to our usual examples, note that following 2 NT—3♣ or 2♣—2◊— 2 NT—3♣, opener's rebids show:

3 NT ... a four-card club suit and no other four-card suit.

3◊ ...... a four-card diamond suit and also possibly any other four-card suit.

3♡ ...... a four-card heart suit and possibly a four-card black suit, though *not* a four-card diamond suit.

3♠ ...... a four-card spade suit, no four-card red suit, but possibly a four-card club suit.

A few examples should show how well this method works.

	N.	S.
♠ A K 9 2	2 NT—	3♣
♡ A Q 6	3◊	—3♡
◊ A J 9 2	3♠	—4♠
♣ K 8		

```
        N
   W         E
        S
```

♠ Q J 6 3
♡ J 10 5 3
◊ 8
♣ 9 6 5 3

With just enough to raise to game, South would clearly prefer a suit contract if a fit can be found. In reply to 3♣ opener bids 3◊—the suit South least wants to hear, but he can next bid 3♡, safe in the knowledge that this will not block a possible final contract of 3 N.T. In the same spirit it costs North nothing to show his second suit also at the three-level, and with a sigh of relief South settles for 4♠.

Facing exactly the same North hand, give South this, and now the bidding goes like this. Opener, having discovered that one ace is missing, leaves the decision to South, who might be weaker for his bidding than he actually is. Note that 5 N.T. from North would force the slam contract, which might be wrong. But South is good for his bidding and, though just below strength for an immediate

South	N.	S.
♠ Q 6 5	2 NT—	3♣
♡ K J 8 5	3◊	—4◊
◊ K Q 8 4	4 NT—	5♣
♣ 9 3	5◊	—6◊

raise of 2 N.T. to 6 N.T., has no inhibitions when it comes to playing in the known diamond fit.

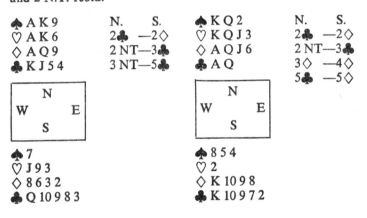

♠ A Q 6
♡ A J 8
◇ K Q J
♣ K J 4 3

N.	S.
2 NT	—3♣
3 NT	—4♣
4 NT	—5♡
5 NT	—6◇
7♣	

Since North's 3 N.T. rebid shows that his only four-card suit is clubs, South confirms trump support in a hand which he does not fancy for No Trumps, whilst he also suggests that the combined hands are worth more than a mere game contract. This time North can follow 4 N.T. with 5 N.T., as a 6♣ king-denial can be left to play. Once South is known to hold a club suit, two aces and a king, the Grand Slam in clubs must be a good proposition.

♠ K 5 2
♡ 6
◇ A 8 7 3
♣ A Q 7 6 5

The same type of sequence can take place after the 2♣ opening and 2 N.T. rebid.

♠ A K 9
♡ A K 6
◇ A Q 9
♣ K J 5 4

N.	S.
2♣	—2◇
2 NT	—3♣
3 NT	—5♣

♠ 7
♡ J 9 3
◇ 8 6 3 2
♣ Q 10 9 8 3

♠ K Q 2
♡ K Q J 3
◇ A Q J 6
♣ A Q

N.	S.
2♣	—2◇
2 NT	—3♣
3◇	—4◇
5♣	—5◇

♠ 8 5 4
♡ 2
◇ K 10 9 8
♣ K 10 9 7 2

The second of the two examples is from a team of four match. One North-South pair played in 3 N.T. which proved disastrous, the opposition making three spades, the ♡A and a club when this suit failed to break. The pair who played in 5◇ were in no difficulty, losing simply to the two major suit aces. Note, by the way, that over South's 4◇ North wisely chose a cue-bid of 5♣, allowing South to cue-bid if he thought the slam contract a good proposition. When South settled for 5◇ North took the hint and passed.

THE 'FLINT' 3◇ CONVENTION

Invented by the British international player Jeremy Flint, this convention is the nearest approach you have to a weak take-out of an opening 2 N.T., or the 2 N.T. rebid in the sequence 2♣—2◇—

2 N.T., as it is a device to allow the combined hands to be played in a part-score.

As a natural bid over 2 N.T., 3♦ is so rarely needed that it is used conventionally as a 'transfer' bid, that is, a bid which asks partner to convert to some specific suit, in this case hearts. So if responder's only asset is a long weak heart suit, the bidding can go 2 NT.—3♦—3♡—No Bid, and *opener* will play the hand in 3♡. If responder's long weak suit is spades, he in turn can convert 3♡ to 3♠, which opener is requested to pass. Alternatively, if his suit is one of the minors and he doesn't think it wise to go to the five-level, he bids it at the four-level over opener's 3♡ and, once more, opener should pass.

When responder has an unbalanced hand with one long weak suit, the border-line between passing the 2 N.T. and using 'Flint' to reach a part-score suit contract is very fine. Some players would elect to play in 3♡, for example, on a blank hand except for a five-card heart suit, and as with so much bidding, you'll never be certain of the best course until you see the two hands together. Similarly, the border-line is fine between hands which will and will not run to more than the part-score. But there will be times when you are in no doubt. Here, for example, facing 22 points,

♠ 8
♡ 10 8 7 6 4 3 2
♦ 7 5
♣ 9 8 6

opener's possible maximum for his 2 N.T. opening, the part-score is your highest ambition. Respond 3♦ and pass opener's conversion to 3♡. Exchange your two major suits and you would take out 3♡ into 3♠, expecting opener to pass.

You will notice that in each case responder's rebid, either a pass or take-out into a suit at the lowest available level, shows weakness. There is one other sequence, designed to show that responder has a genuine diamond suit *and* mild slam ambitions, and that is a responder's rebid of 3 N.T.

♠ K 7
♡ A J 9
♦ Q J 10 7 6
♣ 9 8 7

2 NT—3♦
3♡ —3 NT

Here, for example, responder is not quite good enough for a direct response of 4 N.T. (inviting opener to bid 6 N.T. on a 22-point maximum). True the combined holding might be 33 points, but the slam is more likely to be successful if played in diamonds and if, of course, opener has a good fit for this suit. All this information is conveyed by the sequence shown, and opener can pass the 3 N.T. rebid or himself take further steps. Note that if responder had no ambitions towards the diamond slam he could have raised to 3 N.T. in the first place.

From the other side of the table there may be times when, with a maximum for his opening bid and a strong fit for responder's suit, opener is unwilling to allow the bidding to die after a mere transfer bid and response. He will, of course, have to face responder's wrath if the part-score contract would have been a 'top' while the game goes down, but once having decided on this course here's how he goes about it.

♠ K 6
♡ A K 7 5
♢ A J 7
♣ A K 5 3

If responder bids 3♢ facing this maximum 2 N.T. instead of converting to the requested 3♡ opener rebids 3♠. This shows his maximum count and a big *heart* suit. If responder's suit is hearts he takes out into 4♡. If it is spades he passes instead of himself making the transfer from 3♡ to 3♠.

♠ A K 7 5
♡ A J 7
♢ K 6
♣ A K 5 3

This is the same maximum hand with the suits exchanged. Now opener transfers as requested to 3♡ if responder bids 3♢, but when responder converts this to 3♠, he raises to 4♠. If responder has a six-card suit headed only by the ♠10, this has every chance of bringing in six tricks, in addition to which it only needs a well-placed ♢A to make the game.

♠ A K 7 5
♡ A K 5 3
♢ K 6
♣ A J 7

This time the same points and distribution with a big fit for *either* major. Opener refuses to convert to 3♡ or 3♠ but instead bids 3 N.T., leaving responder to select the suit at the four-level.

The refusal on opener's part to make the requested response does not, of course, cut out the possible four-level minor suit contract.

'GERBER' OVER 2 N.T.

This convention can be used by responder in exactly the same way as when the opening bid has been 1 N.T. It is set out in detail at the end of Chapter 5 so there is no need to repeat it here. The only difference, of course, will be that responder is basing his own bidding on his partner's known 20-22 points, not the lesser number held for a 1 N.T. bid. It is, perhaps, also worth pointing out that responder's 4♣ bid would be 'Gerber' in this sequence, where opener has shown the make-up of his 2♣ by the 2 N.T. rebid. A responder's *natural* rebid of 4♣ here could not conceivably be necessary.

2♣ —2♡
2 NT—4♣

REVISION QUIZ ON CHAPTER 13

1) What do you respond to partner's opening 2 N.T. on the following hands?

   a) ♠ K 8 4: ♡ Q 9 6 3: ◇ 10 4 2: ♣ 9 7 6:

   b) ♠ Q 10 8 4:1 ♡ K 7: ◇ Q 4 2: ♣ K 10 9 4:

   c) ♠ Q 10 9 7 4 3: ♡ Q 4: ◇ J 9 3: ♣ J 4:

   d) ♠ 8 7 6: ♡ 9 8 7 5 4 3: ◇ 6: ♣ 7 5 4:

2) Your partner has opened 2♣, not 2 N.T. on the hands above. What do you respond?

3) Your partner has opened 2♣ to which you correctly respond 2◇. He now rebids 2 N.T. What do you bid next?

   a) ♠ J 7 3: ♡ 10 7 2: ◇ 9 8 7 4: ♣ J 3 2:

   b) ♠ J 7 3: ♡ Q 10 7 2: ◇ 9 8 7: ♣ Q 3 2:

   c) ♠ Q 10 9 6 5 2: ♡ J 4: ◇ J 9 3: ♣ J 3:

   d) ♠ J 10 6 3 2: ♡ Q J 6 5: ◇ 8 4 3: ♣ 6:

   e) ♠ K 10 9 2: ♡ 9 8 7: ◇ K 3 2: ♣ Q 3 2:

   f) ♠ J 9 7 2: ♡ 8 5 3: ◇ 10 7 4 2: ♣ 8 3:

   g) ♠ 8 7 6 5 4 3: ♡ 7: ◇ 9 4 3: ♣ 6 3 2:

4) What opening bid would you make on the following hands?

   a) ♠ A Q 7: ♡ Q J 10: ◇ A K J 3: ♣ K J 3:

   b) ♠ K J 9: ♡ Q 9 6: ◇ A K 9 4: ♣ A Q 9:

   c) ♠ A K J: ♡ K Q 9: ◇ A 10 9: ♣ K Q 10 9:

   d) ♠ A K J: ♡ K Q 9 6: ◇ A Q 4: ♣ A K 10:

   e) ♠ K 10 9 6: ♡ K Q 8: ◇ A Q 4: ♣ A Q J:

   f) ♠ K 10: ♡ A Q: ◇ A K Q J 9 8 3: ♣ K 8:

ANSWERS TO REVISION QUIZ ON CHAPTER 13

1) a) 3 NT With five points opposite a minimum of 20 points you want to be in game, and your hand is evenly balanced.

   b) 3♣ You would prefer a 4♠ contract, but will settle for 3 N.T. if partner cannot show spades.

   c) 3♠ A simple matter of showing your long suit, and whatever opener rebids, you will merely repeat spades—unless, of course, he raises your spades, in which case you will pass.

   d) 3◇ This requests opener to convert to 3♡ which you will pass.

2) a) 2◇ A normal negative response. Your next bid of course, will be conditioned by opener's rebid.

   b) 2 NT A positive response showing at least 9 points and no biddable suit.

   c) 2◇ A negative response to start with, after which you will show your spade suit.

   d) 2◇ If opener rebids 2 N.T. you will rebid a 'Flint' 3◇.

3) a) 3 NT Horrible as it may seem, two knaves, a ten and that 9-8-7 sequence just make this worth a raise.

   b) 3 NT The same raise, though this time without a qualm.

   c) 3♠ Having 'denied' with 2◇, you will show your spades on the next round.

   d) 3♣ Obviously you hope for a major suit contract here.

   e) 3 NT You are too evenly balanced to want to bother with anything but the obvious contract.

   f) Pass The 2 N.T. rebid is not forcing, and even though opener will have 23-24 points, you have not enough to warrant disturbing the 2 N.T. contract in any way.

   g) 3◇ This requests opener to convert to 3♡ which you in turn will convert to 3♠, expecting opener to *pass*.

4) a) 2 NT A typical hand for this powerful opening bid.

   b) 1◇ Just under strength for a 2 N.T. opening bid, but if partner can respond at all—particularly if he chooses 1♡—you will rebid a direct 3 N.T. If he can't make a 'free' response you are probably better out of any higher contract.

c) 2♣   The quality of the intermediates makes this hand worth the 2♣ opening, so you bid 2♣ intending to rebid 2 N.T. You will see that even a couple of knaves in dummy would be invaluable.

d) 2♣   An even stronger hand on which you intend to rebid 3 N.T. even if responder bids 2◇.

e) 2 NT Another typical hand for this bid.

f) 2 NT Some people may not agree with this, but the hand is slightly under strength for a 2♣ opening and if you bid the obvious alternative of 2◇ you risk getting a negative response of 2 N.T. from your partner. If he becomes declarer in a No Trump contract it may be highly dangerous, as your ♡ A-Q and two King-doubletons will be led through. If you open 2 N.T., partner will raise even with a very weak hand, and any lead except a diamond is likely to be helpful to you.

Chapter 14

Pre-Emptive Bidding

No system would be complete without some form of nuisance-bid, designed to make life difficult for the opponents, and the vast majority of Acol players use the highly obstructive opening three-bids on weak hands which appear to contain little or no defence to an opponent's contract. Some players favour weak opening two bids in the majors, but this is not a variation to be undertaken lightly without a very clear partnership understanding, both of the fundamental changes involved in the Acol System itself and of a system of responses to the weak two bids. For a fuller discussion on these points the reader is referred to *Conventions Made Clear* by the same authors but, meanwhile, we need consider opening weak twos only in the light of how to counter them if bid against you. Suffice it to say that they are probably best coped with by your chosen convention for countering weak three openings, which are an infinitely superior weapon—not to mention the fact that the Strong Two opening bids play a big part in the success of most Acol players.

PRE-EMPTIVE OPENING THREE BIDS

A pre-emptive bid at whatever level has one object only, and that is to obstruct the opposition to the limit. An opening at the three-level deprives the opposition of two rounds of bidding space and may well make it virtually impossible for them to discover their best game contract, let alone slam.

Suitable hands for pre-emptive opening bids have the following features:

(a) Clearly practically worthless in defence.

(b) Unlikely to be of value to partner as a supporting hand.

(c) Worth six or seven playing tricks at the suit named if vulnerable, and six if not vulnerable, especially against vulnerable opponents.

This opening bid is, in effect, an immediate sacrifice bid, since if opener finds himself facing a worthless dummy he expects to be defeated by two or three tricks.

The best position for making a pre-emptive opening bid is third-in-hand after two passes. Two passes and third hand suitable only for a weak three frequently add up to a strong fourth hand, the bidding of which may be quite ruined by having to start operations at the three level. (There is no such thing, of course, as a pre-emptive opening three bid fourth-in-hand, as there can be little or no object in trying to shut out opponents who have both passed!)

A hand containing two or more honour tricks is *too strong* to open with a three bid, and it should not contain a four-card major in addition to the long suit opened. The former is not devoid of defensive values, and the latter may furnish excellent support for a partner able to bid the suit—which he probably won't do after the pre-emptive opening, or it may seriously damage an opponent trying to play in that suit. Here are a few typical examples of hands suitable for an opening three bid:

♠ 9 6	♠ A Q 7 6 5 3 2	♠ 9
♡ 9 3	♡ 8	♡ K J 10 9 6 5 3
◇ K Q 10 8 6 5 4	◇ 9 7 2	◇ 8 7
♣ Q 5	♣ 8 6	♣ Q 8 5

♠ 7   Compare the next two examples. This hand is
♡ K Q J 8 6 5 3 too strong to open 3♡, though it is not strong
◇ A 7   enough to open 2♡. The correct bid is 1♡
♣ Q 8 5   followed by a 3♡ rebid.

♠ Q 10 5 4   Here again the hand is unsuitable for an open-
♡ A Q J 6 4 3 2 ing three bid, but for the different reason—it
◇ 3   contains good four-card support for the second
♣ 7   major, spades. Open 1♡ and, if responder
should bid spades, you have an excellent chance for game on 'shape'. If, on the other hand, partner bids a minor and your opponents buy the contract in spades you have an excellent chance of defeating them.

THREE NO TRUMP OPENING BID

There are two versions of the 3 N.T. opening bid in current use, one of which is commonly known as the gambling 3 N.T. This is based on a long and solid minor suit with not better than one king outside. The bid is coupled with a series of responses based on possible developments.

It would be highly unwise to attempt to use this convention except in a practised and accustomed partnership, and even then it can end in disaster.

♠ 7 6
♡ 7
◇ A K Q J 7 3
♣ 7 6 5 4

To open 3 N.T. on a hand like this, for example, could score well against weak opponents, but for our money we'd rather open 3◇, in which suit we'd be likely to make at least six tricks!

Whichever version you use, it must be recognised that the bid is chancy and intended as pre-emptive, for which reason though, as we've said, it may score well, it may equally do you out of a better contract. Used in the version we recommend it has one other object, and that is to *discourage* partner from bidding either of the majors. The bid is most likely to prove valuable third-in-hand after two passes, at which point partner is known to hold even less than an Acol Light Opener. It should be based on a minimum of a six-card minor suit headed by 'tops', with protection in at least two other suits. Clearly to open 3 N.T. is more likely to make life difficult for your left-hand opponent, who may be strong in the majors, than a mere pre-emptive three-bid in the minors would do. Here are two possible examples:

♠ J 7   ♠ K 5
♡ K 8   ♡ A 3
◇ K 7   ◇ A K Q 10 9 2
♣ A K Q 10 8 4 2   ♣ Q J 8

The second of the two may even score you nine tricks as, with the lead coming up to it, you may be able to get your opponents into trouble on discards on the long diamonds whilst having eight tricks 'on top' with a spade lead. From a defensive point of view, remember that the bid is known to be based on a long minor, and it is common practice for the defender on lead to cash an ace—particularly a major suit ace, in the hope of getting a signal from his partner that this is, indeed, the suit missing. To make this point, here are the East-West hands which were actually dealt after South had opened 3 N.T. of the 'gambling' version, with little or nothing outside his minor suit.

♠ A 8 4 3   ♠ 10 7 5 2
♡ A Q 6   N   ♡ K J 10 9 4
◇ 5   W   E   ◇ 7 6
♣ K J 8 7 2   S   ♣ 9 3

West, on lead, did *not* try the fourth best of his longest suit, clubs. Instead he cashed the ♠A which got the discouraging ♠2 from East. West followed with the ♡A, now certain that this must be the suit missing and East played his $\heartsuit$J. As dummy had shown up with three small hearts, East made doubly sure by overtaking West's next lead of the $\heartsuit$Q though, in fact, he need not have done this as West had three and South a singleton. But the net result was six tricks to the defence who could not have scored a game for themselves.

RESPONDING TO OPENING THREE BIDS

If you have passed initially when your partner opens at the three-level there is unlikely to be anything for you to do about it, except possibly to aid and abet him if the opposition looks like finding a good contract against which you think there will be a profitable 'sacrifice'. For example, after two passes your partner opens 3$\diamondsuit$,

♠ 8 4 3 2
♡ 5 3
♢ K J 9 5 4 3
♣ 10

over which your right-hand opponent makes his chosen conventional take-out request. It should be clear to you that you and your partner have virtually nothing between you except diamonds, diamonds, diamonds. Bid 5$\diamondsuit$ or even, at favourable vulnerability, 6$\diamondsuit$. Your judgement must tell you that the less you have, the more they have. When this hand was actually dealt responder bid 6$\diamondsuit$ and the next player was on a guess. He bid 6♠ which was one down when there was no defence whatsoever to 7$\heartsuit$—a very useful gain for the diamond holders!

Sometimes your partner will elect to open with a three-bid before you have had a chance to bid or pass. Inconsiderate though you may feel this to be if you have a strong hand, there are some sound rules to guide you out of your trouble when it is you, rather than your opponents, who are pre-empted!

In the first place, remember that opener will have told you the whole story in one bid, so if you feel that, in spite of this, you still may have a game on, you will have to provide him with the honour tricks he will need. With a minimum of three honour tricks plus something helpful in the distribution line you may raise him to game in his suit—*he* will not bid again himself unless you make a forcing bid or unless he thinks an even higher sacrifice contract is desirable.

♠ A 10 9
♡ J 5
♢ A Q 8 7
♣ K J 10 6

Here you should raise partner's opening 3$\heartsuit$ to 4$\heartsuit$. Your heart support is not all that great, but it will be facing almost certainly a seven card suit, and your outside strength, if it turns out to be well-placed, may help him to make game. If he opens three of any other suit, again, the game raise should be worth while.

A cardinal rule is never to 'rescue' partner's pre-emptive opening bid. He has already announced his desire to play in one specific suit and you should not disturb this unless you are sure that you have something superior to suggest, such as a suit of your own which you are certain will be better to play in than his. For example, if your partner opens 3♣, 3♢, or even 3♠, don't be tempted to take out into hearts on this hand. Your spade support is,

♠ 8
♡ K J 10 7 6 5
♢ A Q 8
♣ Q 7 6

alas, abysmal, but you have no assurance at all that part of his 3♠ bid was not based on a void or singleton in hearts. You have excellent support, however, if he elects to bid one of the minors, and with your help he might even make his contract. If your opponents get together in spades you will have to judge, on the bidding, whether to sacrifice in opener's minor or hope to defeat their contract.

In the past, any response to an opening three bid made below game level has been a mild slam try in the suit opened. That is to say, if your partner opened 3♡ and you responded 3♠, this was a mild slam try in *hearts*. In practice, however, it has been found that this interpretation was frequently misunderstood and abused. We offer you, therefore, the following modifications, which fit in well with the system as a whole, though note that they differ from the instructions in our previous books.

Just as a change-of-suit response at the one-level by a player who has not previously passed, so a new suit response below game-level (i.e., at the three-level in a major or the four-level in a minor, 3♡—3♠ or 3♡—4♣) is a one-round force. Subsequent bidding will show whether responder is 'slamming' but in principle a minor suit response should be regarded as a slam try, and a major suit response as a game force. Thus 3♡—3♠ is game-forcing, and opener should raise to 4♠ on even as mild a fit as a doubleton spade. 3♠—4♡ may be passed by opener as game has been reached and, if responder had intended slam investigations he could have bid 4♣ or 4♢.

A direct jump to game in a new suit by responder is hardly capable of being misunderstood (3♡—4♠ or 3♠—5♢), and needs no explanation other than to point out that responder should feel confident that his hand is likely to be worth the game contract in spite of the weak single-suited hand known to be held by opener.

♠ A K J 8
♡ K J 7
♢ 9
♣ A Q J 7 5

Bid 4♣ over partner's opening 3♡, making a slam try in *hearts*. It would be dangerous to bid 3♠ because, as explained above, opener would be likely to raise to 4♠ on no better than a doubleton. Knowing that his suit is agreed as trumps, opener can show any feature his hand may contain. For instance, he might have opened 3♡ on a seven-card suit headed by the queen and the ♢A, in which case he can cue bid 4♢ over 4♣.

A take-out of the opening three bid into 3 N.T. should not put opener into a panic. Responder knows the type of hand his partner is likely to hold and will himself *either* have a fit with the suit opened, which will assure him of being able to get into what will be his dummy to enjoy opener's suit length without the help of outside entries, *or* he will have a long and solid suit of his own which he will be able to run with more hope of making nine tricks than the greater number required for a game in his suit.

♠KQJ5
♡93
♢KJ8
♣AQ43

If partner opens 3♢ take out into 3 N.T. With any luck you may be able to run nine tricks before the opposition discovers your weakness in hearts. If the hand which will be on lead doubles, you can escape into 4♢, but just for that reason he is unlikely to double if holding the hearts! The hand on your right, if it could take no action over the original opening 3♢, and not being on lead, is unlikely to be able to double.

♠KJ10
♡AQ
♢7
♣AKQJ10 7 6

If partner opens 3♢ take out into 3 N.T. A lead in either major is likely to be helpful, in which case you will have nine tricks 'on top'. Even if opener has not got the ♢A, a suit which can be opened at the three-level is morally certain to provide a good stop!

PRE-EMPTIVE OPENING FOUR BIDS

Opening four bids in any suit can be used effectively on exactly the same type of hand but with a little added length in the suit In the minors nothing is guaranteed except suit length and a desir to make life difficult for any opponent wanting to bid a major sui game or slam. In the majors, though also highly pre-emptive, th bid shows a game-going hand with *not more than two honour tricks* and partner is not expected to disturb or make any sort of a slan try on less than two aces. Here are two examples, the first of a mino

♠87
♡6
♢KJ9865432
♣10

suit opening four bid. It would be equally goo as a 4♣ opening if that were the suit, thoug exchange it for one of the majors and it shoul be opened at the three-level.

♠8
♡KQJ107652
♢9
♣A98

Here is a typical 4♡ opening bid if facin a partner who has already passed. If he ha not yet had a chance to bid there is a dange of shutting him out of the auction by such a opening when there may be a slam availabl and in this context the hand should be opened with 2♡, for which it qualifies.

PRE-EMPTIVE OPENING FIVE BIDS

There is a clear distinction between opening five bids in the minors and in the majors, the latter being conventional. For details turn to p. 257 Chapter 18. Made in the minor suits, however, opening bids of 5♣ or 5◇ are just that much more pre-emptive than bids at either the three or four level. They require somewhat better quality hands with eight or nine playing tricks and a glaring weakness in the majors.

♠ 6
♡ 8
◇ A K J 9 7 6 4 3
♣ K 6 2

Here the two major suit singletons pin-point the danger, and probably the best—and only— way of obstructing your opponents is to open 5◇. Note that the hand is just below strength for a 2◇ opening, which you would use if holding the ◇Q in place of the ◇J facing a partner who had not already passed.

COUNTERING PRE-EMPTIVE OPENING THREE BIDS

In the foregoing pages we have seen the damage an opening pre-emptive bid may do to the opposition's bidding sequence, but all too often you will find yourself in the opposition seats, trying to counter a pre-emptive opening made by your opponent. It is vital to have a clear partnership agreement as to a method of countering such opening bids and there is a wide variety of conventional bids which can be used as a request to partner to take action. One inescapable fact remains—opening three bids were designed for their nuisance-value, and a nuisance they will remain. No counter-measure is perfect and whichever you decide to use you will inevitably meet hands on which one of the others would have proved more satisfactory.

You may take your choice from the six methods set out in *Current Conventions Made Clear* by the same authors, but we give you here details of the well-tried favourite '3 N.T. for a Take-out'.

Three No Trumps for a Take-Out: This was the original Acol convention and it remains popular amongst a very wide field of players. It is still our own choice, having the merit of simplicity in addition to the fact that it eliminates only one bid from the range of natural overcalls, and that is the bid of 3 N.T. itself. It does not even eliminate the possibility of 3 N.T. as the final contract, as responder to it, knowing that his partner is strong in the other three suits, can pass the take-out request if he himself holds a good stop in the suit opened.

Using the conventional 3 N.T. as a take-out request you can, of course, bid any suit over the suit opened at any appropriate level. That is to say, you can bid 3♡ or 3♠ over an opening 3◇, which would indicate to your partner that you were not strong enough to bid direct to game in your suit. You can also make a business double of the suit opened, which obviously shows a good holding in the suit opened plus other goodies and your partner, knowing this, can pass the double for penalties, take out into a suit if his judgement tells him that defence is not likely to be successful, or possibly even convert the double to 3 N.T. if this appears a more profitable chance at the vulnerability existing.

The incidence of hands on which you would genuinely like to bid 3 N.T. to play in that contract is low, and in the majority of even these rare cases you will probably have an alternative natural suit bid or double available. We freely concede that this method of countering opening three bids is not infallible, but nor is any other. Whatever convention you use, whether or not to take any action over the opposing bid will frequently remain a matter of very close judgement. Particularly when your left-hand opponent has not yet passed, bold refusal to be shut out of the auction can cost you a pretty penny, as equally can a decision to remain 'fixed'.

Don't forget that the immediate overcall in the suit opened can be used in conjunction with 3 N.T. for a take-out, on rock-crusher hands where you hardly care what your partner's long suit may be provided he has one! The bid is more generally used, however, to show a two-suiter, probably 6-5 or even more. A player responding to this immediate overcall, therefore, should not leap wildly on just because of strength in one particular suit, remembering that his partner may well be two-suited in the other two.

S.	W.	N.	E.
3◇	4◇	—	4♡
—	4♠		
	or		
3♣	4♣	—	4◇
—	4♡		

In the first sequence, when West takes out his partner's 4♡ reply into 4♠, East can read West for a black two-suiter and might give preference to 5♣ if not strong enough to suggest a slam in either. In the second sequence West can be read as holding a major two-suiter, and East could pass, raise, or convert to 4♠.

♠ K 9 7
♡ A K Q 9 5 4
◇ 7 6
♣ J 9

Let us end this section with our usual selection of examples. On this hand, using 3 N.T. for a take-out you can bid a simple 3♡ over either 3♣ or 3◇.

♠ K Q 5 2
♡ A 7 3
◇ K J 9 2
♣ A Q

Here you can double an opening 3◇ or 3♠ for business. Using 3 N.T. for a take-out you would certainly refuse to remain 'fixed' and would bid 3 N.T. over any suit you felt unable to double.

♠ A K 10 9 6
♡ A Q J 10 8
◇ K 10
♣ 7

Not being quite strong enough for an immediate cue-bid of opponent's suit which might land you in a slam, bid 3 N.T. for a take-out over either 3♣ or 3◇. If partner responds in the other minor (most likely) take out into 4♡ which, by inference, asks for preference between the majors.

♠ A K Q 9 8 6
♡ A Q 10 9 7 3
◇ 10
♣ —

Bid 4♣ over 3♣ or 4◇ over 3◇. If partner responds in the other minor take out into hearts asking for preference between hearts and spades. Note the greater strength held in comparison with the previous example, leaving partner in a good position to judge whether to be content with game or press on to a slam.

♠ A K 8 6
♡ A K Q 7
◇ K Q J 5
♣ 10

Here's the rock-crusher type where you do not really mind what your partner's suit is as long as you find out, and can play in at least a game. Bid 4♣ over 3♣.

COUNTERING PRE-EMPTIVE OPENING FOUR BIDS

The higher the level of the pre-emptive opening, the harder it is to be sure of reaching your own right contract. Over opening bids at the four-level, probably the best method is to bid 4 N.T. for a take-out when the bid has been in a major suit and an optional double over a four-level minor.

When the opening bid has been 4♠, clearly partner will be able to bid his own best suit in reply to 4 N.T. without hindrance, as 4 N.T. is a bid which uses no bidding space in this situation. Over an opening 4♡ there is an inference that 4 N.T. is based on the minors, as the opportunity to bid 4♠ was not taken. In either case the double is left free for 'business'.

The use of 4 N.T. over the minors takes too much bidding space, as it eliminates any chance of playing at the four-level in hearts or spades. For this reason we suggest an optional double, which may be used on a hand with fair defensive values though prepared to play in a major suit game. In this case 4 N.T. becomes natural and may be left to play.

1) At game to your opponents and after two passes, what opening bid would you make?

   a) ♠ K J 9 7 6 4 2: ♡ 9 6: ◇ 10 4: ♣ J 3:
   b) ♠ J 9 6 3: ♡ K Q 10 9 5 4 3: ◇ 3: ♣ 5:
   c) ♠ J 4: ♡ 9 6: ◇ A J 9 6 4 3 2: ♣ 6 4:
   d) ♠ 9 8: ♡ K J 10 9 7 4 2: ◇ 5 4: ♣ 10 6:
   e) ♠ 4 2: ♡ 9 6: ◇ 8: ♣ A J 9 8 6 5 3 2:
   f) ♠ Q 6: ♡ J 10: ◇ K 3: ♣ A K Q 8 7 6 3:

2) At game to your opponents your partner deals and opens 3♣. What action would you take?

   a) ♠ A Q 10 9 6: ♡ A Q 3 2: ◇ 9: ♣ K 10 4:
   b) ♠ 8: ♡ A K J 10 8 4 3: ◇ A 6 4: ♣ 9 4:
   c) ♠ K J 10: ♡ A Q 4: ◇ K 10 9 7: ♣ Q J 3:
   d) ♠ Q 6 3: ♡ A 10 4: ◇ K 9 6: ♣ J 10 6 3:
   e) ♠ 8 6: ♡ 9 5 3: ◇ 10 9 8: ♣ K 10 9 6 4:
   f) ♠ A 10 3: ♡ K 10 5: ◇ Q J 4 2: ♣ K 6 4:

3) Your right-hand opponent deals and opens 3♡ (Acol weak). Using 3 N.T. for a take-out, what would you bid?

   a) ♠ A K 10 4: ♡ K J 9 6: ◇ A 6 4: ♣ 8 3:
   b) ♠ A K Q 9 6 5 2: ♡ 5 4: ◇ A 4: ♣ Q 4:
   c) ♠ 6: ♡ 5 4: ◇ A K Q J 8 4: ♣ K J 4 3:
   d) ♠ A K Q 6: ♡ 4: ◇ A K 10 8: ♣ A K 6 3:
   e) ♠ A 10 6 4: ♡ K J 9: ◇ Q 9 4: ♣ K 3 2:
   f) ♠ A Q J 9 7 6: ♡ —: ◇ A K J 10 6 5: ♣ 6:

4) At Game All your right-hand opponent deals and opens 4◇ (Acol pre-emptive). What would you bid?

   a) ♠ A J 10 7 4: ♡ A J 7 3: ◇ A J 6: ♣ 6:
   b) ♠ A K J 10 6 5: ♡ A 10: ◇ 9 3: ♣ A Q 4:
   c) ♠ A J 7 2: ♡ K J 6: ◇ K 8 4: ♣ Q 9 6:

5) At Game All your right-hand opponent deals and opens 4♡ (Acol). What would you bid?

   a) ♠ A Q 7: ♡ —: ◇ A Q 10 7 2: ♣ A Q 10 9 3:
   b) ♠ A K J 10 6 3: ♡ A J: ◇ 8 5: ♣ A Q 3:
   c) ♠ A K J 9: ♡ 7: ◇ A Q J 5: ♣ K Q J 8:
   d) ♠ A 7 2: ♡ A J 8 4: ◇ K Q 7: ♣ K J 6:

ANSWERS TO REVISION QUIZ ON CHAPTER 14

1) a) 3♠   A perfect pre-emptive opening bid with no support for any other suit or any defensive values.

   b) No.   The four spades rule this out for a pre-emptive opening in hearts, as your support for spades, if partner bids them, is so good.

   c) 3◇   Here again, you have nothing but the diamonds and are uninterested in anything except getting your obstructive bid in as quickly as you can.

   d) 3♡   Another typical opening three bid.

   e) 3♣   A worthless defensive hand and your only hope is pre-emptive action.

   f) 3 NT No one would blame you for opening a simple 1♣ on this hand, but the extreme shortage in both majors, particularly after your partner's original pass, makes the pre-emptive opening of 3 N.T. a very good bet.

2) a) 3♠   A game force. You will be happy to play in 5♣, or in 4♠ if your partner has even a doubleton in support of this suit.

   b) 4♡   An immediate take-out into a game contract in your own suit is your best bet here.

   c) 3 NT With three suits well stopped and a fit in clubs, this contract should be well worth trying.

   d) No.   Just hope that with your support he may even make 3♣!

   e) 5♣   This is a clear case of the less you have, the more they have. As your right-hand opponent passed the opening 3♣, fourth hand is morally certain to hold a big hand.

   f) 3 NT Again here you have a very good chance of bringing in nine tricks at No Trumps. Note the club fit.

3) a) Double. This of course, is a business double which should be more profitable than trying to find a contract for yourself.

   b) 4♠   Bid to the limit of your strength. This should be a very reasonable contract.

   c) 4◇   It's just to prevent you from coming in with this sort of holding that the opening three-bids have been developed.

   d) 4♡   The immediate overcall, seeking the best fitting suit from your partner.

   e) No.   If you miss a good contract by passing, it's just your tough luck that you had Acol opponents!

f) 4♡   Another cue-bid of opponent's suit. If partner bids 5♣ bid 5♢ asking for his preference—if possible at the slam level—between diamonds and spades.

4) a) Double. Clearly you can't let 4♢ go uncontested, and your best bet is to use an optional double with the hope that your partner will pass.

b) 4♠   A natural bid of your own strong suit putting no onus on your partner. He is unlikely to bid unless he has visions of a possible slam.

c) Pass If you feel reluctant to pass, note that you have no 'shape', in addition to which your left-hand opponent has not yet passed and may hold the entire balance of strength facing a very highly distributional opening hand.

5) a) 4 NT For a take-out, though your partner will take the inference that, as you did not bid 4♠, your chief interest is in the minors. However, if he bids 5♠ you will be happy to let him play there.

b) 4♠   A natural bid of your own long and strong suit.

c) 4 NT Here you cannot bid 4♠ as you must seek partner's choice of suit. Notice that your partner must not strain to show a minor if he has a biddable spade suit. If he does bid 5♠ when you are truly two-suited in the minors you can always take out into clubs asking for preference.

d) Double. A business double which partner will not disturb unless he has visions of a slam. A non-vulnerable game for your side is not likely to be worth as much as the penalty from the double.

Chapter 15

The Double

THE Acol System lays no claim to the exclusive use of any of the various types of doubles, though no Acol player's armoury would be complete without a sound knowledge of how to use this valuable weapon, both in attack and in defence.

Doubles can be roughly divided into four groups, penalty or business doubles, take-out or informatory doubles, tactical doubles, and lead-directing doubles, though there are points at which the divisions may appear to overlap as, for instance, when a take-out double has notified partner of a certain amount of strength facing him which in turn enables him to make a subsequent penalty double.

PENALTY OR BUSINESS DOUBLES

A penalty double is, as the name implies, a double made with the express intention of collecting a penalty from the opposition as opposed to a 'positive' score by way of a declarer contract.

When it comes to making a business double of a high level contract, don't double just for the sake of doubling when your opponents have bid up freely and easily. This does not mean, of course, that you must not double if for some reason you are sure they have reached a contract they cannot make—it's not entirely unknown for even experts to bid a Grand Slam missing the ace of trumps! But beware of giving away, by your double, the disposition of your resources. If your partner has been consistently silent during the auction and your opponents have reached their contract with unembarrassed ease, then probably the entire balance of the outstanding strength is in your own hand, and to double may well give this valuable information away, even helping declarer to make his contract.

Another point to bear in mind is that if your opponents have been bidding, perhaps in the two majors, and end in 4♡ which you are certain you can defeat, it may well be wiser to let them play there rather than to double and tip them off to go into spades. Don't talk them out of a contract you can defeat into one you can't, when you have no reason to hope your partner can cope with the switch. Be careful too of doubling in the hope of a penalty when you've a highly distributional hand. The other hands may then well be unbalanced too, and a six or seven card suit headed by K-Q-J may not be worth even one winner in defence, particularly if it has been supported by partner during the auction. The most profitable holding for a business double is a damaging holding in the opponents' trump suit and some top card winners of your own.

It's a different matter, of course, if you know that the opposition have been competing in an effort to push you beyond your own depth, or have in any other way gone beyond what you judge to be their own safe level. If, for instance, you and your partner have bid to 4♡ and have been outbid by 4♠, then you must judge, if you can, what will pay you best. Can they make 4♠? Can *you* make 5♡? Which will pay you best at the vulnerability existing— a double of 4♠ or a bid of 5♡ which may in turn be doubled and go down? These are, and always will be, close and difficult decisions on many occasions. When doubtful as to your ability to make your own contract it is generally wiser to settle for the known plus-score of a penalty double. Sometimes this will turn out to be even more profitable than any positive score you could have made yourselves.

The same strictures, of course, apply to doubling a slam contract. If you are sure you can defeat it, then double by all means, but if doubtful sit back and let declarer do all the work of finding out who's got what without tipping him off. There is one exception here, and that is if you and your partner are using the conventional Lightner Slam Double, for which see p. 211.

Another profitable source of gain can be the double of an opposing low-level contract, but when it comes to this department it is important that you should be able to judge whether a double is intended for a take-out or for penalties. The general rule is that if partner has bid, or has missed a previous chance to double the same denomination on a previous round, the double is for business, and the doubler's partner should only disturb it if his hand is unduly weak for any bid he may have made, is highly unsuitable distributionally for defence, or if he thinks his side has a better contract available.

	N.	E.	S.	W.
1)	—	1♠	2♡	x
2)	1♠	—	2♡	—
	2♠	x		
3)	1♠	x	2♡	x

In the first sequence West's partner having bid, the double is intended for penalties. In the second, also a penalty double, East did not double 1♠ (which would have been for a take-out).

Here again, a penalty double by West whose partner has made a bid, even if it were only a show of strength by an informatory double.

There are situations more difficult to recognise but generally logic will solve them. For instance in this sequence East made a take-out double of the opening bid which West converted to a penalty double by passing, so East's subsequent double of 2♡ is intended as a penalty one.

	N.	E.	S.	W.
4)	1♣	x	—	—
	2♡	x		
5)	1♡	1♠	x	
6)	1♡	2♢	x	

A double of an intervening one-level contract can be precarious. At duplicate where a non-vulnerable game scores 400 points, East-West have to set the contract by three tricks to justify themselves for not bidding if they have a game available, for which reason it seldom turns out costly to slip in a one-level overcall. But a double of a two-level contract, as in No. 6, can reap rich rewards, particularly at favourable vulnerability when two down doubled and vulnerable scores 500, better than the points to be won from a non-vulnerable game. The requirements for a two-level double are in the region of 8-9 honour points plus a damaging holding in the enemy trump suit.

Another point of importance is that this penalty double should *not* be made with good support for partner's opening suit. The more you have in that, the less likely it is to yield defensive tricks, so the mere fact of doubling will warn partner of a misfit, and with this knowledge he can pass the double, take out into his own or another suit if he thinks this wiser, or go for a No Trump game, banking on your holding in the enemy's suit.

♠ 8
♡ K J 9 7 5
♢ A 8 7 6
♣ 10 5 3

On sequence No. 1 on p. 207 West has an attractive double of the 2♡ intervention whatever the vulnerability. The hand is not likely to produce a game unless a heart stop is the only thing needed by East—in which case you will be giving him vital information by the double. But at equal or favourable vulnerability, if he decides to let the double stand, the penalty should be worth more than any positive score.

There is, by the way, a convention which drops the 'business' aspect of West's double in this position. This is the negative or 'Sputnik' double, for details of which see *Conventions Made Clear* by the same authors.

Another double which is always intended primarily for penalties and not for a take-out is one made by a player who has himself opened the bidding in No Trumps. Here North has opened 1 N.T.

N.	E.	S.	W.
1 NT	2♡	—	2♠
x			

and in the second example his original over-call was 1 N.T., the latter always being a *strong* bid in Acol. In both cases North is making a business double, not asking for a take-out. Doubtless he will be equally happy to take care of 2♠ should West try to rescue himself into that suit, or East put him back to it.

and

N.	E.	S.	W.
			1♠
1 NT	—	—	2♡
x			

The most usual moment, however, for making a penalty double is when the auction has been competitive and you are in a position to judge that your opponents have gone beyond their depth.

N.	E.	S.	W.
1♣	1♡	2◇	—
3♣	—	3◇	x

♠ Q J 7 4
♡ 3
◇ A J 9 2
♣ K J 8 2

This West hand would be almost too good to be true. The North-South bidding screams of a misfit, West has a misfit for East's suit with the knowledge that his partner holds enough to make an intervening bid, and any attempt at escape West can double equally well.

If you adopt the attacking policy of doubling part-score contracts you will inevitably on occasions double your opponents into game. But this is not the end of the world, and in the long run you will gain more than you lose. There are, however, a couple of important 'dont's' to bear in mind. Don't double when you have only a slender chance of defeating the contract because, if it is made, you stand to lose more than you gain. Secondly don't make what is often cheerfully called a 'free' double—there is no such thing. What is usually meant by the phrase is a double which, if the contract is made, doesn't give your opponents a game they wouldn't have scored anyway. If they make the doubled contract they will gain more than you could have gained by defeating them one trick, and if they are able to re-double the loss to your side will be even more costly.

TAKING OUT A PENALTY DOUBLE

When your partner has made a penalty double, particularly one of a low-level contract, you will have to judge whether or not to take him at his word, which is that he doesn't care for your suit but *does* care for the enemy suit. If you judge that your hand has good defensive values, then let the double stand unless you are so sure of your own game that you think it best to go for this and not the penalty. But the lack of defensive values in an Acol Light Opener

♠ 8 2
♡ K Q J 8 7 5
◇ A 8 7 6
♣ 7

can make a hand totally unsuited to defence. Here, your opening 1♡ has been overcalled with 2♣ which your partner has doubled. It doesn't take much imagination to see that defensive values are almost nil, so take out into 2♡. Move one of the black cards and make the diamonds into a 5-card suit, and you should take the double out into 2◇, showing the weak red two-suiter since diamonds may fit your partner's hand better than hearts.

DOUBLING AN OPENING ONE NO TRUMP

The double of an opening No Trump bid is always intended primarily for penalties and *not* for a take-out. From this it follows that the doubling hand should be strong—at least the upper limit of the opposing opening bid—and it should ideally also contain a promising suit in which to initiate the attack. Lacking such features it is better to use one of the take-out conventions such as 'Sharples' or 'Astro', details of which you can find in *Current Conventions Made Clear* by the same authors.

Knowing that the double is intended for penalties does not debar the doubler's partner from taking action if he thinks this best. For example, on weakness though holding a five or six-card suit and no entry, take out into the suit. There's little or no chance of having your long suit led so its only value will be if used as trumps for your own side. In other words, make a weak take-out of the double, as you would do if your partner had opened 1 N.T.

Partner of the doubler should also take out by a jump bid if he has a long suit and unbalanced hand and sees prospects of a game or slam which may be more profitable than an attempt to defeat the doubled 1 N.T., particularly when it seems unlikely that your partner will attack in your suit.

If your right-hand opponent has redoubled, it doesn't leave many points for you and you are virtually bound to have a near Yarborough. Take out into your best suit on weakness—a pass would generally indicate that you had just enough to think it possible to defeat the redoubled contract, though you might pass as being possibly a lesser evil than taking out!

The time to pass the double happily is if you hold enough points, well distributed, to know that you and your partner between you have the balance of strength, basing this on the knowledge that the double has promised at least the upper limit of the strength held by opener.

LEAD-DIRECTING DOUBLES

Many players think only of lead-directing doubles in terms of high contracts, but this is quite wrong, and doubles particularly of low-level conventional bids can frequently be made to direct partner's lead. For example in this sequence South's 2♣ bid is a conventional request to North to show major suits, and a double by West would indicate a good club holding. If East is eventually on lead he can produce a club with impunity.

N.	E.	S.	W.
1 NT	—	2♣	x

When a player who will *not* be on lead initially doubles an opposing No Trump contract, this should be taken by his partner as lead-directing. The rules to be followed in selecting the lead are as follows:

1) If the doubler has himself bid a suit during the auction, the double confirms that this is the suit he wants led regardless of the fact that the opponents have bid No Trumps over it.

2) If the doubler's partner has bid a suit during the auction, the double confirms willingness for the suit to be led in spite of the No Trump contract having been bid.

3) If neither defender has bid during the auction, the double suggests the lead of the first suit bid by the dummy.

In each instance the doubler is anxious for the attack to come in the indicated suit, and probably he doesn't want to risk having his only side-entry knocked out by any other lead. A superb example of this came up recently. Here's the bidding and the West hand.

S.	W.	N.	E.
1♡	—	2 NT	—
3 NT	x		

West
♠ 7
♡ K Q J 10 7 4
◇ A 6 3
♣ 8 6 3

As you can see, it was vital to West to get a heart lead whilst his ◇A was intact. South had perfectly correctly opened on a 17-point hand with ♡ A 9 6 3, and without the original heart lead declarer would have been able to knock out the ◇A and run his nine tricks.

The Lightner Slam Double is also lead-directing, and it calls on partner to find an unusual lead.

Unless the slam contract is clearly a sacrifice one, in which case the Lightner inferences do not apply, a double by the defender who will *not* be making the opening lead suggests that the least-likely-looking lead is the one that may hit the jackpot. The lead of a trump or a suit bid by either partner would be quite normal, so must be ignored. So too should the lead of an *unbid* suit, which would also be normal in the circumstances. In the majority of cases a lead of dummy's first bid side-suit or, failing that a side-suit bid by declarer will probably be the required choice. It may well be that the double has been made on the strength of a void in that suit.

From this it follows that unless you are certain of defeating a slam bid against you in any case, you must *not* double if the one lead you want is a normal one of the suit bid by you or your partner. If your only hope lies in a normal lead, then don't double, as you will only be directing your partner's attention to an abnormal lead in another suit.

TACTICAL DOUBLES

Although lead-directing doubles are also tactical, there is another type which operates mainly when the bidding has reached a high level in a competitive auction. Both sides are fighting for the contract and it appears to you that it is time a decision was reached. In these circumstances you can sometimes double in *order to tell your partner to stop bidding.*

N.	E.	S.	W.
		No	No
1♡	2♣	4♡	5♣
x			

Giving North credit for understanding the auction thus far, it is his decision that he neither wants to bid 5♡ nor put the onus of decision on South. He is willing to defend 5♣ doubled though in extreme circumstances South might refuse to be silenced. If he takes out his partner's double he will have to be prepared to face North's wrath if 5♣ can be defeated and 5♡ also goes down!

This brings us to another little item, a 'forcing pass'. Substitute a pass for North's double in the sequence above, and he is saying clearly to South that he does not know which course to take, whether to bid 5♡ or double 5♣. He, therefore, leaves the decision to South.

A FORCING PASS

A forcing pass is one made in a situation where it is clear that partner must choose a course of action other than himself pass. In the bidding sequence above, South could not open, and has only chosen to bid because of his partner's opening bid. North leaves the decision of whether to bid on or double to South.

The situations for a forcing pass are:

1) A decision on whether to sacrifice or bid on.

2) When the opponents have obviously sacrificed, partner's decision on whether to bid on or double is requested.

3) When it is clear from the bidding that partner must take some action. For example, after North's strong opening bid it is

N.	E.	S.	W.
2 NT	—	3♡	4♣
—			

inconceivable that he would be willing to allow West to play in 4♣ undoubled, and it is also obvious that South will be able to take some further action. North does not wish to obscure the issue by bidding, either to double or support South's suit, and so leaves the decision to South.

TAKE-OUT OR INFORMATORY DOUBLE

A take-out double asks partner to take out the suit bid by the opponent into his own best suit, one of the great advantages of the bid being the scope it affords for finding the best contract. It gives the partnership the greatest freedom to explore their resources to the full, and may be used whenever you would like to consult with partner, rather than tell him, the best final denomination.

An ordinary overcall, whether a simple, strong jump, or pre-emptive jump bid in a new suit, definitely points to where the strength of the bidder's hand may be expected. A take-out double, on the other hand, announces that there is strength, though without indicating as yet exactly where it lies, and it asks for information from partner. An overcall in a suit, therefore, *informs* partner of your choice of trump suit. A take-out double asks his opinion on the matter.

When considering making a take-out double, remember that your hand should be qualified for any response your partner may make *including a penalty pass*. This means that the balance of your length should be in the three suits *not* opened against you, so that you can stand a take-out into any of them. Alternatively, with a good No-Trump-type stop in opponent's suit and a shortage in one of the other suits, a double will show whether partner covers your own weakness or whether you will be better off in a suit contract.

'Shape' is important when making a take-out double. Three small cards in the opponent's suit are as good as three losers when you are inviting your partner to pick a suit to play in. Remember too that the double always implies at least good support for any unbid major.

Strong unbalanced hands are best bid by way of either a jump of one level (1♡—2♠) or a cue-bid in the opponent's suit (1♡—2♡) as explained on p. 233, as the latter avoids the risk of partner converting the double to a penalty one by passing.

The general rules for suitable hands are ones containing something in the region of 12 or more honour points with 'shape', which should include support for an unbid major. Other hands may be bid by way of a simple overcall, a jump or a forcing overcall or a cue-bid, as the case may be.

♣ 7
♡ K 10 6 5
◇ K J.8 4
♣ A Q 9 6

An ideal hand for a take-out double of 1♠. It may not be particularly strong, but it is well worth having a competitive go. Change the suits around a bit, and you will see another aspect of the double.

♠ A Q 9 6
♡ K 10 6 5
◇ K J 8 4
♣ 7

When your right-hand opponent opens 1♣, who are you to decide which of these suits to bid? *Ask* your partner which he prefers by doubling—do not try to *tell* him.

♠ K 9 6 3
♡ A Q 10 6 3
◇ 8
♣ A 6 4

Here again, double an opponent's 1◇ opening in preference to bidding 1♡, your most likely means of finding a spade fit. If partner bids 2♣ instead of 1♠ you can now bid 2♡.

♠ 6 2
♡ Q J 9 7 6
◇ A J 5
♣ A Q 8

Double an opening 1♠ in preference to bidding 2♡. This might well catch a disastrous penalty double from your left-hand opponent, whereas the take-out double gives you an excellent chance of finding the best resting place—possibly in 2♣ or 2◇.

♠ A Q 9 4
♡ K J 9 3
◇ 9 6
♣ A Q 10

Double an opening 1♡ and, if partner bids 2◇, bid 2 N.T. If he should bid 1♠ in response to your double, that will surely be the best denomination, and you would also accept his suggestion of a club contract. You have the points but not the distribution for a No Trump overcall in the first place. With diamonds wide open it could be highly dangerous to suggest playing in No Trumps until you know your partner at least stops the suit.

PROTECTIVE DOUBLES

Protective doubles are nothing more than take-out doubles, though made in the 'protective' position, that is, when two passes have followed the opening bid. You will find more about protective bids in Chapter 16 but suitable hands are slightly different in character from those in the normal immediate overcalling position. The reason for this is that there is a quite considerable chance that partner will want to convert to a penalty double by passing so that for a double in the protective position, you should be prepared for a pass. This means that you should have a minimum of 11 or 1 points and the sort of hand on which you will not mind defending

The one thing you know about the deal, other than what you hold yourself, is that opener's partner is too weak even to respond at all, and it may well be that your partner has passed the opening bid because of a good holding in the opponent's bid suit and no sensible alternative to bid himself. He may, therefore, be eagerly awaiting a double which he can pass. On this hand, for example, your left-hand

♠ K J 9 7
♡ K J 9 5
◇ A 8
♣ 10 8 4

opponent deals and opens 1◇ which is passed round to you. You can't let this go uncontested, though you may reach quite the wrong contract if you bid one of your majors. Double. You will be quite happy to defend if your partner passes,

and if he takes out because lacking a good diamond holding, you will also be happy to let him play in any one of the other three suits.

	W.	N.	E.	S.
♠ A Q 10 9 2				
♡ A J 8 7 2	1♣	—	1◇	x
◇ 8				
♣ 6 3				
South				

The double, which is your best bid on this hand, is neither in the immediate overcalling nor protective position, since East has bid. It is, however, still a take-out

double, as South has not yet missed any previous opportunity to double either of the opposition's suits, so it clearly asks North to compete in the better of his two majors. Had South bid 1 N.T. instead of doubling it would have been a natural bid showing 16 or more points with both the opponents' suits stopped. Exchange the suits and, therefore, the bidding sequence, giving South the minors.

	W.	N.	E.	S.
♠ 8				
♡ 6 3	1♠	—	2♡	2 NT
◇ A Q 10 9 2		or		
♣ A J 8 7 6	1♡	—	1♠	2 NT
South		or		
	1♡	—	2♡	2 NT

In the first example it is inconceivable that South's 2 N.T. is natural and strength-showing and a bid of 2 N.T., either here or in the alternative sequences shows South's

wish to compete in the minors. This is, in fact, the Unusual No Trump Convention. for fuller details of which see p. 238 of Chapter 16. Note the difference from the double, no risk being run of a pass by North.

RESPONDING TO PARTNER'S TAKE-OUT DOUBLE

When your partner makes a take-out double in the immediate overcalling position there are three possible situations with which you can be faced; (i) if opener's partner bids in a suit or in No Trumps, (ii) if he redoubles, and (iii) if he passes. If opener's partner takes some action, either to bid or redouble, then you in your turn take the common sense course. That is to say, if you have something sensible or constructive to say, say it, but otherwise regard yourself as having been let off the hook.

Remember that a partner who has made a take-out double is seeking the best spot to play the hand, so if you have a reasonable suggestion, even after an intervening bid, make it, however weak your hand.

♠ Q 10 9 7	W.	N.	E.	S.
♡ 8 6 2	1♢	Dbl	1♡	1♠
◇ K 7 3		or		
♣ 9 5 3	1♢	Dbl	2♣	—
South				

In this sequence it is just worth while for South to show his suit since he can do so at the one-level, but change the bidding, and now South passes because his hand is not good enough to bid voluntarily at the two-level. Change the hand by making the ♣3 into the ♠3, and now the spades are worth showing even at the two-level. Similarly, if opener's partner has redoubled, you should try to be helpful if you can. Remember that if you pass the bidding will almost certainly go round to your partner again, and he may well be groping as to how *he* is to get off the hook if his hand is totally unsuited—as it probably will be—to defending a one-level redoubled contract. If you have a four-card suit you can bid at the one-level, however weak your hand, bid it. If you have a five-card suit show it even at the two-level.

♠ 8 6 3	W.	N.	E.	S.
♡ 8 7 6 3	1♢	Dbl	Redbl	1♡
◇ K 7 3				
♣ 9 5 3				

Even without the ◇K you can bid 1♡ on this hand, but if the opening bid had been 1♠ you could not bid 2♡ after the redouble. But change the hand by making the ♣3 into the ♡2, and now you should bid 2♡ over 1♠ doubled and redoubled. Your partner, the doubler, will not expect much from you. After all, if West has an opening bid, North the values to double and East the values to redouble, there's not much left for South! If by any chance you, as South, find yourself with a good hand, then probably West's opening bid was 'psychic' and you will have to bid strongly to show it up. A cue-bid in the suit opened, passing the choice back to your partner, is one possible method, or alternatively a jump bid in any good suit, which your partner will recognise as showing real strength rather than just trying to help.

When there has been no intervening action at all from your right-hand opponent you have, in honour bound, to take some action, and the only time you can pass is if you feel the best thing you can do is to convert partner's take-out double to a business one. This will be if you have a strong holding in the suit doubled and judge that the resulting penalty will be as good a score as you can get. As always when judgement is needed, it may be difficult

♠ 9 5 4
♡ Q J 10 8 7 6
◇ 6
♣ 8 5 4

to be sure of making the right decision but here, for instance, if your partner doubles an opening 1♡, and this is passed round to you, your best, and possibly only plus score will come from defending, so pass.

Responding to partner's take-out double is another of the departments where recent years have brought modifications. We now cut out mention of specific point counts, and substitute instead general rules. These must be applied with common sense and may be, perhaps, less easy for the learner, but they will be found very adequate indeed once properly mastered.

1) *On very weak hands* the bidding should be kept as low as possible. A four-card suit which can be shown at the one-level should, therefore, be bid in preference even to a five-card suit if that would mean going to the two-level. If this still leaves no sensible bid, then use a weakness response of 2♣. On this

♠ 9 7 2
♡ J 9 8 5
◇ 10 7 6
♣ 9 7 3

hand, for example, if partner doubles 1♣ or 1◇, respond 1♡, but if he doubles 1♡ or 1♠, bid 2♣. Change the distribution, making two of the small clubs into small diamonds (a 5-card diamond suit) and if partner doubles 1♣ you bid 1◇. If he

doubles 1♡ or 1♠ bid 2♣, not 2◇.

2) *On slightly stronger* hands show any suit held as naturally as possible, though preference should be given to showing a four-card major. This is bearing in mind that partner's double will almost certainly be based on a fit for any unbid major.

♠ 9 7 2
♡ J 9 8 5
◇ K 10 7 6 3
♣ 9 7

If partner doubles 1♣ or 1◇, bid 1♡. If he doubles 1♡ (which you are not strong enough to pass comfortably for penalties) or 1♠, bid 2◇. Comparing this with the responses on very weak hands you will notice that the weakness bid of 2♣ was not used, just that one extra ◇K making the hand worth more than a purely negative response.

3) *On stronger hands* containing a good biddable suit jump the bidding by one level. This is *not* forcing but highly invitational, and partner, the original doubler, should make every effort to respond. Again, good judgement will often have to be used.

♠ 9 7
♡ Q J 10 8 6 5
♢ K 9 2
♣ 8 4

Take, for example, this hand. If partner doubles 1♣ or 1♢, it is well worth a jump to 2♡, though if he has doubled 1♠ and you jump to 3♡ you are cramping the auction badly.

If, however, you bid 2♡ your partner will note that you did not use the negative 2♣ reply, so will be able to give you credit for a reasonable suit.

4) *On strong hands* you will have the choice between the double jump and a cue-bid of the suit which has been opened against you. If game is clearly in sight, choose the cue-bid, particularly if you are in doubt as to the best final denomination. Alternatively you can bid game direct if neither the jump bid nor cue-bid seems wise.

♠ A J 7 4
♡ K 10 9 7
♢ K 8
♣ 7 3 2

If partner doubles 1♣ or 1♢, cue-bid that suit, passing the choice—which is virtually bound to be one of the majors—back to him.

Many players use the cue bid of opponents' suit after the take-out double as 'forcing to suit agreement only'. This means that, whilst the cue-bid passes the buck back to the doubler to pick the denomination that suits his hand best, he must not rebid in the firm expectation that the cue-bidder will himself go on. In other words, on a strong doubling hand he must himself now bid strongly. This is not yet standard practice in the Acol System, though by the time this book gets into print it may well have become so. For that reason we draw your attention to it here.

5) *On a balanced hand* which includes a stop in the suit bid against you, respond 1 N.T. but again, only if this is sensible. The 1 N.T. response should seldom be made on a complete minimum, and should always include a guard in the suit opened. Without these the alternatives of a suit bid or 2♣ negative are both available.

♠ 10 9 7 4
♡ Q J 6 4
♢ K 8 4
♣ 9 7

If partner doubles 1♣ or 1♢, bid 1♡. If he doubles 1♡ bid 1 N.T. If he doubles 1♠ the choice is more difficult and probably 1 N.T. is again the best bet. Substitute the ♢9 for the ♢K and you still bid 1♡ over 1♣ or 1♢ doubled, but over 1♡ doubled you should bid 1♠ and over 1♠ doubled the negative 2♣.

RESPONSES FOLLOWING OPPONENT'S TAKE-OUT DOUBLE

Responses to partner's opening bid when there has been an intervening take-out double are quite different from responses in the normal way, so we must go into these in some detail. Such responses are not the exclusive property of the Acol System though like the system itself they are based on common sense, bearing in mind that it is essential to have partnership co-operation and understanding in any situation which may crop up.

The first vital difference is that a simple change-of-suit response made over a take-out double is *not* the one-round force it would be without the double. It is in the nature of a rescue operation which warns opener, your partner, that you are unable to take any stronger action whilst suspecting that the hand will play better in your suit than in his. Other bids are used to show moderate or good responding hands and each one of these will, of course, have a bearing on opener's own rebid in this altered situation. On each of the following hands you are South, bidding after your partner's opening has been doubled by your right-hand opponent.

♠ 9 5 4
♡ Q J 10 8 7 5
♦ 6
♣ 8 5 3

If your partner opens 1♦ or 1♠, in the normal course of events you would pass, not even being strong enough to bid a forcing change-of-suit 1♡ over 1♦, let alone 2♡ over 1♠. If the opening 1♦ is doubled you can bid 1♡ with impunity. This change-of-suit is not forcing, and will warn opener of the situation. If his opening bid is 1♠, however, it is best to pass, as you have a reasonable 3-card fit, not to mention the singleton diamond, which may well help him to make his contract if he is left to play it.

It follows from the above that there must be a replacement bid for the simple change-of-suit, and here a *jump* bid is used, which is merely a one-round force and not a game force as it would be without the intervening double.

This shows an attacking rather than a possibly defensive hand with a good biddable suit of its own, and opener will rebid as he was doubtless prepared to do when he opened the bidding, except at the forced higher level.

♠ K Q J 9 6 2
♡ 5 3
♦ A 5
♣ 9 8 7

Here, for example, your partner's opening 1♡— or one of either minor—is doubled on your right. With no interest in defence you should make the one-round force of 2♠. In addition to being nicely pre-emptive, it will give opener a clear picture of the type of hand held by responder and, whereas he would be reluctant to disturb a one-level rescue-type bid, here he will know that responder has at least ambitions.

If responder has the sort of hand on which he would have made a limit bid response in an uncontested auction, this will doubtless be the best possible bid when a take-out double has intervened. A hand worth a normal raise of a one-bid to the two-level should, however, raise even higher if this seems possible, in an attempt to pre-empt the opponents out of finding their fit. In other words, if responder is dithering on the edge of raising a one-bid to three, he should raise to three without further ado, whilst a hand dithering on whether to pass or raise to two, should raise.

♠ Q 7 5   Here South, without an intervening double, would
♡ Q 6 3 2   pass partner's opening 1♡, merely thankful that
◇ 8 5 3   opener had chosen the best of a sorry bunch. But
♣ 9 5 4   with an intervening double South should stretch to
           the limit and raise to 2♡, which may well make it
difficult for his left-hand opponent to come into the auction. The bid will also, of course, make it easier for opener to judge whether an ultimate sacrifice contract will be worth bidding. Add to this example hand by replacing the ♠Q with the ♠A, and it would have been worth a limit raise of 1♡ to 2♡ so now, over a take-out double, raise to 3♡.

The normal limit level of three having been used up in this pre-emptive manner, it becomes essential to have a different bid to show a full-strength raise from the one-level to three, and this is done by way of a conventional bid of 2 N.T. over any suit opened. On

♠ A 9 6   this hand you would have raised your partner's
♡ Q 10 8 4 opening 1♡ to 3♡ so over an intervening double,
◇ K J 8 7   bid 2 N.T., which carries exactly the same message.
♣ 6 3   Opener will rebid as he would have done in an
           uncomplicated sequence, simply converting to 3♡
if he would have passed a 3♡ raise, bidding 4♡ if he would have done so, or taking any other action for which his hand is suitable in the light of partner's raise. This conventional 2 N.T. bid may be used over either major or minor suit openings from partner, carrying the message of trump fit and limit-bid strength rather than pre-emption. It goes without saying that a highly pre-emptive jump bid to the four-level can, of course, be used effectively on a weak 'shape' responding hand.

Lastly we come to the important *redouble*, a bid which clearly cannot exist at all without the intervening double. This shows a minimum of 9 honour points without guaranteeing any help for partner's bid suit. In other words, as compared with a hand holding good trump support which is not likely to make a good defensive hand, it shows values, but does not show where they are. The implication is that the redoubler may well be interested in making a penalty double of the opponents' next move. It guarantees the ability to make at least one further bid and invites opener to leave this up to the redoubler. Opener should take the hint and pass if he thinks his hand will be helpful from a defensive point of view. He should rebid his hand only if he sees poor defensive prospects, that is, with an Acol light opener, weak except for a long rebiddable suit, or on a two-suiter when he thinks his side's best prospects lie in a declarer contract of their own.

♠ A J 9 7
♡ 10 4
◇ K 10 8
♣ Q 10 9 6

Your partner opens 1♡ which is doubled on your right. Here is a splendid chance to redouble, showing a minimum of 9 points, no particular enthusiasm for hearts, and the prospects of a lucrative penalty double, particularly if the opponents try a black-suit contract. The redouble, of course, lets your left-hand opponent off the hook of responding, though whether he bids or leaves his partner to seek his own salvation, you promise opener that you can yourself make a further bid assuming the auction gets round to you again. The only time you may not be able to do this is in the unlikely event of the take-out double and redouble being passed out, in which case your partner will have to play in 1♡ redoubled, but with your side-suit strength he will have every chance of making it.

A trap pass by opener's partner is a tactical manoeuvre rather than a matter of system, but no description of the available responses after a take-out double would be complete without a word about it. If you remember that a redouble ranks as a bid, which lets the doubler's partner off the hook of having to find a response to the double on what may well be a worthless hand, you will realise that it can sometimes pay to pass, thus forcing him to bid, when you could nevertheless redouble. This can be a particularly effective move at favourable vulnerability, that is, if only your opponents are vulnerable.

♠ Q 7 3	N.	E.	S.	W.
♡ K Q J 5	1◇	x	—	1♡
◇ J 10	—	—	x	
♣ Q 9 4 2				
South				

This is an actual hand from tournament play. The luckless West had a Yarborough and was hopelessly caught for an 800 penalty which no 'rescue' by East would have improved. At the other table, where South redoubled, North-South played in, and made, 3 N.T. for 400 points—hardly as profitable as 800!

REVISION QUIZ ON CHAPTER 15

1)   The opponent on your right deals and opens 1♡. What action would you take on the following hands?

   a) ♠ K Q 10 7: ♡ 9: ◇ A Q 8 4: ♣ A 10 3 2:

   b) ♠ Q 7 4 3: ♡ 3: ◇ A 10 9 8: ♣ A 4 3 2:

   c) ♠ K Q J 10 9 7: ♡ 4: ◇ A Q J: ♣ A J 7:

   d) ♠ Q 10: ♡ J 10 8 7: ◇ A K 5 4: ♣ A 10 6:

   e) ♠ Q 10 9 7: ♡ 4 3: ◇ K Q 10 6: ♣ A K J:

   f) ♠ A 4: ♡ 6 3: ◇ K Q J 10 7 2: ♣ A 4 3:

2)   Your partner, North opens 1♡ and next hand doubles. What do you, South, bid on the following hands?

   a) ♠ Q 10 9 7 4: ♡ 4 3: ◇ J 6 4: ♣ 10 9 7:

   b) ♠ Q J 9 6: ♡ 4 3 2: ◇ K J 9: ♣ K 8 4:

   c) ♠ Q 10 6 4: ♡ 10 3: ◇ J 4 2: ♣ Q 9 6 2:

   d) ♠ A 4: ♡ Q 10 9 6: ◇ 6 3: ♣ K J 6 5 4:

   e) ♠ 9: ♡ Q 10 8 4 3: ◇ J 9 5 3 2: ♣ K 3:

   f) ♠ K J 9 6: ♡ 4: ◇ A 10 9 5: ♣ K J 8 4:

   g) ♠ Q 10 6 2: ♡ 9 4: ◇ J 8 7 6: ♣ A 6 3:

   h) ♠ A 6: ♡ 10 4: ◇ K Q J 10 7 2: ♣ 9 3 2:

3)   West, the dealer, opens 1◇. North, your partner, doubles, and East bids 1♠. What do you, South, bid on the following hands?

   a) ♠ J 4: ♡ J 10 9 6 4: ◇ Q 4 2: ♣ K 7 3:

   b) ♠ Q J 8 6 4: ♡ 10 7: ◇ K 6 2: ♣ 10 9 4:

   c) ♠ A J: ♡ K 10 9 8 4 3: ◇ 4: ♣ Q 8 4 2:

   d) ♠ K J 9: ♡ J 10 9 8: ◇ A Q 10: ♣ 6 4 3:

   e) ♠ Q 10 9 8 4: ♡ J 6: ◇ 9 8 3: ♣ A Q 10:

4)   West, the dealer, opens 1◇. North doubles and East redoubles. What do you, South, bid?

   a) ♠ Q J 10 7 4: ♡ 10 7 4: ◇ 9 8 4: ♣ K 3:

   b) ♠ 10 7 4: ♡ K Q 10 9 7: ◇ Q J 4: ♣ K J:

   c) ♠ 7 4 2: ♡ 9 3 2: ◇ 7 6 5 3: ♣ 8 4 2:

   d) ♠ Q 4 3: ♡ K 7 4: ◇ K 10 9: ♣ 10 9 6 3:

   e) ♠ J 10 9: ♡ K 4: ◇ Q J 9 4: ♣ Q J 4 3:

   f) ♠ K 9 8 4: ♡ K J 10 3: ◇ 9: ♣ K 7 4 2:

5) In the following sequences you are North, the dealer, and have opened 1♡. What would you rebid?

a) 1♡   x   3♡   —
   ?
   ♠ 9 3 : ♡ A Q 10 8 7 6 : ◇ K 7 5 : ♣ Q 8 :

b) 1♡   x   xx   —
   ?
   ♠ 9 3 : ♡ A Q 10 8 7 6 : ◇ K 7 5 : ♣ Q 8 :

c) 1♡   x   xx   2♣
   ?
   ♠ 9 3 : ♡ A Q 8 7 6 : ◇ K Q 9 7 5 : ♣ 8 :

d) 1♡   x   1♠   —
   ?
   ♠ 9 3 : ♡ A Q 8 7 6 : ◇ K Q 8 4 : ♣ K 8 :

e) 1♡   x   2 NT —
   ?
   ♠ A 7 : ♡ A Q 9 8 7 4 : ◇ K 7 5 : ♣ K 8 :

f) 1♡   x   xx   2◇
   ?
   ♠ A 7 : ♡ A K 9 6 3 : ◇ J 8 : ♣ K Q 8 4 :

g) 1♡   x   xx   —
   ?
   ♠ A 7 : ♡ A K 9 6 3 : ◇ J 8 : ♣ K Q 8 4 :

h) 1♡   x   xx   2◇
   ?
   ♠ A 7 : ♡ A K 9 6 3 : ◇ K Q 8 4 : ♣ J 8 :

6) North's opening 1♡ has been doubled by your partner and passed round to you. What would you, sitting West, bid?

a) ♠ J 7 6 4 : ♡ J 10 3 : ◇ 9 8 6 4 3 : ♣ 8 :
b) ♠ 8 6 4 : ♡ J 9 6 2 : ◇ 9 8 6 4 : ♣ 8 2 :
c) ♠ 8 6 4 : ♡ 9 6 : ◇ K 10 8 6 4 : ♣ J 10 5 :
d) ♠ Q J 10 8 6 3 : ♡ 9 2 : ◇ 8 4 : ♣ K 7 2 :
e) ♠ 10 8 5 4 : ♡ Q J 9 3 : ◇ 8 2 : ♣ K 7 2 :

ANSWERS TO REVISION QUIZ ON CHAPTER 15

1) a) Double. Here you have a typical doubling hand—strong in every suit but the one opened and you want to ask your partner, rather than tell him, which suit to play in.

    b) Pass   Exactly the same shaped hand, but not enough playing strength to take action on your own. Pass, and hope to be able to support partner if he can bid.

    c) 2♡   The forcing bid which avoids the danger of partner making a penalty pass of a double.

    d) Pass   Although you have 14 points, too much of your 'shape' is in opponent's suit. Pass and hope that they will try for a high heart contract which you can double, or that your partner may be able to take action. A 'protective' double by him if your left-hand opponent passes would be highly attractive.

    e) Double. You have support for any suit your partner may bid.

    f) 3◇   It is better to jump in your long suit, which is the only one you are really interested in playing in. Compare (c) above, for which you are not quite strong enough.

2) a) 1♠   A warning to your partner that you cannot raise hearts let alone support the suit, and that you have not the values to redouble or jump-bid, whereas you have a reasonable suit of your own which may be an improvement on his.

    b) Redouble. With 10 points you redouble to tell partner that you can take action on the next round, whatever the opposition bids.

    c) Pass   With no constructive bid, or a suit to show, pass and await developments.

    d) 2 NT   A typical hand on which, without the double, you would have bid 3♡.

    e) 3♡   A hand on which, without the double, you would have raised 1♡ to 2♡.

    f) Pass   This is a very good example of a hand suitable for a
    OR   'trap pass'. If you pass West will have to speak, and you
    Redouble   may well get the chance of a highly profitable penalty double when the action gets round to you again.

    g) Pass   Over 1♡ without the intervening double you would bid 1♠. Here take the opportunity to pass telling partner that you cannot raise his suit, bid or jump bid a suit of your own, or redouble.

h) 3♦   A one-round force, which 2♦ would not be once there has been a double on your right. Opener will know that you have an excellent prospective trump suit in a hand unsuitable for a redouble.

3) a) 2♡   You have a very far from worthless hand opposite a double and it is probable that East has bid his 1♠ on something like the hand in 2 (a).

b) Pass Without East's bid you would have liked to have bid 1♠ yourself, but are not strong enough to take any action over East.

c) 3♡   This time both your count and 'shape' are good enough to try for a game.

d) 2 NT With 11 points and good stops in both of opponents' suits, this is your honest bid.

e) Double. Apart from the fact that you would have liked to have bid spades yourself, you hold good defensive values.

4) a) 1♠   The redouble relieves you of the responsibility of bidding, but you have a good five-card suit, so show it.

b) 2♡   If you work it out, there are really not enough points in the pack for the bidding thus far. Tell your partner that you, anyway, are not fooling!

c) Pass Nothing in this hand should induce you to bid once the redouble has absolved you from this responsibility. It has given your partner his chance to speak again.

d) 1 NT This moderate 8-point hand has its values scattered and you will not mind what action partner make take.

e) Pass This really amounts to a penalty pass, though your partner cannot know it. Someone must be fooling and if it is the opposition you must be able to cause great damage. If—as is most likely—partner re-opens with a bid, you can take the appropriate action.

f) 2♦   Telling your partner to take his pick from any of the other three suits, for all of which you have support.

) a) Pass Without East's intervening double you would not go to 4♡ over South's 3♡. Here he will be even weaker than his standard three-level limit bid, so pass.

b) 2♡ You have the same hand as in (a), but though your partner has promised at least 9 points and interest in doubling East-West's final contract, your hand is wholly unsuitable for defence.

c) 2♢ Here again, with a weak two-suiter based on 'shape', the idea of defending a low-level doubled contract is highly unattractive, so show your second suit, putting partner in the picture.

d) Pass South is showing a weak hand with a reasonable suit of his own. His failure to raise hearts or redouble warns you to leave his bid alone. After all, it is no longer forcing.

e) 4♡ Had South, in an uninterrupted sequence, bid 3♡, you would have gone on to 4♡. His 2 N.T. over the double is the equivalent of a full-strength 3♡ limit bid, so bid the game.

f) Pass South has shown his ability to take action on the next round, with the added suggestion that this will be to double the opponents' final contract. With an excellent defensive hand pass, giving him his second chance to bid.

g) Pass The same hand as in (f), and you pass for the same reasons. The fact that West has exercised his right to pass instead of bidding 2♢, as he did in (f), makes no difference.

h) Double. The bid best calculated to put partner in the picture. If he has the values to redouble, suggesting an interest in doubling the final East-West contract, you are in an excellent position to tell him that you approve the idea, particularly if diamonds are to be trumps.

6) a) 1♠ With a suit, even if a miserable one, that you can show at the one-level, bid it.

b) 2♣ The weakness bid, as you have really nothing sensible to say.

c) 2♢ Just good enough for this in preference to 2♣ from which your partner will realise that you have not got a complete 'bust'.

d) 2♠ A non-forcing though invitational bid showing a reasonable trump suit. Note the comparison with (a) above.

e) 1 NT The heart stop makes this worth while and distinguishes the hand from the near 'bust' of (a) above.

Chapter 16

The Competitive Auction

WE have already dealt with the various aspects of the double—
when to double—what it means—how to respond and so on. The
majority of doubles are, of course, part of a competitive auction,
but to group all competitive bids, including the double, together,
would have made such a monstrous chapter that we thought it
better to deal with doubles and redoubles in a chapter of their own.

Not all the bids described in this chapter are essential to the system
and, for instance, you may get along very well without Directional
Asking Bids or the Unusual No Trump. Both, however, are so
widely used nowadays that they are almost an accepted part of the
system, for which reason they are included here. Nor, with one
exception, does Acol lay sole claim to any of the defensive and
intervening bids, so, though they too cannot be classed as being
specifically Acol's own bids, they are essential for any good sound
Acol player who wants to have a solid basis for his bidding in
competitive situations.

In general Acol players continue to carry out their policy that
the best form of defence is attack and, if the opposition has gone
into the attack first, to counter-attack as often and as freely as
possible. The more you intervene, the more opportunities you give
for the opposition to go astray, though bear in mind that if your
intervention is not sound, you can be sticking your neck out in a
big way. It may result in nothing but a huge penalty against you
when there is no chance of any gain.

SIMPLE OVERCALLS

When the bidding is opened by your right-hand opponent you must
decide whether or not to intervene. This decision is a little easier at
duplicate than at rubber bridge because at duplicate each board is
a separate entity, and a disaster incurred on one board at M.P.
Pairs can give you no more than a 'bottom'. At rubber bridge it will have
to be added to any further disasters, and the chance to recuperate
may not come your way. Your aim should always be to avoid
a penalty greater than the points your opponents can gain. A non-
vulnerable game is worth 300 bonus points and a vulnerable game

500 points. So 3 N.T., for example, will score 400 points if not vulnerable and 600 if vulnerable. Obviously, then, to intervene and risk being doubled and incurring a penalty greater than these amounts will do you no good at all!

Playing tricks are of more importance when contemplating an intervening bid than honour points. To make a vulnerable overcall at the one-level you should have the expectation of winning at least four tricks if not vulnerable and five if vulnerable. For an intervening bid at the two-level you should be at least one trick stronger in either case.

The main objects of making an intervening bid are:

a) To compete with your opponents, either to gain the contract for your own side, or to push the enemy too high.

b) To suggest the best suit for the opening lead, or best line of attack should you become the defenders.

c) To pave the way for a possible sacrifice contract, usually when not vulnerable against vulnerable opponents.

Bear in mind as well that it is generally highly unwise to let the bidding go too high before making your intervention. Unless your opponents' bidding is weak and being allowed to die at a low level, when it may well be good policy to take some action, use your common sense. In this auction, for example, had North *opened*

N.	E.	S.	W.
No	1♠	—	2♡
3♣	x		

1♣, he might have got away with the 3♣ rebid. As it was he was known not to be good enough for either a one-level or pre-emptive opening bid in clubs, and this little exercise cost him 900 points. The excuse was that it was to direct his partner's lead, but it was a somewhat costly price to pay when East doubled!

Whether or not an intervening bid is made with the express intention of trying to gain the contract for your own side, it may well have nuisance-value for your opponents by depriving them of a round of bidding. Note the difference between an intervening bid of 1♠ over 1♡ or 2♣ over 1♠, neither of which obstructs opener's partner, and 2♣ over 1♢, the latter making it impossible for him to bid a major suit at the one-level. Keep such considerations very much in mind and try to strike a happy medium between the risk of heavy loss and the chance of gain.

When your only asset is a good holding in the suit opened against you, your best course is generally to pass and await developments. If opener's partner either passes or bids weakly, your partner may be able to take some 'protective' action. Alternatively, not knowing of the bad trump break, your opponents may go too high when, even if you cannot double, you have hopes of defeating them.

Acol players use a *strong* No Trump in the immediate overcalling position so remember that, even if you announce 'weak throughout' or 'variable', this does not apply to an intervening bid of 1 N.T. The hand should contain a minimum of 15 honour points including a good stop in the suit opened, and partner will treat it as he would a strong opening No Trump except that he will now use 2♣ as a weak take-out and not a fit-finding bid.

♠ A 8 4
♡ A 9 2
◇ J 10 6
♣ A 10 8 3

Bearing in mind the need for playing tricks when intervening, compare these two hands. The first, with 13 points and two 10's is a 'must' for a weak 1 N.T. opening bid, but is quite unsuitable for any sort of intervention. The second, though hardly even worth an Acol light opener, is well worth an overcall of 1♠ if any other suit is opened against you.

♠ K J 9 7 5 3
♡ A 6 2
◇ 9 4 3
♣ 8

♠ K 10 7
♡ A J 6
◇ Q 6 5
♣ Q 8 6 5

Here again, though you would certainly open 1 N.T. if not vulnerable, don't be tempted to make any sort of overcall. The distribution is far too balanced to make a good attacking hand though it may well prove declarer's downfall if used in defence. Pass and hope that the enemy will bid too high—to intervene at this stage would probably prevent any chance of this.

♠ A 8
♡ K J 7 5 3
◇ Q 9 5
♣ 9 6 2

If your right-hand opponent opens 1♡, *pass*. A double would be asking partner to take out—the last thing you want—and 1 N.T. would imply a much stronger hand. If 1♣ or 1◇ is opened against you, you can intervene with 1♡. You *might* get doubled and go down but nothing venture nothing win, especially as a one-level contract has to be defeated very heavily to make the penalty worth while, so if they are vulnerable, your opponents are more likely to try for their own game. If the opening bid is 1♠ it would be sticking your neck out in a big way to come in with 2♡, a tempting target for a business double!

♠ K Q 9 8 7
♡ 7 5
◇ Q 8 6
♣ A 9 2

Worth an overcall of 1♠ whatever the vulnerability. Make the suit hearts instead of spades and it is still worth a one-level intervention over 1♣ or 1◇. Over an opening 1♠ an intervention of 2♡ would be highly doubtful if vulnerable. But non-vulnerable 2♡ over 1♠ deprives your left-hand opponent of the chance to show a minor at the two-level so, particularly if your partner has not yet passed, it would be worth the risk.

♠ A Q 9 7
♡ K 7 4
◇ 8 5 3
♣ 9 6 2

Over a minor suit opening bid even this meagre hand is probably worth an intervening bid of 1♠. It may catch a double and prove highly expensive but, on the other hand, it prevents your left-hand opponent from bidding 1♡ and may also make life difficult for him if, with up to 8 or 9 points, he is unable to bid 1 N.T. for lack of an adequate spade guard. Unlike the previous examples on which we advised against taking any action, here you can bid at the one-level in a suit which may get highly in the way of the enemy auction. On doubtful hands, therefore, let your decision hang on three considerations, the vulnerability, whether or not your partner has previously passed, and whether an intervening bid is likely to obstruct your opponents' bidding.

♠ 9 7
♡ K J 7
◇ K Q 10 8 6 3
♣ A J

This hand is worth an intervening bid at the two-level over either 1♡ or 1♠. It has attacking possibilities of its own and an excellent six-card suit.

PROTECTIVE BIDS

A 'protective' bid is one made fourth-in-hand when two passes have followed the opening bid, and is so called because it protects partner's pass. If that sounds a bit mysterious, what it means is that if opener's partner has not even the very meagre quota of 5 or 6 points needed to dredge up a response to an opening one-bid, he must be abysmally weak and your partner may well have passed only because for some reason his hand contains no sensible bid. He may, in fact, hòld something like the hand on p. 229 where he could not overcall 1♡ because of his holding in the suit. In that case he will be waiting and hoping that you will be able to take action. If that action should be a protective double it will be just what he is hoping for, and he will be able to convert to a business double by passing.

The values required for a protective bid are somewhat different from those in the immediate overcalling position. Different pairs will have different agreements on the subject, but the following is more or less standard practice. Remember that they are based on two known facts, opener had no better than a one-level bid, and responder was too weak for any reply at all. Judged against your own hand there may well be a strong assumption that your partner has some values which, added to your own, will produce either a penalty or at least a part-score for your own side.

In Chapter 15 we had a look at the values required for a protective double which should always be moderately strong with a minimum of 11 or more points in a hand on which you will not be unhappy to defend the one-level contract if your partner passes for penalties. Next in line comes a protective 1 N.T., a bid which may be made on as little as 10-11 points with at least a partial stop in the suit doubled. The weakest protective bid is a simple overcall in a new suit which may be made on about 8 points. Next comes a cue-bid in the suit opened and this, according to modern practice, is what is known as 'forcing to suit agreement'. As we saw in the previous chapter when the cue-bid was used in response to partner's take-out double, the cue-bid is forcing only until the best spot in which to play the hand has been found. There is no obligation on either player to go on to game, and either may pass, make a further invitational bid, or jump direct to game if strong enough.

At the lower end of the scale the cue-bid would be used on a hand unsuitable for a double which might be passed for penalties, and where the best final denomination is in doubt. Here, for example,

♠ A 9 7 6	N.	E.	S.	W.
♡ J 7 6 4	1♣	—	—	2♣
◇ K J 6				
♣ 10 9				
West				

though unwilling to allow North's 1♣ opening to go uncontested, and not being enthusiastic about the prospect of defending if East passes a double, West can cue-bid 2♣ to seek the best fit for a part-score contract. He is free to pass East's two-level response. With greater strength, of course, West would be equally free to raise East's response, either invitationally or direct to game.

In between comes a jump bid in a new suit which shows a good hand with a strong suit of its own and a genuine wish to contest for

♠ A Q J 7 6 4	N.	E.	S.	W.
♡ 7	1♡	—	—	2♠
◇ K Q 9				
♣ A 7 5				
West				

a game or part-score. This hand, for example, is quite unsuitable for a protective double as you have no wish to defend if partner decides to pass. It is equally unsuitable for a protective 1 N.T. and too strong for a mere bid of 1♠.

One word of warning here and that is, think carefully before you make a protective bid over an opening 1♣ passed round to you. An opening 1♣ bid is used by many players as a way out of difficulty if too strong to open 1 N.T., and responder's pass has possibly left opener floundering in a three-card suit with no chance of escape into 1 N.T. where he would far rather play. 1♣ is also often the prelude to showing a black two-suiter, and protective action by you may give opener his chance to get out into 1♠ which may well fit responder's hand far better than 1♣.

♠ A J 10 7
♡ J 7 3
◇ J 7 2
♣ Q 10 9

If an opening 1♣, 1◇, or 1♡ is passed round to you, 'protect' with 1♠. You must chance opener getting out into 1 N.T., and he's not likely to be very well off if he rebids 2♣. Add the ◇K and you can double the opening bid, being willing to defend if your partner passes.

In a wider sense 'protection' is often of value later in the auction, particularly at duplicate where every part-score has to be contested if this is possible. On this hand, for example, you will not have

♠ —
♡ A K 6 5 3
◇ 8 7 4
♣ K 8 7 4 2

opened the bidding as dealer. Your left-hand opponent bids 1♠, your partner passes, and your right-hand opponent raises to 2♠. 'Protect' by doubling. This is, of course, a take-out double (Chapter 15, p. 213) which will not mislead your partner. If opener is strong and bids on your partner will be released from any obligation to speak and will only do so with something constructive to say. If the double is passed round to him he may be able to pass for penalties or else bid his own best suit which enables you to contest the part score at the three-level.

You will hardly need reminding that, when responding to a protective bid made by your partner, you must keep in mind the low values required for simple protective bids, and gear down your own enthusiasm accordingly.

JUMP OVERCALLS

Here we come to another of the modifications which most good players use nowadays, many hands which would have qualified for a jump overcall before now being bid by way of a cue-bid in the suit opened by your opponents (see p. 233 in this chapter).

The jump overcall is used largely as a tactical bid and suitable hands will vary according to the vulnerability. A good six-card suit is the least requirement, and this should be in a strong hand unsuitable for a take-out double which partner might pass for penalties, and not good enough for the immediate cue bid.

♠ A K Q 8 6 3
♡ 7
◇ Q J 9
♣ A 7 3

This hand is clearly unsuitable for a take-out double and is too good for a simple overcall of 1♠ after any other suit opened against you. Bid 2♠ at any score. A slightly weaker hand such as this would be worth the jump to 2♠ if not vulnerable against vulnerable opponents. As this is strength

♠ K Q 10 9 5 4   showing but *not* forcing, keep to single-suited
♡ 6   hands for this bid. On two-suiters either make a
◇ Q 7 4   simple overcall and hope for a chance to show
♣ A Q 9   your second suit later or, if strong enough, use the
                 cue bid as explained below.

If the opening bid forces you to make your jump overcall at the three-level (1♠—3♡ or 1◇—3♣) you must, of course, be more wary. Three-level bids are tempting targets for business doubles, which may convert even a one-trick defeat into a good result for your opponents, who may well not have anything 'on' themselves.

FORCING OVERCALLS

Old-stagers will know the immediate cue-bid of the opening bidder's suit as a game force on something like a 2♣ opener but, as we've already said, this has undergone modifications of recent years because of the very low incidence of the need for it. Nowadays it is used as a strong bid, forcing for one round. Partner should respond as he would to a take-out double (Chapter 15) and, thereafter may use his own judgement unless the forcer makes a *repeat* cue bid in the suit opened, when the sequence becomes forcing to game. Judgement does not, of course, include passing with any reasonable values in the hand, though a minimum rebid by the player who has made the cue bid may be passed on complete weakness.

This cue bid has the great advantage of avoiding the danger that partner may pass a take-out double for penalties—in other words, the bid is reserved for strong hands, either single *or* two suited, which are quite unsuitable for defence.

♠ A K Q 9 5 2   If your right-hand opponent opens 1♣, 1◇ or
♡ A 8   1♡, bid two of that suit. Then bid and rebid
◇ 7 6   spades. You don't want to be in game if
♣ K Q 4   partner has a Yarborough, but with anything at
                all he will bid again.

♠ K J 10 9 6   Bid 2♣ over an opening 1♣. If partner bids 2◇
♡ A Q J 6 2   make the repeat force of 3♣, which indicates
◇ K Q 3   a major two-suiter. If instead he bids 2♡ or
♣ —   2♠, raise him.

♠ A K 9 8 7   Bid 2◇ over 1◇ or 2♡ over 1♡. If partner
♡ 5   responds, as he is most likely to do, in a red
◇ A   suit, rebid in clubs, indicating a black two-suiter.
♣ K Q J 9 8 6   He should show preference for spades or clubs or
                jump preference if he possibly can.

♠ 7
♡ A K 10 8 4 3
◇ A Q J 9 7
♣ 8

Over 1♣ bid 2♣ or over 1♠ bid 2♠. If partner responds in your other singleton bid hearts next, showing the red two-suiter. The fact that you don't pass or raise the suit in which your partner responds shows that it is the other suits you are interested in unless, on a single-suiter like the first example, you merely rebid spades again.

PRE-EMPTIVE OVERCALLS

Pre-emptive overcalls are made for just the same purpose as pre-emptive opening bids, to deprive the opposition of bidding space, and pre-emptive overcalls are made by jumping at least one more level of bidding than is needed to show a strong hand, as set out on p. 232. Single-suited hands *only* qualify, and should be otherwise weak except for great length in the suit bid.

♠ 9
♡ K Q 10 8 7 6 4 3
◇ 5 2
♣ 6 4

Particularly at favourable vulnerability this hand would be worth a jump to 3♡ over an opening 1♣ or 1◇, or 4♡ over 1♠. Strengthen the suit by as much as the inclusion of the ♡J in place of one of the other cards and it would be worth 4♡ over any opposing opening. With no defensive values whatsoever your only real hope of a good score is to prevent the opponents from finding their own best spot.

ONE NO TRUMP OVERCALL

As already mentioned, to overcall an opening bid of one of a suit with 1 N.T. requires a balanced hand of a minimum of 15 points, and many people require even 16 points. This is in no way related to the values being used for an opening 1 N.T. The hand should be of No Trump type, that is, more or less evenly balanced, and should contain a sound stop in the suit opened.

It is highly unwise to drop this standard, as you may easily get caught in the sandwich of the opening bid and the remainder of the available strength being on your left and, if that happens, you will have no safe way out of the trap of a business double.

♠ A J 3	♠ K Q 5	♠ K 10 3
♡ K 9 8	♡ Q 10 9	♡ A Q
◇ K Q J 7	◇ Q 10 8 4	◇ Q 7 4
♣ Q 10 7	♣ A Q 7	♣ A Q 10 7 5

All these hands make excellent 1 N.T. overcalls of any suit opened, having 'something in everything' and a good count.

Note, by the way, that the strength of your No Trump overcall is one of the essential details to be disclosed to your opponents. I you have 'Acol' on your system card your opponents will automatically expect a strong hand, and you must have no partnership agreement that the bid may be made on less.

Note also that in response to a 1 N.T. overcall the fit-finding aspect of a 2♣ bid, as explained in Chapter 5, no longer operates. Partner will raise or take out in the knowledge that he is facing a strong hand, though he can be pretty sure that, as the 1 N.T. bidder did not use a take-out double, he is not particularly interested in seeking a suit contract.

TWO NO TRUMPS OVER ONE NO TRUMP OPENING

This is a special Acol conventional bid and may be used in either the immediate overcalling or protective position. It is a game force and shows a two-suited hand. Partner should respond by showing suits of equal length in *ascending* order. With only one suit, of course, he bids that suit.

Without this conventional bid strong two-suiters can be extremely difficult to handle over an opening 1 N.T. from the opposition. A double of an opening No Trump is always primarily for business and will only be taken out by the doubler's partner on weakness or if he anticipates a better result from a different contract, so that a double cannot be used to seek information from partner. The game-forcing 2 N.T. takes the place of a take-out double, and can be used on very much the same lines as the immediate cue bid of an opponent's opening suit bid.

♠ A
♡ A K J 9 7 4
◇ —
♣ A Q 10 7 5 3

If an opponent opens 1 N.T. make the game-forcing overcall of 2 N.T. Partner will respond in his own best suit which will, alas, almost certainly be spades or diamonds. But you can now be certain of reaching game in the best-fitting of your own two suits, as you can rebid 3♡ over his 3◇ or 4♣ over his 3♠, showing that his response has not hit the jackpot and that he must keep the bidding open to allow you to show your second suit after which he will, if necessary, give preference.

RESPONSES TO OVERCALLS

If you have read the previous pages with attention you will know that there are a number of classes of overcall available, and the fact that your partner has chosen one particular one means that his hand is not qualified for one of the others. It may be not strong enough for one bid, too strong for another, or unsuitable in shape but, if he is playing Acol, he should have bid his cards without waiting for you to bid them. You will, therefore, have a fairly clear idea of the sort of hand you are responding *to*, that is, minimum, strong, evenly-balanced, or whatever the overcaller has announced.

If a player has made a minimum overcall there is not the same urgency for *his* partner to 'find a response' as there would be if he were making an opening bid, which does not mean he should pass if he has something constructive to say! Judge your own hand against the type of hand shown by the overcall and act accordingly.

There are, however, various differences between responding to opening bids and responding to overcalls. Remember that an overcall in a suit, generally though not invariably shows a five-card suit at the one-level, and certainly a minimum of a five-card suit and more probably a six-card suit if at the two-level. Couple this with the fact that a change-of-suit bid by the partner of an overcaller is not forcing even for one round, and you will see that direct suit raises can be given much more freely than in responding to an opening bid, where primary, or four-card support is needed. A jump bid in a new suit is a one-round force, and a cue bid in an opponent's suit is a game force.

♠ K J 8 7 5	N.	E.	S.	W.
♡ 7		1♡	2◇	—	?
◇ A J 8				
♣ Q 8 7 5				
West				

If your partner had opened 1◇ you would have responded 1♠ in the hope of finding a major suit fit. Now, however, you know that the hand 'belongs' in diamonds. East will certainly have a five-card suit and probably a six-card one, so raise to 3◇.

♠ K Q 5	N.	E.	S.	W.
♡ 8 7		1♡	2◇	2♡	?
◇ 8 6				
♣ A Q 10 9 7 6				
West				

From the above you will see that a bid of 3♣ from West indicates that he is not 'with' East in diamonds. In fact exchange the ◇8 for a diamond honour and it would be better to bid 3◇ than 3♣. So settle first for a raise in partner's suit if you can manage it, and be prepared for him to pass your change-of-suit response if he does not like the prospects. He should not return to his own suit in the belief that any bid from you shows support for his suit. If your own hand is good enough to fancy the chances of game even when he's made only a simple overcall, then take some strong action, such as a jump in a new suit or a cue bid of opponent's suit. The latter promises no specific holding but your partner should treat it as a Directional Asking Bid (see next section) and respond accordingly, awaiting further developments from you.

DIRECTIONAL ASKING BIDS

The use of a Directional Asking Bid—a DAB for short—is often the only way in which a partnership can reach a No Trump contract in the face of an opponent's opening or intervening bid. There are frequent instances of a hand suitable to play in No Trumps except for a weakness of, perhaps, Q-x only in the suit bid by the opposition. All that is needed is to find out whether partner can supply a 'boost' to the partial stop, such as K-x or J-x-x, which will turn the other partial stop into a sure hold, at least for one round. You don't *have* to use DABs as an Acol player, but you will find them a great asset—as long as you're playing with a partner who knows them too!

♠ Q 8	S.	W.	N.	E.
♡ K J 6	1◇	—	2♣	2♠
◇ A K J 10 6	?			
♣ A 6 3				

As South you open 1◇ and the bidding goes like this. What are you to rebid? Clearly with a marked spade lead to come you dare not play in No Trumps unless your partner has a little something in spades. So bid 3♠, a DAB, *asking* him if he can give help in this department. If North has even a partial spade guard he will bid 3 N.T. Without this he must find another rebid, either in his own suit or perhaps supporting yours.

♠ Q J	N.	E.	S.	W.
♡ A J 9	1♣	—	1♠	2◇
◇ A 8 6	?			
♣ K Q J 9 5				

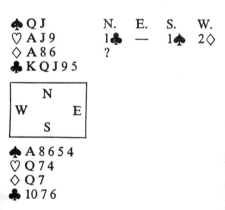

North has a diamond guard, but if South has any honour in the suit, the lead in a No Trump contract will come from East *through* South's holding. On the other hand if South can be persuaded to become declarer, either a diamond lead will have to come from West and up to South's hand, or the defence will have to lose a 'tempo' towards clearing their suit. So North rebids 3◇, asking South if he can help stop the diamond suit, which gives 3 N.T. with South playing the hand a much greater chance of success.

Thus if a player himself holds a certain guard in the suit he's worried about he can still make a DAB with the object of placing the final No Trump contract with his partner as declarer, which can make a single guard into a double stop.

You will realise that DABs are unconditionally forcing for one round, and responder must bid in No Trumps if he can help his partner in this way, or return to the most suitable trump contract available. One other point to note is that there should never be any confusion between DABs and cue bids or strength-showing bids which are used to agree partner's trump suit when a possible slam is being investigated, because the player who uses the apparent DAB can always remove his partner's No Trump response back to the suit, which makés the position clear. In this sequence, for

S.	E.	N.	W.
1♡	1♠	2◊	—
2♠	—	2 NT	—
?			

example, if South is interested in a spade guard for No Trumps he will doubtless raise North's 2 N.T. to 3 N.T. If he has, in fact, strong diamond support and intends to play in a diamond game or slam he will not raise in No Trumps. A jump bid in diamonds would be his most likely bid, if unable to make any other constructive bid which makes it clear that No Trumps is not his final aim.

This is another convention which is not essential to the Acol System but is so widely used nowadays that it is a handicap if it is missing from your repertoire. As the name implies, it is a bid in No Trumps when this cannot really be expected to be genuine. Its most general application is when the No Trump bidder foresees a possibly profitable sacrifice contract.

There are various schools of thought as to the best way of using the convention, but you won't go far wrong if you regard it as a form of take-out double expressing shape rather than strength, though there may be honour strength included as well.

N.	E.	S.	W.
1♡	2 NT		

or

N.	E.	S.	W.
1♡	—	2♡	2 NT

If the opponents have only called, or only had the opportunity to call, one major suit, then a jump bid of 2 N.T. as in the first example, or a bid of 2 N.T. which it would clearly be ridiculous to take as a genuine bid in No Trumps, asks for partner's choice between the *minor* suits.

N.	E.	S.	W.
1◊	—	1♠	2 NT

Any jump bid in No Trumps when the opponents have called two suits asks for partner's choice between the remaining two suits, in this case hearts and clubs. Note that 1 N.T. from West would be a strong natural No Trump bid, and not 'unusual'.

N.	E.	S.	W.
1♣	—	2♡	—
3♡	—	4♣	—
—	4 NT		

Similarly any unduly high level of No Trump bid, as here where it obviously cannot be genuine, is asking for a take-out, this time into partner's better choice between the minor suits. Doubtless East did not come into the bidding at a lower level because he hoped, in vain as it turns out, that North-South would not reach a game contract. Now that they have done so he sees no hope of defeating them but, with length in the other two suits, wants to sacrifice in whichever fits best with his partner's hand.

The player who elects to bid an 'unusual' No Trump should be at least 5-5 and preferably 6-5 in the two suits concerned. Here is a classic example from a recent match:

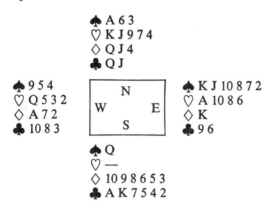

♠ A 6 3
♡ K J 9 7 4
◊ Q J 4
♣ Q J

♠ 9 5 4
♡ Q 5 3 2
◊ A 7 2
♣ 10 8 3

♠ K J 10 8 7 2
♡ A 10 8 6
◊ K
♣ 9 6

♠ Q
♡ —
◊ 10 9 8 6 5 3
♣ A K 7 5 4 2

When the vulnerable East dealt and opened 1♠, South could foresee no defence. He bid an immediate 2 N.T., asking for North's choice between the minors. North, far too good for a mere 'preference' of 3◊, bid 4◊ and South bid the fifth which West, on the strength of his ◊A and partner's opening bid, rashly doubled. There is, of course, no possible way to defeat 5◊ though South, when he bid 2 N.T., was thinking in terms of a sacrifice. A very profitable one it proved too, as East, in the other room, played in 4♠ which he had no chance to make.

♠ 4
♡ J 6
◊ K J 7 6 2
♣ Q J 9 7 6

You can't of course, expect always to have quite such an ideal hand for the bid, and a holding such as this would be very adequate at favourable vulnerability.

In responding to an 'unusual' No Trump bid, show length rather than honour strength, even if this is no better than the choice between a void and a singleton! But honours in one of the two suits and even a reasonable 'fit' in the other can only be helpful.

As in the case of a take-out double, an intervening bid lets responder 'off the hook', and he may use his judgement in preferring to pass rather than show preference for one or other of the 'asked' suits. Thus the decision as to whether to double the opponents' final contract or to seek the sacrifice by another 'unusual' No Trump bid can be left to partner. Here's a sad tale where misunderstanding on this point caused acute disaster. North-South were vulnerable, so when East voluntarily bid 5♣ over North's 4♠, and South still confidently went to 6♠, West was justified in visualising club length

West	N.	E.	S.	W.
♠ 3	1♠	—	3♡	3 NT
♡ —	4♠	5♣	6♠	7♣
◇ A 10 8 7 4 3	X	—	—	—
♣ A 9 7 5 4 3				

with East and a void in the South hand. This meant that his hand was good for one defensive trick only, the ◇A, so he sacrificed in 7♣, doubled and four down when 6♠ could not be made. East instead of taking the opportunity to pass, had bid 5♣ on a 4-3-3-3 Yarborough.

THE GARDENER EXTENSION

You may have noticed from the details at the beginning of this section that a player with an Unusual No Trump bid in mind could not, in the early stages of the auction, take action over a *minor* suit opening bid, so for the gadget-minded we give you here a note of a new aspect of the Unusual No Trump, which has recently been accepted into the ranks of 'permissible' variations. This is the Gardener extension, whereby a bid of 2 N.T. over a minor suit opening requests partner to show his preference between *hearts* and the *other* minor, that is, excluding spades. This seems a useful innovation for various reasons. A player who holds spades will usually elect to bid the suit himself, which he can, of course, do over an opening 1♣ or 1◇ with little danger to himself, and the bid of 2 N.T. would clearly deny any wish to find a spade fit. The partnership is then embarked on a voyage of discovery only into the choice between hearts and the other minor.

REVISION QUIZ ON CHAPTER 16

1) At score Love All, your right-hand opponent deals and opens
1♡. What would you bid on the following hands?

    a) ♠ A Q J 7 4 2: ♡ 9 4: ◇ K 8 2: ♣ 5 4:
    b) ♠ K J 9 8 7 4 2: ♡ 5: ◇ A 9 6: ♣ 10 4:
    c) ♠ Q J 10 9 7 4: ♡ A 3 2: ◇ Q 9 6: ♣ 4:
    d) ♠ A 10 9: ♡ K J 9: ◇ K Q 6 4: ♣ A 10 4:
    e) ♠ K Q J 10 7 4 2: ♡ A: ◇ A 10 4: ♣ K 3:
    f) ♠ 7 4: ♡ 8: ◇ A Q J 9 6 5 3 2: ♣ K 4:
    g) ♠ A 10 9 7 4 2: ♡ —: ◇ Q 4 3: ♣ K 10 6 3:
    h) ♠ A 4: ♡ A K Q: ◇ K Q 10 9 6 4: ♣ K 3:
    i) ♠ K Q 10: ♡ K 10 5: ◇ A 4 2: ♣ K J 6 5:
    j) ♠ K 10 4: ♡ 8 4: ◇ A K J 9 3: ♣ Q 4 3:
    k) ♠ A K Q 6 5 4 3: ♡ K 3: ◇ 8 4: ♣ 3 2:
    l) ♠ A K Q 10 7 5: ♡ —: ◇ A K Q 4 3: ♣ 6 3:
    m) ♠ A 4 3: ♡ 9: ◇ K 9 8 7 4: ♣ K 10 6 3:
    n) ♠ A J 6: ♡ Q J 4: ◇ A Q 4: ♣ K J 3 2:
    o) ♠ 5: ♡ 6: ◇ 7 6 5: ♣ A Q J 9 7 5 3 2:
    p) ♠ K 7 3: ♡ —: ◇ K Q 10 7 4 3 2: ♣ Q 9 6:

2) With North the dealer, the bidding has gone:

          N.   E.   S.   W.
          1♠   No No   ?

What would you, West, bid on the following hands?

    a) ♠ 9 4: ♡ A Q 10 9 4: ◇ J 10 6: ♣ Q 6 4:
    b) ♠ K J 9: ♡ Q 9 6 4: ◇ A J 4: ♣ 10 9 8:
    c) ♠ 10 6: ♡ K Q 9 5: ◇ K J 9 4: ♣ A 4 3:
    d) ♠ 4: ♡ K 10 9 6: ◇ K Q 8 6: ♣ K J 9 6:
    e) ♠ 7: ♡ Q 10 6: ◇ A J 10 9 4 3: ♣ Q 10 5:
    f) ♠ Q 10 6: ♡ K 9 4 2: ◇ K 10 6 2: ♣ J 5:

3) Your right-hand opponent deals and opens 1 N.T. (weak).
What would you bid on the following hands?

    a) ♠ A 4: ♡ K Q J 9 6 3: ◇ K Q 10 9 4: ♣ —:
    b) ♠ A K Q J 9 8 4: ♡ 8 7: ◇ 9 6: ♣ 6 3:
    c) ♠ J: ♡ 8: ◇ A K Q 7 6 4: ♣ A K Q 9 5:
    d) ♠ K J 8: ♡ A Q 7 2: ◇ K 10 6: ♣ Q J 10:
    e) ♠ A K J 7 6 4: ♡ A Q 10 9 3: ◇ 5: ♣ 7:

4) The bidding, with North the dealer, has gone:]

          N.   E.   S.   W.
          1♠   2◇   No   ?

What do you, West, bid on the following hands?
a) ♠ K J 3: ♡ J 9 6 4: ◇ K 10: ♣ Q 10 4 3:
b) ♠ 9: ♡ K 4 3: ◇ Q J 7 6 2: ♣ 10 9 8 2:
c) ♠ Q 9 4: ♡ Q 4 3: ◇ J 7 4 2: ♣ 10 6 2:
d) ♠ A: ♡ K Q 8: ◇ Q J 9 7 5: ♣ 9 8 7 6:

ANSWERS TO REVISION QUIZ ON CHAPTER 16

1) a) 1♠   A simple overcall at the one-level on a hand which would make an opening bid of 1♠ in any case.

   b) 3♠   A weak pre-emptive 'interference' bid.

   c) 1♠   Another perfectly normal overcall at the one-level.

   d) 1 NT An evenly balanced 17 points with a good stop in the suit opened.

   e) 2♡   A forcing overcall on a hand which is unsuitable for a take-out double.

   f) 4◇   Pre-emptive on a hand completely worthless in defence.

   g) 1♠   A simple overcall on a hand just worth an opening bid of 1♠.

   h) 2♡   Forcing again.

   i) 1 NT Another evenly balanced hand typically suitable for this bid.

   j) 2◇   A hand just strong enough for a simple overcall at the two-level.

   k) 2♠   A jump overcall, for which the hand just qualifies as it holds the ♡K over the opening bid.

   l) 2♡   Forcing, to give yourself the certain chance to show both these beautiful suits.

   m) No.   Not strong enough to bid diamonds at the two-level, as even not vulnerable this could cost you a packet.

   n) 1 NT By far the best bid on this hand.

   o) 4♣   Having no defence to either of the major suits and no interest in any other suit as trumps, make the maximum possible interference bid at once.

   p) 4◇   Here again you want to interfere to the limit before the opposition finds its own best contract.

2) a) 2♡   A simple take-out into a new suit.

   b) 1 NT You are justified in re-opening the bidding on a lower point count than normally required for this bid.

   c) Double. If your partner passed with a good holding in spades and can leave the double in, it should prove most profitable.

   d) Double. You do *not* bid 2◇ on a hand like this. If partner passed on good spades, defending should at least be good fun, and you like any suit if he makes a take-out.

   e) 2◇   A take-out into your own good suit.

   f) No.   Here your best bet is to pass. It is unlikely that your partner passed on good spades and a 2♣ response from him would be embarrassing on your hand.

3) a) 2 NT The Acol game-forcing overcall. A double would be 'business', and you want to play this in hearts or diamonds.

b) No.   You will be on lead if the opposition play in 1 N.T. and should take the first seven tricks in spades. If you double they will almost certainly escape into a suit contract.

c) 2 NT Another example of this forcing bid, designed to give you time to show both diamonds and clubs.

d) Double. Your 16 points all lie over the opening bidder who will probably find it quite impossible to make his contract. Your partner will only take out on complete weakness or if he thinks you have a more profitable contract available.

e) 2 NT You do not want to defend a No Trump contract on this sort of hand, but you *do* want to play in spades or hearts.

4) a) 2 NT If partner can overcall at the two-level, you must tell him that your own hand is far from worthless. You would not make this bid without a good stop in the suit opened and some fit with partner's suit.

b) 3 ◇   Your hand is worth this raise and North will probably find it impossible to rebid 3♠ unsupported, whereas he might well bid 2♠ if left to himself. If you then come in, South may be able to compete.

c) No.   Pass and hope that partner is allowed to play in 2 ◇. If North bids 2♠ you can come in with 3 ◇ on the next round.

d) 2♠   A cue bid, 'setting the suit' as diamonds. (It might also be a Directional Asking Bid.)

Chapter 17

Quantitative Bids

It is difficult to know where best to fit in a discussion on the Acol System's quantitative bids, as they can be used equally well, when the right occasion crops up, by either opener or responder. However, perhaps they fall most neatly into place here now that we have covered the fundamental features of the system.

Basically, a quantitative bid is one which is natural, limited, and non-forcing. Thus in a sense all Acol limit bids are quantitative, as they state within narrowly defined limits both the upper and the lower extremes of strength—or weakness—held. The real quantitative bids with which we are now concerned are, however, somewhat different both in content and in character. They *invite* partner to bid on, always to a slam, if certain specific requirements are held by him.

The simplest example of a quantitative raise is one of an opening 1 N.T. or 2 N.T. to the four-level. This shows that responder is interested *only* in whether his partner's opening is minimum or maximum in point-count. If minimum then, of course, the invitation should not be accepted, as responder has said that his own count, facing opener's known *minimum* will not reach the 33-34 points required for a Little Slam in No Trumps. In other words, facing a 1 N.T. opening bid based on 12-14 points, responder will probably hold an evenly-balanced 20 points, bringing the total up to 32 points if opener has his minimum of 12 points, and into the slam zone if he has 13 or 14. Responder's quantitative bid of 4 N.T., therefore, invites him to go on to 6 N.T. if he is better than minimum, and otherwise to pass. The same would apply if the opening bid were 2 N.T., 20-22 points. Here the quantitative raise to 4 N.T. would be based on 12 points, a combined 32 if opener is minimum and at least 33 if he is maximum. These are the situations where a 4 N.T. bid must *not* be confused with a 'Blackwood' request to show aces.

There are, however, other and more important uses for quantitative bids. They may be used—always invitationally—where an expressive bid is difficult to find, or where control of a specific suit is needed. The latter may well be a suit bid by the opposition.

Some examples of these various situations should make the position clear, as well as suggesting the sort of position in which quantitative bids can be used so successfully.

♠ A J 10 8 6 4
♡ 6
◇ A 7 5
♣ A Q 6

♠ K Q 9
♡ K Q J 10 5
◇ 4
♣ K J 5 2

North, the dealer, opens 1♠ to which South responds 2♡. Lacking any first-round control South cannot force on the first round, though he intends to raise to 4♠ (a delayed game raise) if North rebids a mere 2♠—to ensure at any rate that a game contract is reached somewhere. When, however, North makes the strong limit rebid of 3♠, inviting South to bid the fourth if he possibly can, South's hand becomes very much more valuable. He knows, for instance, that North, who is missing his own ♠K-Q, must himself hold at least a six-card suit and much greater power than for a mere Acol light opener. Unable himself to bid a 'Blackwood' 4 N.T., he bids 5♠, by-passing game-level, and inviting North to bid 6♠ if he is fractionally stronger than he need be for his bidding thus far. In fact North is only one trick short of a Strong Two bid, and is able to accept the invitation to bid the undefeatable slam.

The hand above is a wonderful example of invitational quantitative bids, North's 3♠ rebid itself being a quantitative invitation to South to bid to game if he, South, is stronger than he need be for his initial 2♡ response. South is not only stronger, but very much stronger than he need be, in addition to which he has what now becomes more than adequate trump support, though he is clearly in difficulties for an expressive rebid at this point if he cannot make use of a quantitative 5♠ which gets both him and his partner out of difficulties. North will understand that South cannot bid 4 N.T. because he is short of first-round controls, and that as long as North holds these, all should be well. North has three first-round, and one second-round control, the latter in the suit which South himself has bid.

♠ Q 8 5
♡ Q J 9 4
◇ 8 6 3 2
♣ 6 3
South

N.	S.
2♣	2◇
2♠	2 NT
3♡	?

This next example illustrates a point of good judgement. South has responded correctly with not only one, but two negative bids (see Chapter 12). South should reason that apart from the fact that he holds what must be the invaluable ♠Q in his partner's first suit, he also has four to the ♡Q-J (and, therefore, no worse than a strong four-four trump fit) in his partner's second suit, in addition to which North is unlikely to hold *worse* than a losing doubleton in either of the minors. All of this adds up to the fact that if 4♡ can be made, 5♡ is almost certainly equally safe, and the slam should also be made if North can take care of all second-round situations. So instead of a mere raise to 4♡, South should realise that his hand has become a potential gold mine and that he will not be misleading his partner if he now bids a quantitative and invitational 5♡. In the actual event, North held ♠A K J 9 7: ♡A K 10 7: ◇7: ♣A K 4:. He bid 6♡, which contract was, of course, made in comfort.

	N.	S.
♠9 8 6		
♡Q 2	2♣	2◇
◇K 6 4	2♠	2 NT
♣7 6 5 3 2	3♡	3♠
South	4◇	?

This is another hand on the same theme —revaluation in the light of partner's bidding, and the need for an expressive bid which will not mislead partner. Again two negatives have followed the opening 2♣, and South showed mere preference for spades on his third bid. In spite of this North is making a slam try—his 4◇ can be nothing else. Also, in spite of his bidding thus far, South has two cards which North cannot expect him to hold, because he could well have a Yarborough instead of the queen of North's second suit and the ◇K, which must be a key-card in the circumstances. South should bid 5♠, not just 4♠, telling North that he's better than he need be, as well as being fully prepared to allow North to play in spades at the slam level. North turned out to hold ♠A K Q 7 5 4: ♡A K 10 9 7: ◇A 5: ♣—: and bid 6♠, just one trick being lost to a 4—0 trump break.

	N.	S.
♠A J 10 4 3 2	1♠	2♡
♡7	3◇	5♣
◇A Q 10 8	6♣	6◇
♣A 6	6♠	

```
       N
  W         E
       S
```

♠K Q 9
♡A Q 8 5 3
◇K 9 4
♣8 7

Now we come to the situation in which a quantitative bid can be used to pin-point the need for control in a specific suit, as when the partnership has bid three suits, and the slam turns on control of the fourth. On this deal the auction opens with 1♠ from North and 2♡ from South. North then rebids 3◇, a one-round force. As this is a bid reserved for strong hands, it immediately allows South to revalue his own hand upwards. In this particular case a 'Blackwood' 4 N.T. by South would show that North has three aces, but even if he has only two, the important point is to make sure that he doesn't hold a losing club doubleton. A quantitative bid of 5♠ at this point specifically requests second-round control of clubs. Holding even better, the ♣A, not to mention full values for his bidding thus far, North can confirm by cue-bidding the ♣A. South in turn shows the ◇K and North happily bids the Little Slam in spades.

The last situation is where control of the opponents' bid suit is needed. Here is perhaps the ultimate in classic examples, since accepting North's invitation required great courage from South.

♠ K J 4
♡ A K Q J 10 4
◇ 6 4
♣ A 4

♠ A Q 10 9 8 6 5
♡ 8 7
◇ 8
♣ K 5 3

Apart from 'shooting', how else can North be sure of the situation when East deals and opens with a pre-emptive 3◇ over which South bids 3♠? South, of course, is unwilling to be silenced, and even if light in honour points, has magnificent 'shape'. North is even more magnificent, having a full-scale 2♡ opening hand if he'd been the dealer. He also has an extremely good fit for what must, in these circumstances, be at least a six-card suit (and is actually seven). Furthermore he has first-round control of clubs and the sure knowledge that his hearts will provide South with all the discards of losers that he can possibly need *if* the partnership doesn't founder on the rocks of two losing diamond doubletons facing each other. A bid of 5♠, therefore, specifically asks for at least second-round control of the enemy suit, holding which South should trust his partner and raise to 6♠. With a void or the ◇A, South could go even further and confirm first-round control by cue-bidding 6◇.

To sum up, a quantitative bid which carries the partnership above game level, is an invitation to a slam where the player who uses the quantitative bid is in difficulties for an expressive bid to make his needs known. This may be a need for maximum points from his partner (1 NT—4 NT), it may be the need for first-round controls, as in the first example deal. It may be purely invitational, as in the third-round bids following two negatives in the examples on ps. 246-7, simply indicating that responder is stronger than he need be for what he has already said. When three suits have been bid by the partnership it is a direct query as to control of the fourth, and when a suit has been bid by the opposition, it is a query specifically confined to that suit. If the partnership itself has bid only two suits—or even only one suit, as in the last example above— the player responding to the quantitative bid must assume that the other suit or suits are controlled by his partner.

To round off this chapter let's just have a few words on the vexed question of distinguishing between a quantitative (natural) 4 N.T. and when it is one of the slam convention variety. This is a situation open to a good deal of misinterpretation, for which it is difficult to formulate hard and fast rules, and probably common sense allied to partnership understanding will provide the best solution. There are, however, some general rules for guidance.

In the first place a bid of 4 N.T. when neither member of the partnership has bid a suit genuinely is always quantitative. This means that in sequences such as these the 4 N.T. bid is, as explained earlier in this chapter, a quantitative invitation to opener to go on to the slam if holding a maximum for his bid. In No. 3 the 2♣ and 2◇ bids were conventional fit-finding ones, and in No. 4, of course, they were the forcing opening and negative response, not genuine suit bids.

1) 1 NT—4 NT

2) 2 NT—4 NT

3) 1 NT—2♣
   2◇ —4 NT

4) 2♣ —2◇
   3 NT—4 NT

One school of thought decrees that 4 N.T. is always quantitative when no suit has been agreed, either directly or inferentially, but this is not entirely satisfactory. It would mean that the 4 N.T. bid in sequence No. 5 is quantitative, though clearly this could put a responder wishing to use it conventionally into a very difficult position. Sequence No. 6, under the rule above, would also mean that the 4 N.T. bid was quantitative, though this is at variance with the rules laid down by Blackwood himself.

5) 1♠ —2♡
   3 NT—4 NT

6) 1♡ —2 NT
   4 NT

From this you will see that it is not easy to give precise guidance, though there are sequences such as Nos. 7 and where it would be folly not to take the 4 N.T. as conventional. In both cases the 4 N.T. bid follows a strong bid from partner and it is only common sense to assume that slam investigations are now getting under way.

7) 1♡ —3 NT
   4 NT

8) 1♠ —3♡
   3 NT—4 NT

In the final analysis, *if in doubt*, treat 4 N.T. as conventional and not quantitative. After all, a player who bids 4 N.T., even if he actually intends it as invitational, is seeking higher things, and in the long run it will be safer to give him his chance by responding to the 4 N.T. bid rather than passing it.

There is one other quantitative direct raise of an opening No Trump bid, and this also carries with it a conventional significance. It is not very widely used, but the logic of it is clear. It is an immediate raise of either 1 N.T. or 2 N.T. to 5 N.T.

As already explained, the raise to 4 N.T. requests opener to bid 6 N.T. on a maximum, so it would be pointless to use this five-level bid to convey the same message. It is, in fact, a *demand* to opener to bid 6 N.T., even if minimum, and an invitation to bid

7 N.T. if maximum. In other words, responder is strong enough for a jump to 6 N.T. but queries whether the partnership should play at that level or whether the Grand Slam should be bid.

Chapter 18

Slam Bidding

THE possibility of making a slam on any two combined hands may be apparent from the outset of the auction, or it may develop as each member of the partnership looks at his hand in relation to his partner's bids or the other bids around the table. The vital factors needed are, of course, suit control, honour strength and, above all, the right fit. Clearly honour points are the least important of the three—you would make all thirteen tricks on only ten points if you held a thirteen-card suit!—but more often than not the necessary controls will depend on the holding of high honours. It is folly to bid a little slam with more than one first-round control missing, and you must be sure of second round control in any suit of which first round control is missing, or the opposition is more than likely to step in smartly and cash their two winners before you even get under way!

First-round control of any suit is, of course the ace at No Trumps, and the ace or a void at a suit contract. A singleton, as long as an adequate trump fit is held, gives second round control in a suit contract, and a guarded king does the same nineteen times out of twenty in No Trumps. It is frequently possible to discover which of these exist, or are missing, without recourse to any particular slam convention, but there are many special ways and means by which investigations can be made.

We have already examined various sequences such as those involving cue bids or the 'Swiss' convention which show slam interest round about the game level, and now we come on to the slam conventions themselves, for use when one or other member of the partnership has good grounds for suspecting that a slam is in the offing, and will be a good proposition if the essential controls can be located.

Once the trump suit has been agreed, investigations can start by way of cue bids or the like, and it will often become clear that the needed controls are missing, so that the bidding can be dropped in time and below slam level. On many other occasions further in-vestigations will be needed, and here your chosen slam convention will come into its own. There are many to choose from, details of which you can find in *Conventions Made Clear* by the same authors, but your bidding armoury would not be complete without a full knowledge of one of them, so we give you here that trusty and well-tried favourite, 'Blackwood'.

THE BLACKWOOD CONVENTION

This is a device for discovering specifically how many aces and, subsequently, how many kings, one's partner holds when it is clear that a slam is not far away. Before using Blackwood's conventional information-seeking bid, 4 N.T., it is essential that the trump suit should have been agreed, either directly or by inference, or that the 4 N.T. bidder should be prepared to play in a final high-level No Trump contract, because once one member of the partnership has bid a conventional 'Blackwood' 4 N.T., the bidding cannot stop below the five-level. Provided, therefore, a five-level contract seems a good proposition however disappointing the answer to 4 N.T. turns out to be, either member of the partnership may initiate the slam investigations. No specific holdings are required or promised by the bid, and partner must respond as follows:

With no ace	5♣
„ one ace	5♢
„ two aces	5♡
„ three aces	5♠
„ all four aces	5♣

You will note that the response to show all four *or* no aces is 5♣, but this never causes any trouble, as it is hardly likely that the partnership has no aces between them! The reason for this 5♣ four-ace response is that it leaves a subsequent bid of 5 N.T. to ask for kings. In this case 6♣ shows no king and 6 N.T. is used to show all four.

If an opponent intervenes over the 4 N.T. bid, and provided you don't want to double the intervention for penalties, the 'Blackwood' scale of responses is modified as follows:

With no ace	Pass
„ one ace	Bid the suit ranking next above opponent's suit
„ two aces	Jump one step to the *next* higher ranking suit, and so on.

Intervening bids frequently cause complications, and at this high level—if an opponent dares to stick his neck out by bidding over 4 N.T.—although the modified responses are available it may not be wise to use them. You would, for example, have to bid 6♦ over an intervening bid of 5♣ to show two aces. So in these circumstances you will have to let judgement be your guide subject only to the rider that it is generally better to tell your partner the truth, that is, to answer his question about your ace holding.

There is another useful sequence for occasions when the reply to the 'Blackwood' 4 N.T. shows that the partnership is an ace short for slam requirements, yet would like to play the final contract in 5 N.T. The 4 N.T. bidder cannot himself follow with a natural 5 N.T., as this would be interpreted as the conventional request for responder to show kings. He can, instead, bid the lowest available suit *not previously bid by the partnership*, which asks responder to transfer to 5 N.T. For example, the 4 N.T. enquiry has disappointingly revealed that opener has only one ace, whereas two are required for the slam contract. A bid of 5♣, a suit not bid by the partnership, requests partner to bid 5 N.T. which will become the final contract.

1♥ —3♦
4♦ —4 NT
5♦ —5♣
5 NT

A direct raise of an opening 1 N.T. or 2 N.T. to 4 N.T. is always quantitative and not a 'Blackwood' ace-enquiry, the 'Gerber' conventional bid of 4♣, which was set out in Chapter 5, taking the place of 4 N.T. As this has already been explained in detail with examples, there is no need to repeat it here. Before we leave 'Blackwood', however, here is a word of warning about the well-known dangers of 'Blackwood in the minors', that is, when the final contract, either game or slam if one is reached, will be in a minor suit, and most particularly if it is to be in clubs when *any* response to 4 N.T., other than 5♣, the ace-denial, forces the contract to the six-level. If a diamond contract is contemplated, then you can stand a 5♦ response to 4 N.T., which can be passed if one ace is not enough, but if clubs are to be trumps 5♦ drives the partnership into 6♣. As long as you remember this in time to avoid a dangerous 4 N.T. bid, you will find that the necessary information can almost always be obtained by way of cue bids as described in Chapter 10.

Finally, remember that 'Blackwood', as well, indeed, as any other slam convention, is an aid to good bidding and not a substitute for it. Making a slam does not depend solely on the position of aces and kings, so 'Blackwood' should only be used when the information it can provide is really necessary, and once you are sure that partner's ace and king holdings are all you need to know to bid the slam.

THE ACOL DIRECT KING CONVENTION

The Acol Direct King Convention can be used for 'slamming' at any time when partner's specific ace-holding is already known for certain. There are various sequences in which the ace-holding has been clearly stated, and in any of these 4 N.T. asks immediately for kings, the request to show aces not being necessary. For example, in (1) the direct raise of an opening 2♠ to 4♠ guarantees, amongst other things, *no* ace or void. In (2) the jump bid of 3 N.T. shows honour strength but no ace or void again, and (3) is the 'Swiss' conventional response showing two aces. These are only a few of the relevant positions, in none of which would an Acol player be stupid enough to waste bidding space asking a question about partner's aces when he already knows the answer!

1) 2♠ —4♠
2) 2♡ 3 NT
3) 1♠ —4♣

In No. 1, therefore, opener asks how many kings, not how many aces, responder holds. No. 2 must be noted, as 4 N.T. is conventional and *not* a quantitative raise of 3 N.T., because the 3 N.T. response itself is conventional. It is only common sense, therefore, to regard opener's 4 N.T. rebid as the conventional request for kings just as it is in No. 3, where opener has already been told that his partner holds two aces.

1) 2♠ —4♠
   4 NT—?
2) 2♡ —3 NT
   4 NT—?
3) 1♠ —4♣
   4 NT—?

FOUR NO TRUMP OPENING BID

Used in conjunction with the Acol System, this is a rare conventional opening bid, though it is invaluable when the occasions for it arise. It should be used when opener's *only* interest centres on any ace or aces held by his partner, and particularly when a positive response to a 2♣ opening might obscure the subsequent issue of which ace, if he has only one, responder holds. The 4 N.T. opening bid is, of course, unconditionally forcing and the responses are as set out below, after which opener will make the decision as to the best final contract *which responder must not disturb.* Kings and queens galore will be of no help to opener and his only interest is in aces.

Responder bids:

1) With two aces ....5 N.T.
2) With the ♣A ....6♣
3) With the ♠A, ♡A or ◇A ......Five of the ace-suit
4) With no ace ....5♣

♠ —
♡ 8
◇ A K Q J 10 7 6 5
♣ A K Q J

Here opener intends to play in 6◇ whether he is facing a Yarborough or not, but for the Grand Slam it is vital that responder should hold the ♡A, not the ♠A. Open 4 N.T. and, if responder has both aces, he will bid 5 N.T., after which you can bid 7◇ at rubber bridge (for the honours) and 7 N.T. at duplicate (for the highest M.P. score). If he has one ace he will name it. A 5♡ response you would convert to 7◇, and a 5♠ response you would convert to 6◇.

♠ A
♡ A
◇ K Q J 10 7
♣ K Q J 8 6 5

Here again, open 4 N.T. If partner responds 5♣ showing no ace, pass. If he responds 6♣, showing the ♣A, pass. If he responds 5◇, showing the ◇A, raise to 6◇, and if he makes the miracle response of 5 N.T., we leave the rest to you!

If you are ever lucky enough to be contemplating the choice between a 4 N.T. opening and 2♣ followed by a jump bid as described on p. 172, bear in mind that the 2♣ opening will ensure a lower contract if one vital ace is missing. The 4 N.T. opening, on the other hand, means that in no circumstances can the hand be played below the five-level, and the bid is, therefore, best reserved for hands on which a positive response to a 2♣ opening might confuse the issue, or when opener needs to make it clear that his *only* interest is in aces.

♠ K Q J 6
♡ A K Q J 10 8 7 6
◇ —
♣ A

This hand reached us from a correspondent recently, with a query as to the correct opening bid in view of the fact that the hand contained a void. It is, in fact, just about the most perfect example of an opening 4 N.T. hand that could be found. Opener is prepared to play in 6♡ whether or not his partner has a Yarborough and, therefore, no response to 4 N.T. can embarrass him. If partner has the ◇A, a 5◇ response, he will merely convert to 6♡. If partner has the ♠A (as he had!), then opener converts to 7♡. Only the ♠A is needed for the Grand Slam, but if partner gives a positive response to a 2♣ opening bid, how are you to be certain whether he has the vital ♠A or the useless ◇A?

In some earlier books it was stated, quite wrongly, that the 4 N.T opening should not be used if the hand contains a void. This should have been no more than the warning one gives to learners about the dangers of 'Blackwood in the minors' which is that if, for example, the hand is to be played in clubs, a 5◇ (one ace) response to 4 N.T. drives declarer to 6♣ whether he likes it or not. In the same way, if you decide to open 4 N.T., you must be prepared for any response your partner may make. Intending to play, perhaps,

in diamonds on a hand containing a club void, you may want to go
no further than 5♢ unless partner has the ♠A. An opening 4 N.T.
risks a 6♣ response, which would drive you to slam level whether
you like it or not. On this hand, if you open 4 N.T. and partner

♠ A
♡ —
♢ K Q J 10 7 5
♣ K Q J 8 6 5

bids 5♡ you can't stop lower than the little
slam level, though you're missing both minor
suit aces, so it is not a hand suitable for a 4 N.T.
bid, even though it differs by one card only from
our second example hand in this section. Change
the suits by making the clubs into hearts, and still you don't want to
hear a 6♣ response, but give it the same cards except with a
diamond void and you could afford to convert a 5♢ response to 5♡
or a 5♡ response to 6♡, or to pass a 6♣ response. All that is
necessary, therefore, is to be awake to the responses you may get,
and not to bid 4 N.T. with a void in your hand if the *wrong* answer
from partner might leave you in trouble.

MODIFIED GRAND SLAM FORCE

This is another useful convention which can be used with the Acol
System and is something of an improvement on the original Grand
Slam Force. Using it, a bid of 5 N.T. when not preceded by 4 N.T.,
asks partner *how many* of the three top trump honours he holds.
The responses to 5 N.T. are:

With none (i.e., no better than a knave-high suit)............6♣
With one (either ace, king or queen)............Six of the agreed
trump suit.
With any two of the top three............Seven of the agreed
trump suit.

The great advantage of this modification is that it allows a
player who himself holds one of the three top honours to discover
whether his partner has the other two or only one of them. This
actual example cropped up in a match:

West	East	West	East	
♠ A K Q 8 4 2	♠ 7	2♣	3♢*	*Positive response
♡ A Q	♡ J 9 8 5	5 NT**	6♢	with a diamond
♢ A Q 10 7	♢ K J 9 8 2	7♢		suit
♣ K	♣ A 9 8			**Simply to discover
				whether East has
				the ♢K or is only
				knave-high.

FIVE OF A MAJOR OPENING

This is another rare though occasionally useful opening bid, and shows an extremely powerful hand missing *only* the two top trump honours. Responder should raise to six even with the bare ace or king of the suit opened and, of course, direct to seven if he should happen to have both. On this hand, for example, a typical 5♡ opener, only the ♡A or ♡K will help towards the slam, and if responder holds even the bare ♡K and otherwise a Yarborough, he should bid 6♡. With the ace and king he should bid 7♡, and missing both he should pass, however many other aces or kings he may hold.

♠ A K
♡ Q J 10 9 8 6 4 3
♢ —
♣ A K Q

Similarly, of course, an opening bid of six of a major requires partner to raise to seven if holding *one* of the two top honours—opener will have two of them himself.

This convention can be extended to opening bids of six in either minor, requiring a raise to seven on the ace or king, but opening five-bids of clubs or diamonds are pre-emptive and not conventional in this sense.

QUANTITATIVE RAISES OF NO TRUMP OPENING BIDS

In previous chapters it has been mentioned that any direct raise of an opening No Trump bid, whatever the strength, is quantitative and not conventional, and that the 'Gerber' 4♣ replaces 4 N.T. as the ace-request when the opening bid has been either 1 N.T. or 2 N.T. The quantitative raise to the four-level is based on the fact that a No Trump slam, given reasonable breaks, requires 33-34 points, and when responder bids 4 N.T. he calculates his own hand in combination with opener's known point count. If the combined total is in the Little Slam range he bids it direct. If it requires opener to hold his maximum rather than his minimum, he bids an invitational and quantitative 4 N.T., inviting opener to bid 6 N.T. on a maximum.

FIVE NO TRUMP RESPONSE TO NO TRUMP OPENING

There is one other conventional direct raise of a No Trump opening bid, and that is a direct raise to the five-level (1 N.T.—5 N.T. or 2 N.T.—5 N.T.). Clearly, as 4 N.T. is used as the direct invitation to the Little Slam, 5 N.T. must have a different meaning. It is, in fact, a demand to opener to bid 6 N.T. whether minimum or maximum, and a request to him to bid 7 N.T. if maximum. For example, opener bids 1 N.T. on an agreed 12-14 points and responder holds 24 points. This is clearly enough for the Little Slam as the combined total will be 36 points, but if responder bids a direct 6 N.T. the Grand Slam may be missed. He bids 5 N.T., demanding that opener should bid 6 N.T. on 12 points, and 7 N.T. on a *good* 13 or his full 14 points.

Epilogue

THERE, dear reader, you have the Acol System complete; if you have assimilated the pages of this book and made a successful job of your answers to the Revision Quizzes, you will be equipped to go out into the big wide world of Contract Bridge with the knowledge that you play sound, efficient, and straightforward Acol. Admittedly we have included some of the 'frills' which are not essential to the system as a whole, but only as many of them as are likely to be an asset, either from the point of view of playing them or understanding them when you meet them in opposition.

The Acol System has enough rules to guide you and keep you from disaster, even with an unaccustomed partner, and it also gives you the greatest possible latitude for the use of individual flair and judgement as your experience grows.

It would be foolish to pretend that ours is the only version of the system you will ever meet. There are many variations, and you may even like to experiment with some of them at a later stage. Before you tamper with the basic structure of the system, however, make sure you fully understand the implications of the proposed changes. For example, if you find yourself with a partner who wants to play 'weak twos in the majors', you will have to work out a complete sequence of replacement opening bids and responses for the occasions on which you want to open a Strong Two. Or perhaps you will find a partner who doesn't consider Strong Twos forcing for even one round, in which case you may have to lower your standards for a Two Club opening, to guarantee yourself a second chance to bid. Indeed the variations can go further than that, and you may well hear bidding sequences so complicated that they baffle even the experts who dream them up!

The best possible advice we can give you is to avoid pointless elaborations. Learn the system thoroughly, which should be simple enough as it's based entirely on common sense. Learn to bid your own hand to the full, and not to wait for your partner to bid it for you, and also learn not to bid your cards twice. Learn to value—and revalue—your hand in the light of the development of the auction. The terms 'devaluation' and 'revaluation' are not the sole prerogatives of the economists, and that good-looking king for which you counted three points as opener must be devalued considerably when its suit is bid on your left—until you can discover that your partner holds the ace, when up goes its value again!

Acol is a middle-of-the-road system designed to give its users the soundest possible results on the largest possible number of hands. Apart from some highly distributional or freak deals, you will inevitably find that missed contracts are the fault of underbidding, either because you or your partner have not bid your cards to the full, or because you have failed to revalue them, as the auction proceeds. Similarly, a costly penalty may be incurred by failure to devalue, to recognise a danger-spot, or a refusal to drop the bidding when it is obvious that there is a complete misfit with your partner's hand.

Used wisely and accurately, and coupled with common sense and sound judgement, the Acol System will steer you safely through any situation which may arise. We wish you, therefore, good bridge and better bidding.

Index

GEORGE ALLEN & UNWIN LTD

Head Office:
40 Museum Street, London WC1
Telephone: 01-405-8577

Sales, Publicity, Distribution and Accounts Departments:
Park Lane, Hemel Hempstead, Hertfordshire HP2 4TE
Telephone: 0442 3244

Argentina: Defensa 681-5J, Buenos Aires
Australia: Australasian Publishing Company Pty Ltd,
Corner Bridge Road and Jersey Street, Hornsby, N.S.W. 2077
Bangladesh: Provincial Book Depot,
Empire Buildings, Victoria Park South, Dacca
Canada: Methuen Ltd,
2330 Midland Avenue, Agincourt, Ontario
East Africa: University of London Press Ltd,
P.O. Box 30583, Nairobi, Kenya
Europe: Rock House, Edington, Nr. Bridgwater, Somerset
Greece, Turkey and The Middle East: I.P.R.
3 Mitropoleous Street, Athens 118
India: Blackie & Son Ltd,
103/5 Walchand Hirachand Marq., P.O. Box 21, Bombay 1 BR
285J Bepin Behari Ganguli Street, Calcutta 12
2/18 Mount Road, Madras 2
4/21-22B Asaf Ali Road, New Delhi 1
Japan: Eastern Book Service
29/13 Hongo 5 Chome, Bunkyo ku, Tokyo 113
Malaysia: Eastern Book Service
Resident Office, 54 Jalan-Pudu, Room 303, Kuala Lumpur
New Zealand: Book Reps (N.Z.) Ltd,
46 Lake Road, Northcote, Auckland 9
Pakistan: Hamiedkhan Ltd,
22 Faletti's Hotel, Egerton Road, Lahore
Karachi Chambers, McLeod Road, Karachi
Philippines: Eastern Book Service
U.P., P.O. Box 10, Quezon City D-505
Singapore & Hong Kong: Eastern Book Service
53L Anson Road, 11th Floor Anson Centre, Singapore 2
South Africa: Macmillan (S.A.) Ltd,
P.O. Box 31487, Braamfontein, Johannesburg
South America: Oxford University Press Ltd,
Ely House, 37 Dover Street, London W.1.
Thailand: Eastern Book Service
P.O. Box 6/1, Bangkok
West Africa: University of London Press Ltd,
P.O. Box 62, Ibadan, Nigeria
West Indies: Rockley New Road, St Lawrence 4, Barbados